W9-AFB-267

WITHDRAWN

RIDGEMONT PUBLIC LIBRARY
MT. VICTORY, OHIO

THE THANKSGIVING BOOK

THE
THANKSGIVING
BOOK

A Companion to the Holiday
Covering Its History, Lore, Traditions, Foods, and Symbols,
Including Primary Sources, Poems, Prayers, Songs,
Hymns, and Recipes, Supplemented by a Chronology,
Bibliography with Web Sites, and Index

By Laurie C. Hillstrom

Omnigraphics

P.O. Box 31-1640
Detroit, MI 48231-1640

Omnigraphics, Inc.

Cherie D. Abbey, *Managing Editor*
Helene Henderson, *Editor*
Allison A. Beckett, Mary Butler, and Linda Strand, *Research Staff*

Peter E. Ruffner, *Publisher*
Matthew P. Barbour, *Senior Vice President*

Elizabeth Collins, *Research and Permissions Coordinator*
Kevin Hayes, *Operations Manager*
Barry Puckett, *Librarian*
Cherry Stockdale, *Permissions Assistant*
Shirley Amore, Martha Johns, Kirk Kauffman, and Johnny Lawrence, *Administrative Staff*

Copyright © 2008 Omnigraphics, Inc.
ISBN 978-0-7808-0403-6

Library of Congress Cataloging-in-Publication Data

Hillstrom, Laurie Collier, 1965-
    The Thanksgiving book : a companion to the holiday covering its history, lore, traditions, foods, and symbols, including primary sources, poems, prayers, songs, hymns, and recipes : supplemented by a chronology, bibliography with web sites, and index / by Laurie Hillstrom.
        p. cm.
    Summary: "Provides information about the history, lore, traditions, foods, and symbols of the Thanksgiving celebration. Features include narrative overviews and primary source documents, chronology, and resources for further information"--Provided by publisher.
    Includes bibliographical references and index.
    ISBN-13: 978-0-7808-0403-6 (hardcover : alk. paper) 1. Thanksgiving Day.
I. Title.
    GT4975.H55 2007
    394.2649--dc22
                                                                                    2007025708

All rights reserved. No part of this publication may be reproduced or transmitted in any form or by any means, electronic or mechanical, including photocopy, recording, or any information storage and retrieval system, without permission in writing from the publisher.

The information in this publication was compiled from sources cited and from sources considered reliable. While every possible effort has been made to ensure reliability, the publisher will not assume liability for damages caused by inaccuracies in the data, and makes no warranty, express or implied, on the accuracy of the information contained herein.

∞™

This book is printed on acid-free paper meeting the ANSI Z39.48 Standard. The infinity symbol that appears above indicates that the paper in this book meets that standard.

Printed in the United States of America.

CONTENTS

New England Thanksgivings

Thanksgiving Spreads beyond New England

The Civil War and Creation of the National Holiday

Thanksgiving in the Early 20th Century

Thanksgiving in Wartime

Native American Perspectives on Thanksgiving

Thanksgiving in Modern Times

RECIPES

PREFACE

Thanksgiving is an American holiday that reveals many of the qualities that we value as a nation. It encompasses a variety of themes, foremost of which are the expression of gratitude and the importance of home. To be sure, food, parades, and sports are longstanding staples of the occasion, though their precise incarnations have varied over the centuries. Yet ever since Americans have strayed far from their places of origin across the wide continent, each year, they flock back to homesteads to gather with family members and old friends for the special feast held on the last Thursday in November. It is a fitting form of commemoration, given that the historical event memorialized in the holiday is one in which a group of persecuted immigrants sought a new home, in a land where they would be free to practice their religion of choice and govern themselves.

Scope

The Thanksgiving Book: A Companion to the Holiday Covering Its History, Lore, Traditions, Foods, and Symbols, Including Primary Sources, Poems, Stories, Hymns, and Recipes, Supplemented by a Chronology, Bibliography with Web Sites, and Index traces the history, customs, symbols, and foods of the Thanksgiving holiday, from the earliest European explorers and settlers to the early 21st century.

Audience

This book is intended for a general audience, including students and teachers as well as interested adults. Those researching various aspects of Thanksgiving will find pertinent information, and general readers will find engaging narratives, first-person accounts, tales, and facts.

Organization

The main body of *The Thanksgiving Book* is organized into three sections: Essays, Recipes, and Primary Sources.

Essays

The two essays in the first section provide narrative overviews of the holiday. The first essay, Thanksgiving: History and Observance, provides information about the history of the holiday as well as the history of its meaning and observance through the centuries. The second essay, Thanksgiving: Holiday Food from the 17th to the 21st Centuries, examines the history of foods served on the holiday, from the first meal at Plymouth Plantation to the modern Thanksgiving table. The essays contain cross references to selections in the Primary Sources section that illuminate the discussion of the holiday's history, history of observance, and foods.

Primary Sources

This section gathers more than 50 historical documents, essays, stories, poems, articles, proclamations, and hymns shedding light on a range of themes associated with Thanksgiving, from the Mayflower Compact to modern observances. Each document is introduced with annotation that serves to put the document in context. Primary sources are grouped under the following headings:

The Pilgrims and the First Thanksgiving
The Revolutionary Period
America Embraces the Pilgrims
New England Thanksgivings
Thanksgiving Spreads beyond New England
The Civil War and Creation of the National Holiday
Thanksgiving in the Early 20th Century
Thanksgiving in Wartime
Native American Perspectives
Thanksgiving in Modern Times

Recipes

This section contains 41 recipes for a Thanksgiving meal, including safe turkey preparation guidelines from the U.S. Food and Drug Administration. Recipes are grouped under the following headings:

Appetizers
Turkey and Gravy
Stuffings
Side Dishes
Breads and Rolls
Desserts
Beverages
Leftover Ideas

Other Features

Chronology

The Chronology lists important events in the history of the Thanksgiving holiday.

Bibliography

The Bibliography lists all books, articles, and web sites consulted in the preparation of this volume.

Index

The Index lists people, places, customs, symbols, foods, and other topics discussed in the text.

Comments and Suggestions

We welcome your comments on *The Thanksgiving Book*, including suggestions for topics that you would like to see covered in future editions. Please address any correspondence to:

Editor, *The Thanksgiving Book*
Omnigraphics, Inc.
P.O. Box 31-1640
Detroit, MI 48231-1640
Email: editorial@omnigraphics.com

ESSAYS

THE LANDING OF THE PILGRIMS AT PLYMOUTH, MASS. DEC. 22ND 1620.

The MAYFLOWER left Delft Haven in Holland Sept. 6th 1620, and after a boisterous passage of Sixty three days anchored within Cape Cod. In her cabin the first Republican Government in America was solemnly inaugurated. That vessel thus became truly the "Cradle of Liberty" rocked on the free waves of the Ocean.

This print, titled *The Landing of the Pilgrims at Plymouth, Mass. Dec. 22nd, 1620,* was produced by Currier & Ives around 1876.

Thanksgiving: History and Observance

The contemporary American holiday of Thanksgiving means many things to many people. For some, the strongest association with the special day is a huge, home-cooked meal consisting of turkey, stuffing, mashed potatoes, and pumpkin pie. Others appreciate the holiday as a long weekend off work that gives them a valuable opportunity to travel homeward and be reunited with distant friends and family. Some people spend the day watching parades or football games, either live or on television, while others eagerly anticipate the start of the Christmas shopping season the following day. Many Americans attend church on Thanksgiving to express gratitude for the blessings they received during the previous year. Still others mark Thanksgiving by collecting canned goods or serving meals at soup kitchens to help those less fortunate than themselves. Finally, some Americans view Thanksgiving as a patriotic holiday—a time to reflect on the basic principles and values that made the country great.

Both the meaning and the means of celebrating Thanksgiving have changed from generation to generation throughout U.S. history. From the time of the Pilgrims through America's colonial days, Thanksgiving was a solemn and prayerful occasion when people expressed their gratitude to God for fruits of the harvest and instances of good fortune. During the revolutionary period, Thanksgiving evolved into an annual New England tradition and took on patriotic significance. Thanksgiving observances gradually spread westward and southward in the mid-1800s, especially after President Abraham Lincoln declared it a national holiday during the Civil War.

By the early 20th century, Thanksgiving had also become a tool to teach new immigrants about American history and values. Over the course of the 20th century the holiday took on a more celebratory, festive atmosphere with the gradual addition of football games, parades, and Christmas sales to the annual observances. Despite its complicated history, however, Thanksgiving has remained a beloved institution in American life for more than three centuries.

ANCIENT HARVEST FESTIVAL AND THANKSGIVING TRADITIONS

Thanksgiving has been described as "the quintessential American holiday," yet it has its roots in other cultures. In fact, the tradition of giving thanks to a higher power for instances of good fortune has existed in various parts of the world since ancient times. People have long held celebrations, for example, to express their gratitude for successful harvests of food. The purpose of many of these early harvest festivals was to appease the gods or spirits that were believed to control the growth of corn and other crops. A number of early cultures believed that if the gods were happy, the harvest would be plentiful; but if the gods were angry, crop failure—and possibly starvation—would follow.

The ancient Egyptians celebrated a festival in April, the time of the grain harvest, to honor Min, the god of fertility. The festival began with a procession to Min's shrine—in which the Pharaoh often took part—followed by religious ceremonies, music, dancing, and a feast.

Similarly, the ancient Greeks held the festival of Thesmophoria every autumn to honor Demeter, the goddess of corn. Married women built leafy shelters to begin the three-day event. People fasted on the second day, and then they feasted and made offerings to Demeter on the third day. The Greeks also held occasional days of thanksgiving to express their appreciation to the gods for specific positive events, such as a successful battle or journey.

The ancient Romans honored Ceres, the goddess of cereal crops, on April 19, with games in the Circus Maxima. They also observed the Consualia each August 21 in honor of Consus, the god who protected the grain harvest. The Consualia was a harvest festival celebrated with horse and chariot races.

The Chinese celebrate Chung Ch'ui—also known as the Mid-Autumn Festival—during the full moon that occurs in the eighth month of the year, according to the Chinese lunar calendar. The feast associated with this festival features specially baked moon cakes. According to one legend, the baking of moon cakes began during a time when China had been conquered by the Mongols. The Chinese made secret plans to attack the invaders and spread the news among the people by distributing moon cakes with messages hidden inside. The element of surprise helped the Chinese defeat the invaders and regain control of their country.

The Cornucopia

One of the most recognizable symbols of Thanksgiving is the cornucopia—a horn or basket filled to overflowing with fruits, vegetables, grains, and sometimes flowers. It is an ancient symbol of the harvest or of general abundance that dates back to Greek and Roman mythology. Its name comes from the Latin term *cornu copiae*, meaning "horn of plenty."

The ancient Romans believed that the cornucopia originated with Achelous, a river god who took the form of a bull to do battle with Heracles. When Achelous lost a horn in the fight, female water spirits filled it with fruit and flowers. The Romans also associated the cornucopia with Flora, the goddess of plants and flowers, and Fortuna, the goddess of good fortune.

According to Greek mythology, the horn of plenty originated with Amalthea, a nymph who took the form of a goat to nurse the infant Zeus. She may have broken off one of her horns to give Zeus, or he may have presented a cornucopia to her as a token of his appreciation. In both the Greek and Roman versions of the myth, the horn provided an endless supply of food.

The cornucopia later became a symbol of America, which many hopeful immigrants viewed as a land of plenty. A common feature of Thanksgiving decorations in modern times, it often serves as the centerpiece of tables set for the holiday meal.

The Jewish holiday of Sukkot—also known as the Feast of the Tabernacles (or Booths) and the Feast of the Ingathering—is a thanksgiving harvest festival celebrated since ancient times. It also commemorates the 40 years during which Moses and the Israelites wandered in the desert after leaving Egypt. During this period, they built temporary huts, or sukkah, out of branches to provide shelter at night. The modern holiday begins five days after Yom Kippur and lasts for eight days. Many Jews observe Sukkot by building small huts out of branches and hanging fruits and vegetables inside them.

Western Europeans also have traditions of giving thanks for a successful harvest. Since medieval times, people in rural England have celebrated an annual rite of autumn known as Harvest Home. When the last load of grain had been placed on a wagon and was ready to be brought in from the field, local villagers decorated the wagon with ribbons and flowers, danced around it, and

A traditional cornucopia.

sang songs of thanks. After the grain had been put away and all of the season's work completed, many villages held a feast.

*E*ARLY CELEBRATIONS IN NORTH AMERICA

Long before European explorers, fishermen, and traders began arriving in North America in the 1500s, Native American peoples established their own thanksgiving and harvest festival traditions. Many Native cultures made it a regular part of daily life to express gratitude for such necessities as food and shelter (*see the Primary Sources section for the text of a Native American Thanksgiving address*). "We have lived with this land for thousands of generations, fishing in the waters, planting and harvesting crops, hunting the four-legged and winged beings and giving respect and thanks for each and every thing taken for our use," explained Nanepashemet, former director of the Wampanoag Indian Program at Plimoth Plantation, in *1621: A New Look at Thanksgiving.*

The Wampanoags, whose name means "People of the Light" or "People of the First Light," have inhabited the area comprising present-day southeastern Massachusetts and eastern Rhode Island for 12,000 years. They have traditionally offered thanks not only to the Creator, but also to the spirits of all the animals killed and plants harvested to provide food and clothing for their people. Expressing gratitude and humility also forms the basis of the festival known as Nickommo, which is still celebrated by the Wampanoags in the 21st century. Nickommo observances include giving away material possessions, feasting, dancing, and playing games.

Early European explorers and settlers carried their traditions of giving thanks with them to the New World. For instance, historical evidence suggests that an exploring party led by Juan Ponce de León held a special mass to give thanks upon reaching North America in 1521. Similarly, a group of 1,500 Spaniards, led by explorer Francisco Vasquez de Coronado, held a service of thanksgiving in the area of the present-day Texas Panhandle on May 23, 1541. A small settlement of French Huguenots held a thanksgiving service on June 30, 1564, near present-day Jacksonville, Florida. Unfortunately, the French settlement was wiped out a decade later by Spanish raiders.

Most of these early thanksgivings tended to be prayerful occasions, but a few European settlers in the New World also included a feast as part of the observance. On September 8, 1565, for instance, a group of about 800 Spanish colonists led by Pedro Menéndez de Avilés shared a feast of thanksgiving in St. Augustine, Florida, with the local Seloy Indians. Historians of the American Southwest also claim that explorer Juan de Oñate and 400 colonists celebrated thanksgiving along the Rio Grande in April 1598. The Oñate Thanksgiving, which is marked by a festival and reenactment in modern-day El Paso, Texas, included a mass and a feast of goat, fish, corn, and cactus.

A few groups of English colonists also observed thanksgiving in America. One group of settlers held a service to express their gratitude upon reaching the coast of Maine on August 9, 1607. The Berkeley Hundred settlement in Virginia, founded by John Woodleaf, held a thanksgiving service upon reaching the James River on December 4, 1619. The colonists made plans to turn it into an annual event, as their proclamation makes clear: "Wee ordaine that the day of our ships arrival at the place assigned for plantacon in the land of Virginia shall be yearly and perpetually kept holy as a day of thanksgiving to Almighty God." The custom ended abruptly, however, when the settlement was destroyed by Indians in 1622. The founders of the first permanent English colony in America, at Jamestown, Virginia, suffered through a terrible famine during the winter in 1609. When a ship arrived carrying supplies from England in the spring of 1610, they celebrated with a feast of thanksgiving.

Some historians question why one of these occasions has not been recognized as the "First Thanksgiving" celebrated by European immigrants to America, since they occurred before the much more famous harvest feast that was shared between the Pilgrims and the Wampanoag Indians at Plymouth, Massachusetts, in 1621. Residents of Virginia, especially, claim that their state should be honored as the site of the historic event. But many experts argue that none of these occasions—the Pilgrims' feast included—can claim a direct connection with the national Thanksgiving holiday that is celebrated today. "However satisfying it would be to point to a particular day and say, 'This was the first Thanksgiving,' it would not be accurate," Diana Karter Appelbaum wrote in *Thanksgiving: An American Holiday, An American History.* "Thanksgiving was not a New England Athena, springing full grown and completely armed with roast turkey and cranberry sauce from the head of a Pilgrim Father."

THE PILGRIMS

Even if the Pilgrims did not intend to launch a national holiday, there is no doubt that their story—the perilous journey to North America in 1620, the hardships suffered during the first year in the New World, and the feast held in 1621—has contributed a great deal to the modern understanding of Thanksgiving. For many Americans, the connection between Thanksgiving and the Pilgrims has added to the holiday's historic importance and meaning, lending it associations with the values of perseverance, freedom, and democracy.

The English men and women that history remembers as the Pilgrims, because they made a journey for religious reasons, were known during their own time as Separatists. They acquired this name because of their brave decision to separate from the Church of England. During the early 1600s, the Church was the official religion of England and thus had a great deal of control over people's daily lives. The king or queen of England ruled the Church as well as the country, and top Church officials held positions of influence in politics. Although this arrangement added to the Church's wealth and power—allowing Church leaders to build beautiful cathedrals, wear ornate robes, and fill worship services with organ music—some people felt that it also detracted from the Church's mission of serving God.

This engraving, based on a painting by T. H. Matteson and published around 1859, shows the Pilgrims below deck on the *Mayflower* signing the Mayflower Compact.

The Separatists complained that the Church placed too much emphasis on superficial displays and not enough on Christ's teachings. These reformers left the Church of England and formed their own congregations, which held solemn worship services in plain buildings and focused on doing God's work by helping the poor, sick, and elderly. In those days, however, the practice of other religions was banned in England, and opposition to the Church was considered an act of treason against the king. Faced with persecution in their home country, the Separatists decided to immigrate to Holland in hopes of finding an environment where they could practice their religion freely.

The Separatists left England in the spring of 1608, despite several attempts by the British government to stop them. After a brief stay in Amsterdam, they settled in the town of Leiden. The Separatists remained in Holland for twelve years, during which time the Dutch government did not interfere with their religious practices. After a while, though, the English immigrants noticed that their children were beginning to adopt the language and customs of their host country. They decided to seek a new home where they could enjoy religious freedom and still maintain their English identity.

By this time, European explorers had brought back many enticing descriptions of the bounties of the New World. A small group of Separatists made the bold decision to sail across the Atlantic Ocean and try to establish a colony in America. They found sponsors willing to loan them money for the journey, and they made arrangements to repay the loan with money earned from fishing and fur-trapping in the New World. The Separatists set sail from Holland to England on July 22, 1620, in two ships, the *Speedwell* and the *Mayflower*. Unfortunately, the *Speedwell* proved barely seaworthy enough to make the four-day trip to England, so only one ship remained to make the journey to America.

After being stocked with provisions, the *Mayflower* left England for America on September 6, 1620. A total of 102 passengers made the trip, including a group of Separatists and an assortment of others. They took only necessities with them, including warm clothes, furniture, food, cooking utensils, tools, guns, books, and such domestic animals as cats, dogs, pigs, goats, chickens, sheep, and rabbits. During the 66-day voyage they endured cold, wet, cramped, and unsanitary conditions, and both food and water were strictly rationed. One person died along the way, and one baby was born on board the ship.

The *Mayflower* arrived in North America on November 11, 1620, first making landfall near the tip of Cape Cod, Massachusetts. The original charter that the passengers had received from their sponsors had granted them the right to settle on land further to the south, near the Hudson River in present-day New York City. With winter fast approaching, however, the passengers on the *Mayflower* felt that they had to find a place nearby to establish their colony. Since their charter did not cover their present location, they drew up a new charter before leaving the ship. This document, known as the Mayflower Compact, included provisions that allowed them to elect leaders and to make and enforce laws. Some historians consider it to be the first instance of a democratic government being established in America (*see the Primary Sources section for the text of the Mayflower Compact*). John Carver was elected to serve as the first governor of the new colony.

After the 41 adult male passengers had signed the Mayflower Compact, some of them went ashore and began exploring their surroundings under the guid-

Myths about the Pilgrims

A number of commonly held beliefs about the Pilgrims and the 1621 feast known as the "first Thanksgiving" have little basis in reality. Contemporary historians have traced the origin of many of these fictitious beliefs to the work of early authors and artists, who tended to use their imaginations to fill in gaps in the historical record. Here are the facts behind some popular myths about the Pilgrims:

The Pilgrims almost certainly did not land on Plymouth Rock. They never made reference to the rock in any of their writings, and it seems likely that they would have avoided it for fear that it would puncture the hull of the small wooden boat they took ashore. The 12-foot-wide boulder that once sat 40 feet from shore in Plymouth Harbor may have served as a landmark for early European explorers, but it was not anointed as the landing spot of the Pilgrims until a century later.

The Pilgrims did not really wear somber black clothing with white cuffs and square metal buckles. They used vegetable dyes to make clothing in a variety of colors—including red, yellow, purple, and green—and the buckles so often included in artistic renderings of the Pilgrims were not introduced until later in the 17th century.

The 1621 feast did not take place with all participants sitting around a groaning board, or a long wooden table draped in a white linen tablecloth. "Even if all the Pilgrims' furniture was brought out into the sunshine, most of the celebrants stood, squatted, or sat on the ground as they clustered around outdoor fires," historian Nathaniel Philbrick wrote in his book *Mayflower.*

There is no record of what foods were served at the 1621 feast, but the Pilgrims' meal certainly lacked several of the mainstays of modern Thanksgiving dinners. They may have eaten turkey, but they did not have access to the materials needed to make mashed potatoes, cranberry sauce, or pumpkin pie.

The Pilgrims are often depicted as male-female couples, perhaps reflecting the popular view of them as "parents" of the nation. But the reality was far different than this romantic image at the time of the 1621 feast. Of the 54 *Mayflower* passengers who survived the first year in America, only four were adult women, and nearly half were children under the age of 16.

ance of Captain Miles Standish. One of the passengers, William Bradford, described the area in his diary as "a hideous and desolate wilderness, full of wild beasts and wild men." Although the explorers found many signs of Native American inhabitants—including an abandoned village, tilled fields, and stockpiles of food and seeds—they did not make contact with many people. They searched the area for a month before finding a suitable site for their settlement, which they named Plymouth. They rushed to build a common house and several sod-covered dugout shelters and then hunkered down to try to survive the winter.

THE "FIRST THANKSGIVING"

The Pilgrims endured a very harsh first winter in the New World, and 46 colonists died from disease or starvation. Yet when the *Mayflower* returned to England that April, all of the surviving settlers decided to remain in America.

The Pilgrims' first formal introduction to the Native American peoples who lived in the region occurred in the early spring of 1621. On March 16, an Abenaki Indian named Samoset came to visit the Plymouth settlement. Samoset, who had learned the English language from visiting fishermen, arrived carrying two arrows—one pointed and the other blunt—to symbolize the choice his people and the newcomers faced between war and peace.

Samoset and some other Native American leaders of the region felt a strong inclination to make peace with the Pilgrims. Beginning in 1617, a plague had swept through the Native American communities of southern New England, wiping out around 90 percent of the population. Never having been exposed to European diseases like smallpox and chicken pox, the Indians had no natural immunity to them. Their diminished numbers put the tribes of southern New England in a relatively weak position compared to their neighbors, and thus increased their willingness to welcome the English settlers to their territory. The Pilgrims also benefited from the situation by locating their settlement on the site of the former Wampanoag village of Patuxet, which had been abandoned during the plague.

Shortly after his first visit, Samoset returned with Massasoit, the sachem or leader of the Wampanoag tribe. Massasoit and John Carver signed a peace treaty in which they agreed to come to each other's defense if they were attacked by the Narragansett Indians or other powerful rivals (*see the Primary Sources section for the text of the peace treaty*). Massasoit also left one of his people behind to keep an eye on the newcomers. Tisquantum, known to the Pilgrims as Squanto, knew how to speak English and served as the Pilgrims' interpreter and guide. He showed them how to plant corn, identify edible plants, and find and catch fish. Squanto's assistance proved invaluable to the colonists. According to William Bradford's *History of Plimoth Plantation,* the Pilgrims considered Squanto to be "a spetiall [special] instrument sent of God for their good beyond their expectation."

By the end of the summer of 1621—thanks in part to Squanto's assistance—the Pilgrims had built eleven strong houses and collected plenty of food to last through the winter. They had harvested such crops as corn, squash, beans, barley, and peas, and they had also caught good quantities of fish and shellfish. William Bradford, who had been elected governor of Plymouth Colony in April upon the death of John Carver, suggested that they celebrate their good fortune. He sent four men out "fowling," or hunting the ducks and geese that were then migrating through New England, and within a few hours

MASSASOIT AND HIS WARRIORS.

Wampanoag Indian leader Massasoit met with the Pilgrims in March 1621 and signed a peace treaty with them. This 1877 engraving, depicting a gathering of the two groups, was produced by Alfred Bobbett, based on a painting by Felix O. C. Darley.

Squanto (c. 1590-1622)

Tisquantum, more commonly known as Squanto, was born around 1590 in Patuxet, the Wampanoag Indian village that later became Plymouth, Massachusetts. In 1614 he and at least 28 other Wampanoag men were kidnapped and taken to Europe by the famous English explorer and trader Captain John Smith. Squanto was sold into slavery in Malaga, Spain, but he soon escaped and made his way to England.

After living in London for several years and learning the English language, Squanto agreed to serve as an interpreter and guide for Captain Thomas Dermer on an expedition to New England. Upon returning to his homeland in 1619, Squanto found Patuxet—once a thriving village of 2,000 people—abandoned due to a plague that had wiped out 90 percent of the Native American inhabitants of the region.

The following year, a small group of English men, women, and children arrived and began building a settlement on the site of Squanto's former village. Squanto served as a diplomat and interpreter during negotiations between the Wampanoag leader Massasoit and the newcomers. Once the two groups signed a peace treaty, Squanto agreed to remain with the Pilgrims to help them learn to plant crops and live off the land. His assistance proved crucial in ensuring the survival of the colony.

In the late summer of 1621, Squanto was taken prisoner by a rival tribe that hoped to disrupt the friendly relations between the Wampanoags and the Pilgrims. The Englishmen launched a successful armed rescue, demonstrating the strength of their alliance with Massasoit. Over the next year, Squanto used his influence with the colonists to increase his own power among the Wampanoags and neighboring tribes. By the time he died of disease in November 1622, however, his scheming had caused him to become estranged from his people.

---

they had killed enough birds to feed the settlement for a week. Then the Pilgrims began preparing a feast.

The Pilgrims had brought two separate traditions with them from England: the secular Harvest Home festival and the religious holy day of thanksgiving. The former was an annual celebration of a successful harvest that usually featured singing, dancing, games, and a hearty feast. The latter was an occasional solemn day of prayer and religious devotion that was intended to express gratitude for God's providence. The Pilgrims also recognized a related holy day of fasting and humiliation, which they viewed as a way to regain God's favor and obtain relief from misfortunes.

The exact date of the Pilgrims' feast is not known. It almost certainly took place sometime between September 21 and November 9, 1621, and most likely in early October. In many ways, the celebration that has been immortalized as the "First Thanksgiving" marked a new kind of holiday that departed from their earlier traditions. The Pilgrims never used the word "thanksgiving" to describe the event; since it included non-Christian guests and secular forms of recreation, it did not meet their definition of the term. It was not exactly a harvest festival, either, because the Pilgrims did not intend to make it an annual event. Although they gave thanks to God, it was mostly a joyous celebration of the survival of their colony against long odds.

This illustration depicts Squanto guiding one of the Pilgrims at Plymouth Colony.

The only information available to historians regarding the Pilgrims' 1621 feast comes from two surviving accounts of the event. Governor William Bradford described the celebration in his journal, and Edward Winslow, the colony's Indian ambassador, mentioned it in a letter to a friend back in England. Winslow's letter appeared in a collection of writings about the founding of Plymouth Colony called *Mourt's Relation*, which was published in London in 1622. Bradford eventually published his journal as a book called *Of Plimoth Plantation, 1620-1647* (*see the Primary Sources section for Bradford and Winslow's recollections*).

Winslow's account makes it clear that Massasoit and about 90 other Wampanoag Indians attended the feast. Some historians claim that the Pilgrims invited the local tribe to share in their celebration, as a way of expressing gratitude for the Indians' assistance to the colony. Other scholars, though, believe that the Wampanoags came to investigate when they heard the Pilgrims shooting their guns while "fowling." Upon learning that the colonists planned to host a celebration, Massasoit sent out a hunting party that soon returned with five deer to contribute to the feast.

The celebration lasted for three days. The Pilgrims and Wampanoags feasted on venison, wild fowl (possibly turkey, but more likely ducks, geese, and other migratory birds), fish and shellfish, wild berries, boiled pumpkins, corn cakes and puddings, and stews consisting of meat and vegetables. Their meal did not include potatoes, which had not yet been introduced to New England, or cranberry sauce, because they did not have any sugar to sweeten the tart berries. The celebrants also played games and engaged in diplomacy. The Englishmen performed military drills and showed off their marksmanship, while the Native Americans demonstrated traditional dances.

An Annual Holiday in New England

On November 10, 1621, shortly after the Pilgrims had held their famous harvest celebration, another ship arrived at Plymouth Colony. The *Fortune* brought 37 English passengers, nearly doubling the population of the settlement. Unfortunately, it did not bring many provisions, so the Pilgrims were forced to divide their hard-earned food stores in half in order to feed the newcomers.

The first recorded instance of the Pilgrims holding a religious thanksgiving, in accordance with their own definition of the term, took place on July 26, 1623. That summer had been hot and dry, and the near-drought conditions threatened to destroy the colonists' corn and other crops. Governor Bradford set aside a special day of fasting and prayer in hopes of gaining God's mercy. A short time later, as he recalled in his journal, it began "to rain with such sweet and gentle showers as gave them cause of rejoicing and blessing God's help; For which mercy, in time convenient, they also set apart a day of thanksgiving." This thanksgiving was a solemn, religious occasion and did not involve a feast.

In the decades following the arrival of the Pilgrims, English settlements in the New World underwent a rapid increase in number and size. The population of Plymouth Colony, for instance, grew from 300 in 1630 to reach 2,000 a decade later. By 1675 there were more than 100 English towns and villages in New England. During these years, the thanksgiving tradition spread beyond Plymouth and was adapted to local conditions. The colonies held public thanksgiving days for many different reasons at various times of the year. These occasions could be proclaimed by a colony's civil authorities or pro-

King Philip's War

The expansion of English settlements in New England created increased demand for land and other resources, which led to tension and armed conflict between the colonists and Native American peoples of the region. The 54-year peace between the Pilgrims and the Wampanoag Indians was but one casualty of these changing circumstances.

In June 1675 the Wampanoag leader Metacom, a son of Massasoit who was known to the colonists as Philip, led an alliance of Native American nations to war against the English. His goal was to drive the colonists out of his homeland. The bloody, 14-month-long conflict, which became known as King Philip's War, took the lives of an estimated 5,000 people, or about seven percent of the population of New England at that time. Native Americans accounted for up to three-quarters of those killed, and thousands more Indians were captured and sold into slavery in the West Indies.

During this violent struggle, the governor of Connecticut failed to proclaim an annual Thanksgiving Day for the first time in 25 years. When the colonial forces finally prevailed over the Indians, the white leaders of Connecticut declared August 12, 1676, a day of public thanksgiving to celebrate the end of the war. Connecticut has celebrated Thanksgiving without interruption every year since. A few days after the 1676 observance, colonial soldiers carried Philip's severed head into Plymouth and placed it on the palisades of the fort that had been built to protect the town; it remained on display in the town for more than 20 years. (*See the Primary Sources section for a proclamation in gratitude for the end of the war, issued by the governing council of Charlestown, Massachusetts.*)

King Philip's War marked the first chapter in a long history of conflict between European settlers and Native American peoples. In fact, many contemporary Native Americans associate the arrival of the English colonists with violent conquest and genocide, rather than peaceful cooperation. As a result, the Thanksgiving holiday has taken on a different meaning for them. Beginning in 1970, hundreds of Native Americans have gathered at the statue of Massasoit in Plymouth, Massachusetts, on Thanksgiving Day each year to raise public awareness of their alternative interpretation of the holiday.

posed by a church leader to a local congregation. They usually recognized specific positive events rather than general good fortune.

Within a generation, however, the longstanding European harvest festival and thanksgiving traditions began to evolve into an annual American holiday that

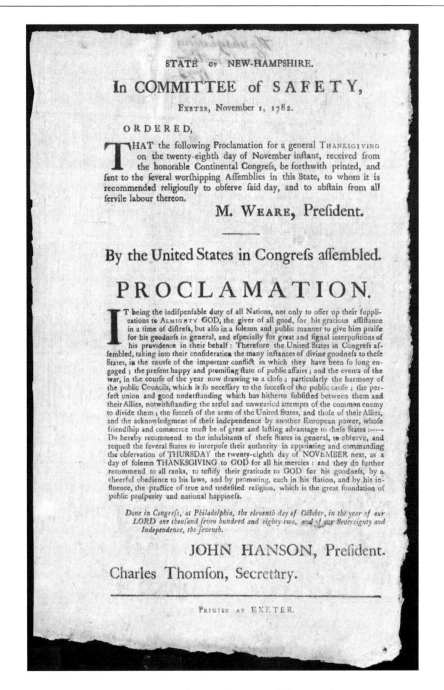

In gratitude for the successful conclusion of the Revolutionary War,
the Continental Congress issued this proclamation on October 11, 1782.
It set aside the following November 28 as a day of thanksgiving for all the states.

included elements of both. Some historians claim that this change originated in Connecticut during the 1640s, when the colonial governor started proclaiming a day of thanksgiving every autumn in gratitude for all the blessings the colony had received throughout the year. "This was the crucial innovation," Appelbaum wrote in *Thanksgiving*. "When Connecticut made Thanksgiving Day an annual festival for general causes ... a new holiday was born. Thanksgiving in Connecticut was held every autumn, not for special reasons, but in gratitude for the ordinary blessings of the 'year past' and for the 'fruits of the earth.' It was held whether the harvest was abundant or meager and regardless of events that had befallen the colony since the previous Thanksgiving Day."

By the 1680s Thanksgiving Day had evolved into an annual holiday throughout the English colonies in the New World. Most colonial governors proclaimed a special day every fall to thank God for the year's blessings. Since harvest time varied in different geographical areas, however, the colonies did not attempt to coordinate their celebrations. Thanksgiving Day observances generally began with a church service, during which the congregation would eagerly anticipate the reading of the governor's proclamation. Then everyone adjourned to their homes for a festive dinner with family and friends.

The Revolutionary Period

The colonies continued to observe an annual Thanksgiving Day into the 1700s. Among the earliest surviving printed proclamations dates back to 1723, when Governor William Dummer of Massachusetts Bay Colony set aside November 28 for residents to celebrate the holiday (*see the Primary Sources section for the text of Dummer's proclamation*). The colonies also continued to observe days of fasting during this period (*see the Primary Sources section for a proclamation of a fast issued by the governor of Massachusetts Bay Colony*). Some governors proclaimed an annual day of fasting every spring, while others proclaimed special days of fasting in response to specific misfortunes. On October 30, 1727, for example, frightened residents of Massachusetts Bay Colony held a special day of fasting and prayer following an earthquake. In general, though, Thanksgiving gradually became less solemn and more celebratory during the 18th century, and feasting assumed a more prominent role in the observance.

As the American colonies moved toward seeking independence from England, the annual Thanksgiving proclamations took on political overtones.

Loyalists used the occasion to praise the king and plead for his favor, while Patriots used it to criticize the crown and the various taxes and restrictions it had placed on the colonies. On October 22, 1774, the Massachusetts colonial assembly broke the tradition of proclaiming a day of thanksgiving under the authority of the King of England. Instead, Massachusetts declared December 15 a day of thanksgiving by the order of John Hancock, president of the provincial congress, without any British input or approval. Most significantly, it was the first colonial thanksgiving proclamation that did not conclude with the words "God Save the King."

During the Revolutionary War, the American colonies often proclaimed days of thanksgiving for victories in battle. On November 1, 1777, for example, the Continental Congress proclaimed a day of thanksgiving to be held on December 18 in gratitude for the Patriots' victory at Saratoga. This historic proclamation, written by Samuel Adams, was the first holiday to be designated by a national authority for all 13 American states (*see the Primary Sources section for the text of the proclamation*). Rather than creating an annual holiday, however, it followed in the tradition of proclaiming special days of thanks for positive events.

General George Washington's troops celebrated the Thanksgiving holiday of 1777 at their winter encampment at Valley Forge. One of his soldiers, Lieutenant Colonel Henry Dearborn, remembered the occasion in a diary entry: "This is Thanksgiving Day, but God knows we have very little to keep it with, this being the third day we have been without flour or bread and are living on a high uncultivated hill, in huts and tents, lying on the cold ground. Upon the whole I think all we have to be thankful for is that we are alive and not in the grave with many of our friends."

The rebellious colonies observed Thanksgiving as an annual event throughout the remainder of the war years. The Treaty of Paris ended the Revolutionary War in 1783. The following autumn, the Continental Congress set aside October 19, 1784, as a national day of gratitude for peace. But no further Thanksgiving Days were proclaimed until the Constitution created the United States government.

The first Congress of the United States considered adopting a proposal calling for a national Thanksgiving holiday. The effort to create such a holiday was led by Elias Boudinot of New Jersey, who had served as president of the Continental Congress during the Revolution. But the proposal met with stiff resistance from some members of the legislative body, especially Thomas

In this illustration from *Harper's Weekly*, November 20, 1869, cartoonist Thomas Nast celebrates the U.S. Congress' ratification of the 14th Amendment to the Constitution, which guaranteed citizenship rights to all Americans, no matter their country of origin.

Tucker of South Carolina (*see the Primary Sources section for the text of the arguments before Congress*).

The arguments against creating a national Thanksgiving holiday varied. Some members of Congress argued that the power to proclaim holidays belonged to the states, and that the creation of a national Thanksgiving Day would amount to federal government interference in local affairs. Others declared that Thanksgiving Day was a religious observance, and thus fell outside the control of the secular government. Finally, some members claimed that thanksgiving was an English tradition that should be discontinued in the independent United States.

Shortly after taking office as the first U.S. president under the Constitution, George Washington issued the first Thanksgiving proclamation for the new nation, setting aside November 26, 1789, as a national holiday (*see the Prima-*

ry Sources section for the text of Washington's proclamation). Although Wash-
ington continued to proclaim an annual Thanksgiving Day throughout the
remainder of his presidency, many prominent people still objected to the idea.

Later presidents disagreed about whether Thanksgiving should be a federal
holiday and, if so, when it should be observed. Thomas Jefferson refused to
proclaim a national Thanksgiving Day during his presidency because he felt
that it violated the constitutional separation of church and state. "Civil powers alone have been given to the President of the United States, and no
authority to direct the religious exercises of his constituents," he explained in
a draft of his famous 1802 letter to a group of Baptists (*see the Primary Sources
section for the final text of Jefferson's letter*). James Madison, on the other hand,
believed that a national Thanksgiving was acceptable under the Constitution,
as long as the federal government did not require citizens to participate in
religious services. He proclaimed a national holiday in 1815 in gratitude for
the U.S. victory in the War of 1812.

*T*HANKSGIVING IN THE STATES

As lawmakers and officials within the federal government argued about the
propriety of making Thanksgiving a national holiday, many states took the
initiative and established an official date for their own residents to give
thanks. By 1800, Thanksgiving Day was observed annually throughout New
England. In 1817 New York became the first state to adopt it as a legal
statewide holiday, and the governors of several other states in the region soon
followed suit. In addition, many local areas continued to hold annual harvest
festivals in the fall.

In the early 19th century, a typical New England Thanksgiving began with a
morning church service. The reading of the governor's proclamation was the
highlight of the service for many people. Some proclamations addressed con-
tentious political issues, while others discussed general causes for gratitude.
Northern governors and preachers often used the occasion to speak out
against the evils of slavery, for example.

After the conclusion of the church service, most New England families gathered for a large meal. The men might take part in a turkey shoot afterward,
while the children played outdoors or went sledding. The evening's festivities
might include attending a dance or playing parlor games like charades or

Thanksgiving in Hawaii

Despite their great distance from the mainland, the people of the Hawaiian Islands celebrated Thanksgiving earlier than many U.S. states and territories. When Protestant missionaries traveled to the islands from New England in the early 1800s, they brought the tradition with them. Historians claim that the first observances of the holiday in Hawaii took place among these missionaries on December 6, 1838.

Over the next decade, Thanksgiving celebrations became larger and more elaborate and involved the participation of increasing numbers of Hawaiians. In 1849 King Kamehameha III set aside December 31 as a national Thanksgiving Day for Hawaii. Observances included a performance by students from all of the Protestant schools and a festive luau featuring a meal of fish and tropical fruits.

As the nation of Hawaii increased its ties to the United States, American citizens there maintained the tradition of Thanksgiving, especially after President Abraham Lincoln declared it a national holiday in 1864. The holiday has been celebrated annually by Hawaiians since the islands were annexed by the United States in 1898.

blind man's bluff (*see the Primary Sources section for stories of early 19th-century Thanksgiving celebrations in New England by Harriet Beecher Stowe and Louisa May Alcott*).

Even though Thanksgiving was not a national holiday at this time, the tradition gradually spread westward as people carried it with them from New England to frontier states and territories. Michigan proclaimed its first Thanksgiving holiday in 1824, followed by Ohio, Wisconsin, and Illinois in 1839. Regular Thanksgiving observances spread to Iowa in 1844 and to California in 1847 (*see the Primary Sources section for recollections of Thanksgiving observances in California during the 1850s and in Nebraska during the 1870s*). Many residents of the South resisted the holiday, however, because of its origins in New England and its association with the abolitionist movement. The first southern state to celebrate Thanksgiving was Louisiana, which adopted the holiday in 1846.

The celebration of Thanksgiving was not well coordinated during the first half of the 19th century. In some states, governors issued a proclamation one year but not the next. Furthermore, the date set aside for the holiday differed from state to state, making it hard for families to time their celebrations. By the 1850s, Thanksgiving had attained the status of an annual legal holiday only in New England, a few mid-Atlantic states, and Texas.

CREATION OF THE NATIONAL HOLIDAY

Disagreements over the issues of slavery and states' rights created a rift between the northern and southern parts of the United States in the mid-1800s. Many people in both sections of the country viewed this situation with alarm. They looked for any sort of common cause that could unite Americans and help them overcome their differences.

Sarah Josepha Hale, the editor of the leading women's magazine of the day, strongly believed that the creation of a national Thanksgiving holiday would serve such a purpose. If the entire country—North and South—could be prevailed upon to celebrate the nation's many blessings together, she argued, then it might be possible to avoid a civil war.

In 1846 Hale launched a determined campaign to make Thanksgiving a legal holiday throughout the United States, which would be celebrated annually on a uniform date. She wrote hundreds of letters to prominent people across the country—from politicians and religious leaders to writers and other opinion makers—in an attempt to generate support for her cause. She also promoted Thanksgiving in the pages of her magazine, *Godey's Lady's Book,* through editorials, recipes, and sentimental stories about long-lost relatives returning to the family home (*see the Primary Sources section for the text of one of Hale's editorials*). Some historians claim that Hale's efforts helped Americans in various parts of the country to understand and appreciate the traditional New England-style Thanksgiving celebration.

But Hale did not succeed in convincing the president to create a national holi-

Sarah Josepha Hale

Sarah Josepha Hale (1788-1879)

The person most responsible for turning Thanksgiving into a national holiday was Sarah Josepha Buell Hale. She was born on October 24, 1788, near Newport, New Hampshire. At a time when educational opportunities were limited for women, she received a solid education at home from her mother and her college-educated brother. Around 1806 she opened a private school, and she taught there until she married lawyer David Hale in 1813.

Upon the death of her husband in 1822, Hale was forced to find work in order to support their five children. Her lifelong love of books and reading led her to become an author herself, and she was soon contributing articles and poetry to popular magazines. In 1827 Hale published her first novel, *Northwood: A Tale of New England,* which contrasted the lifestyles and values of Americans living in the North and South. One chapter provided a sentimental description of a Thanksgiving celebration in a New Hampshire farm family. In 1830 Hale published a collection of poetry called *Poems for Our Children,* which featured the perennial favorite "Mary Had a Little Lamb."

In 1837 Hale accepted a position as editor of a women's magazine called *Godey's Lady's Book.* She shifted its focus toward more intellectual topics, and it soon became the most widely circulated American magazine of its time. Hale featured literary contributions from major authors and published editorials on a number of social reform issues, especially those of special concern to women. For instance, she denounced the wearing of tight corsets as harmful to women's health.

Hale also used her position of influence to campaign for the creation of a national Thanksgiving holiday. She pleaded her case in hundreds of letters to the president of the United States and the governors of every state. She also published editorials, stories, and recipes in her magazine to encourage readers across the country to celebrate Thanksgiving in traditional New England style. Hale published her last column as the editor of *Godey's Lady's Book* in December 1877. The woman recognized today as the "mother of Thanksgiving" died on April 30, 1879, at the age of 90.

day before 1861, when the South seceded from the Union to start the Civil War. As the war dragged on, both sides proclaimed special days of thanksgiving to express their gratitude for successes in battle. On September 18, 1862, for example, President Jefferson Davis issued a national Thanksgiving proclamation for the Confederate States of America following the southern victory in the Battle of Bull Run (*see the Primary Sources section for the text of Davis's first Thanksgiving proclamation*). Many people in the South, who had rejected Thanksgiving as a northern holiday in the past, then rushed to embrace the occasion with patriotic zeal (*see the Primary Sources section for the text of a Confederate Thanksgiving sermon*).

Hale continued her letter-writing campaign during the war years, and one letter finally succeeded in convincing President Lincoln to adopt her recommendation (*see the Primary Sources section for the text of Hale's letter*). On October 3, 1863, following the Union victory in the Battle of Gettysburg, Lincoln declared that the last Thursday of November should be set aside each year as a national day of Thanksgiving. The proclamation emphasized the president's wish that the holiday be celebrated by all Americans, whether they lived in the North or the South, in gratitude for the country's many blessings. Although the text was actually written by Secretary of State William Seward, who had issued four Thanksgiving proclamations when he had served as the governor of New York, Lincoln's signature appeared on the document (*see the Primary Sources section for the text of the proclamation*).

Thanksgiving thus became a national holiday in the United States, 242 years after the Pilgrims' feast. By creating the holiday in the middle of the Civil War, Lincoln imparted it with new meaning and increased its significance in American life. For many people, Thanksgiving gained associations with hope, patriotism, and national destiny.

From 1863 onward, every U.S. president has respected Lincoln's precedent and proclaimed a national Thanksgiving holiday in November of each year. The governors of most states followed the lead of the federal government and established the same day as a legal holiday. Immediately after the Civil War, however, a few southern states continued to resist what they viewed as a northern tradition. For example, Texas Governor Oran Milo Roberts famously refused to proclaim a Thanksgiving holiday for his state in 1879, declaring that "it's a damned Yankee institution anyhow." Over time, though, as the nation's wounds began to heal, Thanksgiving gained popularity in the South as well.

THE "FIRST THANKSGIVING" REDISCOVERED

Throughout the 18th and early 19th centuries, the story of the Pilgrims and their 1621 harvest celebration was largely forgotten and did not play a role in popular celebrations of Thanksgiving. Instead, most Americans simply observed the holiday in the New England tradition, with church services, family reunions, and large meals. The only place where the Pilgrims received much attention was in Plymouth, Massachusetts. Beginning in 1769, the town's residents held an annual celebration of the Pilgrims' landing on December 21. This holiday, known as Forefathers' Day, featured an elaborate dinner and cannons firing in tribute. Forefathers' Day was discontinued during the Revolutionary War, but observances resumed in 1793.

The Pilgrims first began claiming a place in the public imagination in 1820, when the famous orator Daniel Webster presented a moving tribute to them at a bicentennial celebration of their arrival in the New World. Webster's speech helped elevate the Pilgrims to iconic status as "forefathers of the nation" in the eyes of many Americans. Although the English colony at Jamestown, Virginia, had been established earlier, Webster helped draw people's attention toward the founders of Plymouth Colony instead (*see the Primary Sources section for an excerpt of Webster's speech*).

The 200th anniversary of the Pilgrims' landing also inspired the residents of Plymouth to organize the Pilgrim Society and the uniformed Standish Guards. The Pilgrim Society was instrumental in preserving Plymouth Rock as a symbol of the Pilgrims' landing. The society also played a role in building Pilgrim Hall—a museum of Pilgrim history that was dedicated in 1824—and the National Monument to the Forefathers. This 81-foot statue features a central figure of Faith, which inspired the Pilgrims' journey to America, surrounded by four smaller figures representing the values of Morality, Education, Law, and Liberty.

The Pilgrims' reputation grew following the bicentennial celebration and Webster's speech, but their connection with the Thanksgiving holiday remained distant for another two decades. In 1841, though, historian Alexander Young published a book called *Chronicles of the Pilgrim Forefathers*. This work contained Edward Winslow's account of the Pilgrims' 1621 harvest celebration. The Winslow letter had been published before, but Young clarified its authorship and identified the feast it described as the predecessor of New England's Thanksgiving holiday tradition.

In an explanatory footnote, Young referred to the Pilgrims' celebration as the "first Thanksgiving" and speculated that their feast had included turkey (*see the Primary Sources section for an excerpt from Young's book*). Historians have since determined that this marked the earliest scholarly reference to any event as the "first Thanksgiving." As it turned out, Young's rediscovery and interpretation of the 1621 event had far-reaching effects. Nancy Brennan, executive director of Plimoth Plantation, described the impact of Young's work in *1621: A New Look at Thanksgiving:* "Back in the nineteenth century, one paragraph of only 115 words in one letter written in 1621 about a harvest gathering inspired the growth of an American tradition that became a national holiday: Thanksgiving."

AMERICA EMBRACES THE PILGRIMS

In the aftermath of the Civil War, the story of the Pilgrims provided the reunified country with a valuable sense of shared history. "The states needed heroes, myths, and legends to make them one nation," Appelbaum noted. "To fill this need, New England offered the Pilgrims and the first Thanksgiving. Here was a third holiday for the nation to celebrate together along with Washington's birthday and the Fourth of July."

By the 1890s, two more historic events had helped to cement the bond between the Pilgrims and Thanksgiving in American culture. First, the Indian Wars came to an end and America's western frontier was declared closed. When stories about violent confrontations between pioneers and Native Americans in the West no longer dominated the news of the day, the image of the Pilgrims and the Wampanoags sharing a peaceful meal at the "first Thanksgiving" began to seem more plausible.

Second, immigration to the United States increased dramatically and underwent some fundamental changes in character. In the early 1800s, the vast majority of the U.S. population hailed from western Europe or Africa. The late 1800s, however, saw a tremendous wave of immigrants from other parts of the world. Between 1880 and 1920, for instance, more than 27 million people entered the United States from such previously underrepresented areas as southern and eastern Europe, the Middle East, and Mexico. These new immigrants introduced new languages, religions, and customs to their adopted homeland. This situation stirred up anti-immigrant feelings, even among people who had arrived in the United States only a generation or two earlier. Around the same time, the Industrial Revolution drew the U.S. population away from rural areas and into large cities with the promise of jobs in mills and factories.

All of these changes caused many Americans of longer standing to worry about the loss of their cultural traditions and way of life. Some people responded by emphasizing their roots to the nation's founders. A number of patriotic societies formed during this period, including the Daughters of the American Revolution and the General Society of Mayflower Descendants. These and other organizations soon engaged in efforts to "Americanize" the new immigrants by assimilating them into the established culture.

In this environment, the Pilgrims became a valuable tool to help teach new immigrants about American history, culture, and values. They were often portrayed in secular terms as the nation's original immigrants to America, shaped by many of the same goals and experiences as later generations of immigrants. Education reformers, in particular, latched onto the story of the "first Thanksgiving" as a way to impart a sense of history, patriotism, and citizenship to schoolchildren.

As the Thanksgiving holiday approached each November, schools across the country began to focus lesson plans and class projects on the Pilgrims. Children recited Felicia Hemans's famous poem about the Pilgrims' landing in Plymouth, constructed Pilgrim hats out of paper, made dioramas of the 1621

A poor immigrant family eating Thanksgiving dinner on a park bench in New York City, as drawn by artist William St. John Harper for *Harper's Weekly,* November 29, 1884.

feast, sang songs like "We Gather Together" and "Over the River and through the Woods," or performed in Thanksgiving plays and pageants (*see the Primary Sources section for the text of Hemans's poem and the lyrics to these songs*). The reformers hoped that generating enthusiasm for Thanksgiving among children would encourage their parents to adopt American holiday customs as well.

Over time, many of these school activities became holiday traditions, and the Pilgrims became the most recognizable symbol of Thanksgiving. In the face of the rapid changes taking place at the turn of the 20th century, many Americans embraced the Pilgrims and the "first Thanksgiving" as a way to create a sense of stability and connection with the past. "From a tool used to teach schoolchildren and immigrants, this simplified view of Thanksgiving has become a familiar symbol in American culture, used in all sorts of media from cartoons to greeting cards," Karin Goldstein noted on the Plimoth Plantation Web site. "It is important to remember that this view is part of the history of the holiday, rather than historic fact."

Events surrounding the 1921 tercentenary celebration of the Pilgrims' arrival demonstrated the level of national reverence for the early English colonists. The United States government issued three commemorative postage stamps to mark the occasion: a one-cent stamp bearing a likeness of the *Mayflower;* a two-cent stamp depicting the Pilgrims' landing at Plymouth; and a five-cent stamp illustrating the signing of the Mayflower Compact. By this time, the story of the Pilgrims was so well known that these stamps were the first ever issued without the words "United States" or the initials "U.S." on them. The government also issued a special Pilgrim Tercentenary half-dollar coin, with a portrait of William Bradford on the front and a depiction of the *Mayflower* on the back.

Plymouth organized a number of events to mark the anniversary. The town undertook a waterfront beautification and renewal project, for instance, that involved tearing down a wharf and restoring Plymouth Rock, complete with a new portico. The ceremonies also included speeches by Massachusetts Governor Calvin Coolidge and U.S. Senator Henry Cabot Lodge, and a pageant titled *The Pilgrim Spirit* by Harvard drama professor George Pierce Baker.

Parades and Public Celebrations

Although Thanksgiving became more closely associated with the Pilgrims in the late 1800s, it also lost some of its religious elements around this time. As the holiday expanded outside of New England, many Americans wanted to

This photo depicts the "Royal Progress" segment of a pageant held in Plymouth, Massachusetts, to celebrate the 300th anniversary of the Pilgrims' landing.

create their own traditions. In addition, a growing number of people worked long hours in the nation's factories and urban centers, and Thanksgiving was one of only four legal holidays that were recognized by employers (the others were George Washington's Birthday, Independence Day, and Christmas). With so little time off, many Americans viewed Thanksgiving as a rare opportunity for travel and recreation. As a result of these factors, the holiday generally became less of a holy observance and more of a festive and fun-loving celebration toward the end of the century.

Thanksgiving had begun to develop a rowdy side as early as the 1840s, when poor and working-class Americans in some areas used the holiday as an excuse to make mischief. Children in large cities often wore masks or dressed in old, ragged clothes and paraded from house to house, demanding candy or coins from residents. Historians believe that this custom may have derived from the English tradition of "mumming," or going door-to-door in costume begging for treats.

Among the predecessors of the modern-day Thanksgiving parade were the Fantastical parades of the second half of the 19th century. Groups of working-class men in urban areas formed companies known as Fantastics or Fantasticals. The members of these companies dressed up in flamboyant costumes of women's clothing and paraded through the streets of several major cities on Thanksgiving and other holidays. The largest parades took place in New York City, where more than 50 Fantastical companies—known by such colorful names as the Ham Guard Warriors, Oli Bolis, Sleetville Slenderfoot Army, and Gilhooley Musketeers—marched through the streets during the 1870s and 1880s. The cities of eastern and central Pennsylvania were also home to many Fantastical companies. The parades usually ended in city parks, where the men held picnics or gala balls that lasted late into the night.

Groups of children known as Ragamuffins often followed behind the Fantastical parades. The Ragamuffins wore masks or dressed in rags and paraded through the streets blowing horns and begging for change from passersby. While observers generally accepted the Fantasticals as a harmless form of merriment, many people objected to the participation of children in the parades. Reformers argued that allowing children to beg in the streets instilled poor values.

Military parades also made a brief appearance among the Thanksgiving festivities during the late 1800s. Historians speculate that this custom grew out of the longstanding tradition of declaring special days of thanksgiving in gratitude for victory in battle. In New York City, middle- and upper-class men formed groups known as target companies. These groups dressed up in fancy uniforms and paraded to the outskirts of town, where they held marksmanship contests for prizes. Unlike the Fantasticals, who usually partied late into the night, these men usually rejoined their families in time for Thanksgiving dinner. Military-style parades also took place in such cities as Philadelphia and Pittsburgh, Pennsylvania; Savannah, Georgia; San Francisco, California; and Honolulu, Hawaii.

Public tolerance for drunken, rowdy Thanksgiving celebrations declined in the 1890s, as the nation suffered through a period of high unemployment and violent labor disputes. The Fantastical parades gradually declined in popularity until they finally disappeared in the 1910s. Despite the efforts of reformers, however, the Ragamuffin parades continued until the 1930s. At that time, Halloween emerged as the holiday in which wearing costumes and begging for treats was deemed acceptable.

The 1920s saw the introduction of formal Thanksgiving Day parades organized by major retailers as a way to generate enthusiasm for Christmas shopping. Gimbel's department store in Philadelphia started the tradition by hosting a parade on Thanksgiving Day in 1921. The J. L. Hudson Company

Wartime Thanksgivings

For many Americans, the Thanksgiving holiday takes on added significance during times when the United States is at war. Such times of national challenge and unity encourage people to appreciate the American principles and values that the military is charged to defend. As a result, some of the most memorable Thanksgiving celebrations in U.S. history have taken place during wartime.

During World War I, the American people were asked to contribute to the war effort by rationing certain materials. The Thanksgiving meal underwent adjustments during the war years, as Americans tried to reduce their consumption of meat, fat, wheat, and sugar in order to make these items available to feed the troops. Many families grew their own vegetables in "victory gardens" and incorporated these foods into their Thanksgiving meals. On Thanksgiving Day of 1917, thousands of Americans across the country gathered at 4:00 P.M. Eastern time to sing "The Star-Spangled Banner" (see the Primary Sources section for the text of President Woodrow Wilson's Thanksgiving proclamation following the World War I armistice).

During World War II, the Defense Department worked hard to ensure that all U.S. soldiers received real turkey dinners on Thanksgiving, no matter where they were stationed, to reinforce the idea that they were fighting for the American ideals of freedom and democracy. In 1942 hundreds of U.S. soldiers gathered in Plymouth, England, to pay homage to the Pilgrims, and hundreds more attended a Thanksgiving service at Westminster Abbey that featured the singing of hymns and a reading of President Franklin D. Roosevelt's proclamation. King George and Queen Elizabeth also invited 200 American officers to Buckingham Palace that year for the first official British recognition of the U.S. holiday. One of the most memorable Thanksgiving celebrations in history took place in 1945, when the nation expressed gratitude for peace and welcomed millions of American soldiers home from the war (see the Primary Sources section for President Harry S. Truman's proclamation following the end of the war).

sponsored a parade in Detroit beginning in 1923, and Macy's department store launched a competing parade in New York City in 1924.

Many employees at Macy's were first-generation immigrants to the United States, and they wanted to celebrate American holidays in the same festive style that they had enjoyed in Europe. For the first few years, the Macy's parade consisted of floats pulled by teams of horses, marching bands, employ-

RIDGEMONT PUBLIC LIBRARY
MT. VICTORY, OHIO

ees dressed up in costumes, and an assortment of live animals. In 1927 Macy's added the most distinctive feature to its parade: giant helium balloons in the likeness of popular cartoon characters, such as Felix the Cat. Created by the famous puppeteer and cartoonist Tony Sarg, the giant character balloons increased the popularity of the parade and helped make Macy's the world's second-largest consumer of helium (after the United States government). The 1928 parade inaugurated a long tradition of releasing hundreds of smaller balloons that earned the bearer a cash reward if they were found and returned to the department store (*see the Primary Sources section for a more detailed account of the history of the Macy's Parade*).

The appearance of Santa Claus, usually in a sleigh pulled by reindeer, is the highlight of Thanksgiving Day parades that continue to be held in modern-day Baltimore, Chicago, Detroit, and New York City. A total of over four mil-

The "Super Grover" balloon at Macy's Thanksgiving Day Parade in 2005.

lion spectators attend these parades each year, and 100 million more people watch them on television. They have come to symbolize the bounty of the holiday season in the minds of many Americans. The parades were originally held in the afternoon, but they soon moved to the morning hours in order to accommodate another relatively new addition to Thanksgiving observances: football games.

Sports on Thanksgiving

Sports have been a part of Thanksgiving celebrations since the Pilgrims' time. Historians speculate that the "first Thanksgiving" may have featured marksmanship contests and games like stool ball, in which one player defends a stool while other players throw balls at it and try to knock it over. Later celebrations of the holiday in New England included a wide variety of sporting activities, from horse, foot, and bicycle races to turkey shoots and sledding.

Football began its long association with Thanksgiving in the 1880s, when a number of college teams started scheduling their games to coincide with the holiday. The Intercollegiate Football Association, for instance, scheduled its first-ever championship game on Thanksgiving Day of 1876 (Yale defeated Princeton for the title). By the turn of the century an estimated 10,000 high school, college, and athletic club football teams played games on Thanksgiving. Many of these games featured hotly contested match-ups between traditional rivals. Tulane University often played Louisiana State University in a battle of New Orleans rivals, for instance, while the University of Kansas played the University of Missouri for bragging rights in Kansas City. Neighborhood football games also became popular around this time (*see the Primary Sources section for an article on the modern resurgence of this tradition*).

The decision to schedule football games on Thanksgiving Day, however, often aroused controversy. Some people complained about the rowdy atmosphere it created in college towns over the holiday weekend. Others felt that it detracted from the meaning of the holiday, which had traditionally centered around the expression of gratitude for the blessings of home and food and family.

By the 1920s, however, commercial radio was able to broadcast football games into people's homes. Football soon came to be regarded as an important part of Thanksgiving observances, particularly among men. While women gathered in the kitchen to cook, serve, and clean up after the family

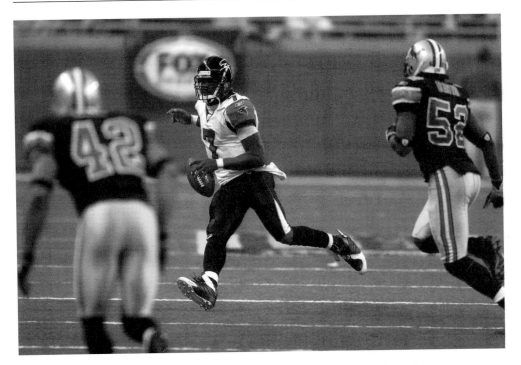

Nationally televised professional football games, such as this
2005 contest between the Atlanta Falcons and Detroit Lions, have become
a fixture of modern Thanksgiving celebrations.

meal, men held their own gatherings—around the radio to listen to the day's football game. Some contemporary historians claim that football thus gave the holiday new meaning as a social bonding event for men, especially after the arrival of television.

The National Football League (NFL) became part of America's holiday football tradition in 1934, when the Detroit Lions hosted the Chicago Bears in the league's first-ever Thanksgiving Day game. The new owner of the Lions, George A. Richards, came up with the idea as a way to earn more money from his investment in the franchise. The Lions have hosted a game on Thanksgiving almost every year since (except when play was suspended during World War II), making it one of the NFL's longest-standing traditions.

The first television broadcast of the Lions' Thanksgiving game took place in 1956. A decade later, the Dallas Cowboys began hosting an annual game on Thanksgiving Day as well. NFL owners have occasionally proposed rotating hosting duties for the lucrative Thanksgiving games among all the teams in the league. Since the Lions have long ranked among the worst NFL teams, some football fans have also favored this idea. As of 2007, though, the league had steadfastly refused to change the time-honored tradition.

COMMERCIALISM AND FRANKSGIVING

By the turn of the 20th century, Thanksgiving had completed its transition from a regional to a national holiday. Americans across the country enjoyed celebrating the holiday with family reunions and feasts, as well as parades and football games. People in the South who had long resisted what they viewed as a Yankee tradition adopted Thanksgiving and made it their own. As the formerly Protestant holiday became more festive and less religious, increasing numbers of American Catholics and Jews felt comfortable observing it as well. Finally, enthusiasm among schoolchildren helped spread the tradition to new immigrant families. Many of these families incorporated their own foods and customs into Thanksgiving celebrations.

After going through its rowdy phase of the late 1800s, the Thanksgiving holiday also became a quieter, domestic observance in the early 1900s. The growth of commerce and industry drew many Americans into urban areas and away from family farms during this era. These changes contributed to a growing sense of dislocation and nostalgia for a simpler, more whole-some existence. Thanksgiving helped many people address these feelings by giving them a chance to travel home and spend quality time with their loved ones.

Thanksgiving also became associated with the start of the Christmas shopping season in the first few decades of the 20th century. Thanksgiving itself had been a minor gift-giving occasion a hundred years earlier, with books and especially Bibles often serving as tokens of the holiday. That custom disappeared by the mid-1800s, however, when Christmas evolved into an occasion for bestowing an abundance of gifts, particularly on children.

By the early 20th century, Christmas had become very important to the fortunes of America's retailers. Christmas advertisements dominated newspapers and magazines in the weeks before the holiday, and several major department stores began sponsoring Thanksgiving Day parades—complete with appearances by Santa Claus—to generate excitement about Christmas shopping. So

The Presidential Turkey Pardon

Of all the customs surrounding the Thanksgiving holiday, one of the most lighthearted is the official turkey pardon. In a special ceremony held in the Rose Garden of the White House each year since 1982, the president of the United States has offered one lucky bird a reprieve from being served up as a holiday dinner.

No one knows for certain how the tradition got started, or when the first unofficial turkey pardon may have occurred. Some historians claim that Abraham Lincoln once agreed to spare the life of a turkey that had become like a pet to his son Tad. It is known that the National Turkey Federation launched its annual tradition of presenting a live turkey to the resident of the White House in 1947. There is no evidence that President Harry S. Truman issued that bird a pardon, and the fate of the live turkeys presented to his successors is uncertain as well. In 1982 President Ronald Reagan bestowed what is thought to be the first turkey pardon since Lincoln, and the custom has continued every year since then.

The turkeys that appear in the annual Rose Garden ceremony are specially raised breeder toms (male turkeys intended for breeding purposes rather than for human consumption). They generally hatch the preceding April and spend their first few months living in an air-conditioned barn. In August, when the toms weigh about 25 pounds, the National Turkey Federation selects a half-dozen candidates based on their excellent coloring, plumage, and temperament. These birds then undergo several months of training to familiarize them with things they might encounter at the White House, such as men in business suits, camera flashes, clapping sounds, and petting.

A few days before Thanksgiving, the chairman of the National Turkey Federation selects two birds—the presidential turkey, and an alternate that can be substituted if necessary—to make the trip to Washington. After appearing in the White House ceremony and receiving the presidential pardon, the turkeys are sent to a local petting zoo, Frying Pan Park at Kidwell Farm in Herndon, Virginia, to live out their lives. Visitors to the farm often expect to see a large flock of pardoned turkeys, but the birds' enormous weight (around 50 pounds) usually causes them to die of natural causes within a year. Still, the presidential turkeys are more fortunate than the 50 million birds that Americans consume annually for Thanksgiving dinner.

many retailers began holding sales on the day after Thanksgiving that many Americans came to consider it as the official start of the Christmas season. In fact, the day after Thanksgiving became known in the retail industry as Black

This turkey was presented to President Lyndon B. Johnson for Thanksgiving 1967. It is likely that this bird ended up on the White House dinner table that year. It was not until 1982 that presidents began pardoning turkeys as an annual tradition.

Friday, because it marked the point in the year when many retailers' annual income shifted from red (the color bookkeepers use to show a loss) to black (the color used to show a profit).

The growing economic importance of the holiday season was underscored during the Great Depression, which placed a terrible financial burden on the American people in the 1930s. The reduction in consumers' income levels during these years limited their spending on non-essential goods. This, in turn, took a heavy toll on the nation's retailers. In 1939 a major industry group, the Retail Dry Goods Association, came up with an innovative scheme to increase holiday sales and thus stimulate the U.S. economy. The group suggested moving the date of Thanksgiving—which was scheduled to fall on November 30 that year—forward one week in order to extend the holiday season and give consumers more time for Christmas shopping.

At this point in history, the national Thanksgiving holiday was established each year by presidential proclamation. Beginning with Abraham Lincoln in 1863, every president had followed tradition and set aside the fourth Thursday in November as Thanksgiving Day. But this date was not fixed by law, so the president could use his own discretion and proclaim a different date for the national holiday. In hopes of lifting the U.S. economy out of the Depression, President Franklin D. Roosevelt went along with the plan advanced by the Retail Dry Goods Association. On October 31, 1939, Roosevelt announced that the federal government would recognize Thanksgiving on November 23, rather than November 30, that year (*see the Primary Sources section for the text of Roosevelt's proclamation*).

The president's decision to change the date of Thanksgiving appeared on the front pages of newspapers across the country. For the most part, the American people reacted negatively to the announcement, which created confusion and turmoil among many segments of the populace. Many colleges and universities had already scheduled football games for the original Thanksgiving Day, and schools across the country had already arranged vacations to coincide with the usual date of the holiday. The White House received thousands of letters and telegrams from angry citizens protesting the change. Republicans in Congress seized on the controversial decision and condemned the Democratic president for being disrespectful of long-held traditions. Pundits soon coined a new term for Roosevelt's holiday: Franksgiving.

The governors of some states responded to the president's unpopular decision by declaring November 30 as a holiday in their states. In all, 23 states went along with the president and celebrated Thanksgiving on November 23, while 22 states defied the president and celebrated the holiday on the fourth Thursday in November. This situation created problems for some families, as members living in neighboring states were unable to spend Thanksgiving Day together. Three states—Colorado, Mississippi, and Texas—observed both November 23 and November 30 as government holidays.

Despite the protests and confusion, Roosevelt proclaimed the earlier Thanksgiving Day again in 1940 and 1941. By this time, polls showed that 62 percent of the American people disapproved of the change. Furthermore, surveys conducted by the U.S. Commerce Department showed no increase in retail sales that could be attributed to the earlier date of Thanksgiving. Confronted with this information, Roosevelt acknowledged that moving the holiday had been a mistake. On November 26, 1941, the U.S. Congress passed a law establishing Thanksgiving as a federal holiday to be held annually on the fourth Thursday in November (*see the Primary Sources section for the text of the law*). Roosevelt signed the law, and it took effect in 1942. Most states immediately changed their state laws to coincide with the federal definition of Thanksgiving. The last state to make this change was Texas, which observed Thanksgiving on the last Thursday of November (the same date as the federal holiday in five out of every seven years) until 1956.

Protests and Counter-Observances

The United States experienced a great deal of social upheaval and change in the 1960s and 1970s. African Americans sought equal rights and opportunities through the civil rights movement, women broke out of traditional roles through the women's liberation movement, and many people became more politically active as a result of the Vietnam War. As these events raised public concern about such issues as racism and diversity, a number of American cultural institutions came under increasing scrutiny, including the Thanksgiving holiday.

Some people, especially Native Americans, began to challenge the prevailing view of Thanksgiving as a celebration of the Pilgrims' heroic quest to establish freedom and democracy in the New World. Instead, they offered another perspective, which held that the founding of Plymouth Colony marked the beginning of the European settlers' long history of racism, brutality, and conquest of indigenous peoples in America (*see the Primary Sources section for articles on Native American perspectives on Thanksgiving*).

The Pilgrims' rise to iconic status in American culture had begun in the early 19th century. Daniel Webster, who was widely considered to be the greatest orator of his day, helped create the mythology surrounding the Pilgrims with a famous speech at an 1820 bicentennial celebration of their landing. In honoring the English colonists, however, Webster claimed that they had courageously settled a wilderness "peopled by roving barbarians" and had overcome "the violence of savages" to bring "Christianity, and civilization" to America.

Webster's negative characterization of the indigenous peoples of America, as much as his positive depiction of the Pilgrims, reflected the views of the dominant culture. A decade later, the Indian Removal Act of 1830 forced the last remaining Native American tribes in the southeastern United States onto federal reservations west of the Mississippi River.

Although organized protests against the popular conception of the Pilgrims and Thanksgiving did not occur until the 20th century, a number of people expressed opposing perspectives earlier. In 1836, for instance, a Pequot Indian minister named William Apess spoke out during a lecture on King Philip's War in Boston. Apess angrily declared that "every man of color" should mourn the arrival of the Pilgrims, and he suggested that Native Americans express their outrage by burying Plymouth Rock.

During the 1970s, Plymouth emerged as the center of a culture war over the legacy of the Pilgrims and the meaning of Thanksgiving. This conflict first erupted in 1970, when Plymouth held a banquet to celebrate the 350th anniversary of the landing of the Pilgrims. Organizers of the banquet wanted to feature a Native American speaker as a way to honor the early cooperation between the Pilgrims and the Wampanoags. They invited Wamsutta (Frank) B. James, president of the Federated Eastern Indian League, to appear at the event.

James prepared a speech that challenged mainstream views of the Pilgrims and offered a Native American perspective on history. "It is with mixed emotion that I stand here to share my thoughts," the speech read. "This is a time of celebration for you—celebrating an anniversary of a beginning for the white man in America. A time of looking back, of reflection. It is with a heavy heart that I look back upon what happened to my People." Upon reviewing the remarks James had prepared, the organizers decided that his message was too confrontational and refused to let him deliver the speech at the banquet.

Many Native Americans were upset when James was not allowed to speak at the banquet. The United American Indians of New England (UAINE) responded by organizing a protest in Plymouth. Hundreds of Native Americans from across the country gathered at the statue of the famous Wampanoag leader Massasoit to sing songs and hear speeches, including the one that James wrote.

Various Native American groups have held protests in Plymouth on Thanksgiving Day every year since. Known as the National Day of Mourning, this counter-observance of the holiday is intended to raise public awareness of alternative interpretations of history. The protesters have employed controversial, and sometimes violent, methods to gain attention for their message. In 1994, for instance, protesters forced their way into Plymouth's First Parish

Participants in the annual National Day of Mourning observance gather around the statue of Massasoit in Plymouth, Massachusetts, on November 26, 1998.

Mark Twain's Perspective on Thanksgiving

Although Native American groups did not launch organized Thanksgiving counter-observances until 1970, a number of prominent people had expressed opposing viewpoints on the holiday before that time. Mark Twain (1835-1910), a great American author who wrote *Huckleberry Finn* and many other classic works of literature, provided a satirical perspective on the Thanksgiving holiday on several occasions during his lifetime. The following quotation comes from *Mark Twain's Autobiography,* which was first published in 1924:

> Thanksgiving Day, a function which originated in New England two or three centuries ago when those people recognized that they really had something to be thankful for—annually, not oftener—if they had succeeded in exterminating their neighbors, the Indians, during the previous twelve months instead of getting exterminated by their neighbors, the Indians. Thanksgiving Day became a habit, for the reason that in the course of time, as the years drifted on, it was perceived that the exterminating had ceased to be mutual and was all on the white man's side, consequently on the Lord's side; hence it was proper to thank the Lord for it and extend the usual compliments.

Unitarian Universalist Church and demanded to air their grievances. Other methods commonly employed by the protesters include disrupting the annual Pilgrim Progress parade and burying Plymouth Rock under mounds of dirt, leaves, and garbage.

Since the annual Native American protests began, the Plimoth Plantation living history museum has made a dedicated effort to provide visitors with multiple perspectives on the Pilgrims and other aspects of early American history. "We at Plimoth Plantation work very hard to peel away layers of inaccuracies and sift through centuries of misconceptions and misrepresentations," wrote Linda Coombs, associate director of the Wampanoag Indigenous Program, in an article for the Plimoth Plantation web site called "Holistic History: Including the Wampanoag in an Exhibit at Plimoth Plantation." "Why is this important? Because to represent, by whatever means, any group as accurately as possible is to show respect. It shows respect for people—both those of the past and those of today."

Historians such as Jill Lepore, author of *The Name of War: King Philip's War and the Origins of American Identity,* applaud this approach. "It is our obligation to examine our American heritage in all its wonder and brutality," she declared in a 1998 *Boston Globe* article. "We have to find a way to acknowledge that both cultures—the Native Americans who lost their land and the Europeans who settled here—are constituent of what it is to be an American."

THANKSGIVING IN MODERN TIMES

Thanksgiving celebrations in the 21st century still maintain many of the same elements that were present in the celebrations of yesteryear: the harvest provides a theme for holiday decorations; presidents and governors make proclamations expressing gratitude for the year's blessings; people attend church services; and extended families come together to share a festive meal. Americans of centuries past would recognize all of these Thanksgiving traditions. Parades and football games are relatively recent additions to the holiday observances, but they also have historic precedents in the military drills and games that were part of the Pilgrims' celebration.

For many contemporary Americans, homecoming is the most important feature of Thanksgiving. This tradition dates back to the 18th century, when families began dispersing outside of New England. It continued through the 19th century, when the Gold Rush and the promise of open farmland drew people westward across the frontier. Then, as now, Thanksgiving served as a time for family reunions.

Into the early years of the 21st century, the weekend of Thanksgiving has ranked among the busiest travel times of the year. More than 10 million Americans typically take commercial airline flights during the four-day holiday, while another 40 million people drive 100 miles or more. An estimated 90 percent of Americans sit down each year to a traditional Thanksgiving dinner that includes some combination of turkey, mashed potatoes, gravy, stuffing, cranberry sauce, and pumpkin pie. Salads and side dishes provide the main sources of variation from this traditional menu, but regional, ethnic, and gourmet specialties have earned a spot on many Thanksgiving dinner tables as well.

Besides being a time when Americans feast and count their blessings, Thanksgiving is also an occasion when many contemporary Americans offer food and other forms of assistance to those less fortunate than themselves. A U.S. Department of Agriculture study released in 2005 found that 38.2 million Americans, including 13.8 million children, are "food insecure," meaning that they do not have enough food to meet their basic nutritional requirements. Mindful of this problem, many people spend a portion of the Thanksgiving holiday serving dinner to strangers at homeless shelters, veterans hospitals, or senior citizen centers.

Some critics have questioned whether the American tradition of feasting on Thanksgiving is appropriate at all, given the large number of people around the world facing poverty, hunger, and homelessness. Since 1973, the international relief agency Oxfam has attempted to raise public awareness of this issue through its annual Fast for a World Harvest campaign. This program encourages Americans to fast on the Thursday before Thanksgiving and donate the money they would have spent on food to organizations that fight world hunger.

Thanksgiving gained new significance and meaning in the lives of many Americans in 2001, following the September 11 terrorist attacks against the United States (*see the Primary Sources section for the text of President George W. Bush's 2001 proclamation*). This shocking event caused many people to reevaluate their priorities and values. It also increased the level of appreciation many people felt for family, community, and country. When the Thanksgiving holiday arrived 10 weeks after the attacks, many Americans embraced it for its emphasis on communion with friends and relatives, its traditional menu of comforting foods, and its nostalgic evocation of a safer, simpler time. "This is the kind of holiday we need right now, an intrinsically complicated one that comes at the end of a bitter harvest and yet finds something sweet to celebrate," said a 2001 *Time* magazine cover story on Thanksgiving (*see the Primary Sources section for an article describing some New York City firefighters' first Thanksgiving after the attacks*).

The meaning and means of celebrating Thanksgiving thus continue to evolve in modern times. Yet somehow, despite all of the changes that have occurred through the centuries, the basic sentiment behind the holiday remains simple and universal: gratitude. "Regardless of how it came to us, Thanksgiving is now a quintessential American day devoid of religious affiliation and ethnicity," Brian Floyd Alward wrote on the *National Geographic* web site. "People of all races and religions celebrate it in a truly independent way with one purpose in mind: to focus on the nation's many blessings."

CONTEMPORARY ANNUAL PUBLIC OBSERVANCES

A number of historic sites offer special programs at Thanksgiving time each year. These programs generally feature reenactments of colonial life and early celebrations of the holiday. Here is a sampling of such observances:

Thanksgiving Movies and Specials

Thanksgiving has not served as the centerpiece of nearly as many movies or television specials as some other holidays, such as Halloween and Christmas. Still, dozens of films have used Thanksgiving as a backdrop to explore themes of gratitude, homecoming, and family dynamics. In addition, a number of popular TV shows have created memorable episodes that take place on Thanksgiving. Here is a list of some well-known examples:

The classic 1947 film *Miracle on 34th Street* is often associated with Christmas, but it actually takes place on Thanksgiving and features the Macy's Thanksgiving Day Parade.

The 1970s family TV series "The Waltons" gave rise to two holiday specials that aired regularly over the holiday weekend for many years: "A Day of Thanks on Walton's Mountain" and "A Walton's Thanksgiving Reunion."

One of the most popular TV specials concerning the holiday is "A Charlie Brown Thanksgiving," which first aired in 1973. When the whole Peanuts gang invites themselves over for Thanksgiving dinner, Charlie Brown and Snoopy prepare a feast of popcorn, toast, and jellybeans.

In director Woody Allen's 1986 film *Hannah and Her Sisters*, the very different members of a family gather to celebrate Thanksgiving in an upscale New York City apartment. Allen won an Academy Award for best screenplay for the film.

The 1987 comedy *Planes, Trains, and Automobiles* stars Steve Martin and John Candy as a pair of mismatched businessmen who encounter an endless series of transportation problems as they try to return home for Thanksgiving.

In the 1994 drama *Nobody's Fool,* Paul Newman stars as a down-on-his-luck construction worker who uses a Thanksgiving visit to attempt to reconcile with the family he abandoned years earlier.

Home for the Holidays, released in 1995, features Holly Hunter as a recently unemployed art dealer who must endure a visit with her dysfunctional family at Thanksgiving.

In the 2003 independent film *Pieces of April,* Katie Holmes stars as a young woman struggling to make it on her own in the big city who invites her estranged family to Thanksgiving dinner.

Berkeley Plantation, Virginia: On the first Sunday in November each year, this historic site hosts an annual First Thanksgiving Festival and reenactment of the 1619 arrival of settlers at Berkeley Hundred. Contact Berkeley Plantation, 12602 Harrison Landing Rd., Charles City, VA 23030, 888-466-6018 or 804-829-6018, fax: 804-829-6757, http://www.berkeleyplantation.com.

Old Sturbridge Village, Massachusetts: On Thanksgiving each year, costumed interpreters recreate a variety of activities from a typical holiday observance of the 1830s, including a dinner cooked over an open hearth, a Thanksgiving sermon, and a turkey shoot. Contact Old Sturbridge Village, 1 Old Sturbridge Village Rd., Sturbridge, MA 01566, 508-347-3362, http://www.osv.org.

Plimoth Plantation, Massachusetts: The living history museum of the Pilgrims offers a reenactment and a harvest feast at Thanksgiving time. Contact Plimoth Plantation, P.O. Box 1620, Plymouth, MA 02362, 508-746-1622, http://www.plimoth.org.

Parades take place on and around Thanksgiving in several cities. Here is a sampling of such events:

Baltimore, Maryland: The annual Thanksgiving Parade is held the Saturday before Thanksgiving. Contact Baltimore Office of Promotion and the Arts, 7 E. Redwood St., Ste. 500, Baltimore, MD 21202, 877-Baltimore (225-8466) or 410-752-8632, fax: 410-385-0361, http://www.bop.org.

Chicago, Illinois: The State Street Thanksgiving Parade takes place on the morning of Thanksgiving. Contact Chicago Festivals Association, 111 N. State St., 11th Fl., Chicago, IL 60602, 312-781-5681, fax: 312-781-5407, http://www.chicagofestivals.org.

Detroit, Michigan: America's Thanksgiving Parade takes place on Woodward Avenue on Thanksgiving morning. The Turkey Trot Fun Run is held earlier that morning. Contact The Parade Company, 9500 Mt. Elliott, Studio A, Detroit, MI 48211, 313-923-7400, fax: 313-923-2920, http://www.theparade.org/parade/index.shtml.

New York, New York: Macy's Thanksgiving Parade is held on Thanksgiving morning. Contact the parade hotline: 212-494-4495, http://www.macys.com.

Plymouth, Massachusetts: Observances include a parade of "pilgrims, patriots, and pioneers," followed by the New England Food Festival on the Saturday before Thanksgiving. Contact Plymouth Rock Foundation, 800-532-1621 or 508-746-1818, http://www.usathanksgiving.com.

A traditional thanksgiving table.

Thanksgiving:
Holiday Food from the 17th to the 21st Centuries

More than any other American holiday, Thanksgiving centers around food. Across the country, around the world, and sometimes even in outer space, Americans gather on Thanksgiving Day to share a feast. Some of the foods and dishes featured in the contemporary meal—including turkey and winter vegetables—have been associated with the holiday for three centuries. Many regional and ethnic specialties, on the other hand, joined the menu more recently. Although celebratory traditions may have changed over the years, Thanksgiving has retained its basic emphasis on food and family—as well as its important role in American life. "Thanksgiving Day, the emotions we attach to the holiday, the people we share it with, and the foods we eat on it are hopelessly bound together," Diana Karter Applebaum wrote in *Thanksgiving: An American Holiday, an American History*. "Every slice of turkey is a serving of tradition, each ladle of cranberry sauce a pouring out of American history, each slice of pie an offering of love, of family, of tradition, of—Thanksgiving."

Foods Available to the Pilgrims

Although the tradition of giving thanks for the harvest and other blessings has its roots in ancient cultures, the American Thanksgiving holiday is most often associated with the English colonists known as the Pilgrims. When the Pilgrims settled in Plymouth, Massachusetts, in December 1620, they had three main sources of food available to them: supplies they brought with them from England on the *Mayflower;* foods native to the area that they obtained by hunting, fishing, and gathering; and food crops that they planted and harvested in their new home. Since the Pilgrims arrived at the onset of winter, however, the weather made hunting and gathering difficult, and agriculture impossible, until the following spring.

For the first several months in America, therefore, the Pilgrims were limited mostly to consuming their own meager supplies. Records show that they brought casks of flour and oats, smoked or salted meat and fish, and kegs of beer, brandy, and wine. They also brought a variety of spices that were not available in the New World, such as cinnamon, ginger, mustard, nutmeg, pepper, and salt, as well as lemon juice to prevent scurvy. A number of domesticated animals made the voyage on the *Mayflower,* including dogs, cats, goats, sheep, rabbits, and chickens, giving the colonists access to milk, eggs, and fresh meat. The Pilgrims also brought some furniture, including tables, chairs, and cupboards, as well as cooking utensils, pots, pans, skillets, plates, mugs, knives, spoons, buckets, and candlesticks.

During the Pilgrims' harsh first winter in New England, 46 people lost their lives to disease, starvation, or exposure. Historians believe that the colonists consumed virtually all of the food they had brought on the *Mayflower* during this period. But the arrival of spring brought a quick reversal in their fortunes. In March 1621 they forged an alliance with Massasoit, the sachem or leader of the local Wampanoag Indians. Massasoit sent one of his people, Squanto, to live among the colonists and serve as an interpreter and guide. Squanto taught the Pilgrims some of the hunting, fishing, and agricultural techniques long used by the Wampanoags and other Native Americans of the region.

Indigenous peoples lived in New England for more than 10,000 years before the first Europeans arrived. They subsisted by hunting wild game in the forests, fishing in the rivers and ocean, and collecting wild fruits, berries, nuts, and roots. They also developed many agricultural techniques and food crops. For instance, the Wampanoags had been growing corn and beans for 500 years by the time Squanto shared their system with the Pilgrims. Native Americans also practiced their own harvest festival traditions, in which they expressed gratitude for the bounty of the land.

Squanto showed the Pilgrims how to catch the herring that spawned each spring in Plymouth's Town Brook. Rather than eat the small fish, however, Squanto advised the colonists to use it as fertilizer for their crops. Using mattocks, or hoes with stone heads and wooden handles, they made mounds of earth about three feet wide. In each mound they buried several herring, then used seeds obtained from Indian stockpiles to plant corn—the multi-colored, hard-kernel variety known as northern flint corn or Indian corn. Once the corn had sprouted, they added seeds of beans and squash to the mounds. As the corn grew tall, the other vegetables attached creepers to the stalks, which provided shade for the roots and discouraged the growth of weeds.

Stewed Pompion

Some of the recipes used by early English colonists are featured in the 1672 cookbook *New Englands Rarities Discovered* by John Josselyn. The following is the author's colorful description of the process of preparing—and the likely gastronomic consequences of eating—stewed pompion or pumpkin:

> The Housewives manner is to slice when ripe, and cut them into dice, and so fill a pot with them of two or three Gallons, and stew them upon a gentle fire a whole day, and as they sink, they fill again with fresh Pompions, not putting any liquor to them; and when it is stew'd enough, it will look like bak'd Apples; this they Dish, putting Butter to it, and a little Vinegar, (with some Spice, as Ginger, &c.) which makes it tart like an Apple, and so serve it up to be eaten with Fish or Flesh: It provokes Urin extreamly and is very windy.

The Pilgrims also planted gardens from seeds that they had brought with them from England. Although these seeds did not fare as well as native plants in the rocky New England soil, they probably cultivated some combination of barley, cabbage, carrots, chard, collards, cucumbers, endive, fennel, leeks, lettuce, marjoram, mint, onions, parsnips, peas, radishes, sage, spinach, thyme, and turnips.

Pumpkins grew so well in New England that they became a dietary staple for the early colonists. The Pilgrims called them pompions—from the French word for melon, *pompon*—and prepared them in a variety of ways, including boiling or stewing. A 1672 cookbook describes stewed pumpkin as an "Ancient New England standing dish" that was probably featured at most meals.

Foods Collected by Hunting and Gathering

Throughout the spring and summer of 1621, the Pilgrims collected a variety of foods native to New England. Fish were so abundant in the ocean and the inland lakes and rivers of the region that the Pilgrims managed to catch good quantities of bass, bluefish, cod, herring, and shad, despite their modest fishing skills. Shellfish, including clams, lobsters, and mussels, were easily gathered along the shoreline. Both the English colonists and the Wampanoag people also enjoyed eating eels. In a 1623 letter, colonist John Pory described the eels available along the New England coast as "passing sweet, fat and wholesome, having no taste at all of the mud." He added that the region's lobsters were "so large, so full of meat, and so plentiful in number as no man will believe that hath not seen."

Deer, wild fowl, and other animals in the forests surrounding the Pilgrims' new home provided food as well. Deer had long been vital to the Wampanoag way of life, serving as food as well as a source of clothing and tools. It is unlikely that the Pilgrims had hunted for or eaten deer before they arrived in the New World. They hailed from a country in which deer were only found in parklands and estate holdings of the upper classes. Since it was illegal for anyone but the landowners to buy or sell venison, the meat was not available to common English citizens. Once the colonists came to America, however, venison became a highly valued part of their diet.

The Pilgrims also hunted a variety of wild birds in New England, including ducks, geese, turkeys, cranes, swans, grouse, quail, partridges, and passenger pigeons. Wild fowl were particularly abundant in the fall, when thousands of ducks and geese migrated through the rivers and marshes of New England. Turkeys filled the woods of the region year round, but the Pilgrims hunted them mostly in winter, when the fast-moving birds could be tracked through the snow. In addition to these wild animals and birds, the Pilgrims probably ate some of their own domesticated animals and chickens.

To round out their diet, the Pilgrims also collected seasonal fruits and nuts throughout the year. Some of the wild fruits and berries native to New England include blueberries, cranberries, gooseberries, raspberries, strawberries, cherries, grapes, and plums. Most of these fruits were gathered in spring and summer, but they could be dried for later use. The Pilgrims also had access to several varieties of nuts, such as acorns, chestnuts, hickory nuts, and walnuts. In addition, the Wampanoags introduced the colonists to a number of other wild plants and herbs, including onions, garlic, leeks, watercress, and Jerusalem artichokes.

The First Thanksgiving Feast

Thanks to their own efforts at hunting and gathering, as well as Squanto's invaluable farming advice, the Pilgrims had collected plenty of food by the fall of 1621. They decided to celebrate their good fortune with a harvest festival

This painting, imagining the scene at the first Thanksgiving, was created by
J. L. G. Ferris sometime between 1900 and 1920.

and feast. The only information available to historians regarding the Pilgrims'
1621 feast comes from two brief surviving accounts of the event. Governor
William Bradford mentioned the celebration in his journal, and Edward
Winslow, the colony's Indian ambassador, described it in a letter to a friend
back in England. The limited historical record makes it impossible to know
exactly what occurred during this celebration, which nonetheless was later
immortalized as the "First Thanksgiving." "The only written record of the celebration mentions just two food items—deer and wildfowl—and doesn't give a
hint about what else was eaten or how the food was prepared or served," Kathleen Curtin and Sandra L. Oliver wrote in *Giving Thanks: Thanksgiving Recipes
and History, from Pilgrims to Pumpkin Pie.* "For that information, we need to
look to other seventeenth-century sources—European paintings and drawings,
period cookbooks, artifacts, Wampanoag oral histories, archaeological evidence, and the journals and writings of the colonists themselves—to make
educated guesses about the details of the celebration."

Indian Corn and Corn Dollies

The northern flint or Indian corn that the Pilgrims learned to cultivate and eat in America has small, knobby ears with hard kernels of various colors, including red, yellow, blue, green, and black. Although ground corn of this type is no longer part of the Thanksgiving menu, the multi-colored ears remain a favorite household decoration for the holiday, as well as a more general symbol of the harvest.

Small dolls made from corn husks are another popular type of Thanksgiving decoration. The custom of making "corn dollies" has its roots in ancient European harvest rituals. Some cultures believed that spirits inhabited corn and other crops. As the corn was harvested, the corn spirit would move from sheaf to sheaf ahead of the sickle. By preserving the last sheaf of the season as a doll, people thought they could catch the spirit and retain its magical powers. The corn dolly was typically displayed as a decoration until it was time to plant the following year's crops, when it was destroyed in a symbolic manner in an effort to ensure a plentiful harvest.

Winslow's account of the 1621 celebration notes that Governor Bradford sent four men out "fowling," or hunting the ducks and geese that were then migrating through New England. Within a few hours they had killed enough birds to feed the settlement for a week. Winslow also mentions that Massasoit and at least 90 Wampanoags showed up—either by invitation or to investigate the sounds of shooting—and stayed for the celebration. These visitors contributed five deer to the feast. All of the meat was most likely cooked whole, with head and feet still attached, on wooden spits over outdoor fires. The "humbles" or innards were generally cooked and eaten as well, often serving as ingredients in stews called pottages.

In addition to venison and wild birds, the Pilgrims and Wampanoags probably ate some of the crops that had been harvested in Plymouth Colony, including corn, squash, and beans. The hard kernels of corn were ground into cornmeal, which the Pilgrims used to make familiar English dishes like corn pudding, cornbread, and fried corncakes. The Wampanoags boiled ground corn in water to create a thick porridge called Nasaump. They often added seasonal berries, herbs, or shellfish to this dish. The Pilgrims were not accustomed to eating raw foods, so they typically boiled vegetables in large brass pots to make stews or sauces. Pumpkins were either stewed in this manner or cooked whole in a fire.

The 1621 feast probably also included fish and shellfish, as well as an assortment of wild fruits, berries, and nuts. Most fruits were no longer in season by fall, but the Pilgrims almost certainly had stores of dried berries available. Grapes were usually harvested in the fall and might have been used to make wine. Beer was the favorite drink of the English colonists, but it was probably not available at the first Thanksgiving feast. The Pilgrims had long exhausted the kegs they brought with them on the *Mayflower*. Even if they were able to grow enough barley over the summer to make more beer, it most likely did not have enough time to ferment before the harvest celebration.

MISCONCEPTIONS ABOUT THE FIRST THANKSGIVING

A number of popular misconceptions surround the manner in which the Pilgrims' 1621 feast was prepared, served, and eaten. Many artistic renderings of the first Thanksgiving depict a number of English women placing platters of food before English and Wampanoag men gathered around a long groaning board or table. In reality, only four of the 20 adult women who had set sail on the *Mayflower* survived the first year in Plymouth Colony. It is highly unlikely that these four women took sole responsibility for preparing and serving a feast for 50 other colonists and around 100 Wampanoag guests. Instead, English men and children probably contributed to the meal preparation by butchering the deer, plucking the birds, gathering shellfish, and grinding corn. It is unclear whether Wampanoag women attended the celebration, but if so they may have provided another source of labor.

Contrary to popular belief—and modern practice—the first Thanksgiving was not a single large meal shared by all celebrants at a large table covered with a white tablecloth. According to Edward Winslow, the Pilgrims and the Wampanoags spent three days feasting, playing games, demonstrating military drills and traditional dances, and engaging in diplomacy. Massasoit and the leaders of Plymouth Colony may have eaten together at one table, where they would have received their choice of the best available foods. Some of the other colonists probably ate at tables, either outdoors or indoors, while others sat on the ground or crouched around cooking fires.

It seems likely that the 1621 meal was served and eaten less formally than many people assume. The Pilgrims did not have china, silver, or linens. Instead, they had plates and mugs made of tin or pewter, and they ate with

Reenactors recreate the first Thanksgiving at the Plimoth Plantation
living-history museum in Plymouth, Massachusetts.

knives, spoons, and their fingers (forks did not arrive in New England until the early 1700s). The Wampanoags ate with their fingers out of wooden or earthenware bowls.

Modern Favorites Missing from the Feast

Although the historical evidence is limited as to what foods the Pilgrims actually served at the 1621 feast, it is known that a number of dishes associated with modern Thanksgiving celebrations were not available at that time. "Generations of Americans have been taught that the Thanksgiving meal of today not only celebrates that feast, shared with the Indians, but replicates its menu," historian Godfrey Hodgson wrote in *A Great and Godly Adventure: The Pilgrims and the Myth of the First Thanksgiving*. "It is clear that none of these beliefs is true. What we are seeing, when we sit down to a Thanksgiving turkey, is a prime example of what historians have called 'the invention of a tradition.'" In fact, the main connection between the 21st-century Thanksgiving menu and the 1621 harvest feast is that both meals incorporate foods native to New England.

One example of a popular Thanksgiving food that was missing from the Pilgrims' feast is cranberry sauce. Wild cranberries grew in the swamps and bogs of New England, where they provided food for cranes and other birds. But the berries were too bitter for humans to eat without sugar—an exotic spice that was not available in America at that time. The early colonists never mention cranberries in their writings, and it took another 50 years before anyone in New England made a sauce by boiling cranberries with sugar.

Mashed potatoes is another example of a dish that was conspicuously absent from the 1621 feast. Although potatoes had been cultivated in South America by the 1600s, they were unknown to the Pilgrims and did not become available in New England until the 18th century. In addition, the Pilgrims did not serve pumpkin pie at the first Thanksgiving. Although the English colonists grew and ate pumpkins, they lacked wheat to make pie crusts and ovens to bake pies.

Other popular holiday foods that were almost certainly missing from the first Thanksgiving feast include bread and rolls; popcorn and corn on the cob (the type of corn grown in Plymouth Colony was unsuitable for these purposes); and apple pie and cider (apples were not introduced to the Americas until a few years later).

THE HOLIDAY MENU EVOLVES IN NEW ENGLAND

For many years following the Pilgrims' 1621 harvest celebration, various colonies proclaimed occasional days of thanksgiving to recognize specific instances of good fortune. During the late 1600s and early 1700s, however, Thanksgiving Day evolved into an annual holiday that was celebrated throughout the English colonies in the New World. Most colonial governors proclaimed a special day every fall to thank God for the year's blessings. Thanksgiving Day observances generally began with a church service, during which the congregation would eagerly anticipate the reading of the governor's proclamation. Then everyone adjourned to their homes for a festive dinner with family and friends.

Over time, New England became a land of prosperous farmers. The colonists maintained barnyards full of domesticated animals—including cows, pigs, goats, sheep, turkeys, geese, and chickens—that provided a ready supply of meat for Thanksgiving dinner. They also gained the resources to buy imported sugar, spices, molasses, tea, and other foods that had been out of reach for their Pilgrim ancestors. The introduction of these materials added more flavor and variety to the holiday meal.

By the time of the American Revolution, many New England families enjoyed three or four different kinds of meat at Thanksgiving dinner. Roast turkey—which was considered a festive dish and a symbol of the holiday—usually held a place of honor at the head of the table. Rather than wild turkey, however, most American families consumed domesticated birds that had been raised on their own farms. Other popular meat dishes of this era included roast duck and goose, and joint of mutton, pork, and beef.

In those days, most meat was roasted over an open fire, either by suspending it from a hook or by turning it on a spit. A tin oven or piece of sheet metal might be used to catch the drippings, which could be used for basting or other purposes. Some meat dishes of this era were also cooked in a sort of primitive Dutch oven. The meat was placed in a heavy metal roasting pan—along with an assortment of vegetables, herbs, and spices—covered with a tight lid, and set into the fire, with hot coals piled on top.

In addition to generous quantities of meat, a typical Thanksgiving meal in the 1700s featured boiled seasonal vegetables, such as squash, turnips, potatoes, and cabbage. The feast might also include a variety of sweet treats prepared weeks or months in advance, such as apple butter, currant jelly, gooseberry

This undated photo shows a man selecting a turkey for Thanksgiving dinner.

jam, pickled pears and peaches, and cranberry sauce. "On an ordinary Sabbath, one or two of these delicacies might grace the table," Applebaum wrote in *Thanksgiving.* "But on Thanksgiving, the best of everything the farm could offer was spread on the table in generous quantity."

PIES BECOME A HOLIDAY TRADITION

After the United States gained independence from England, the Thanksgiving feast took on a more distinctly American character. In the early to mid-1800s, for instance, pies emerged as an important part of the holiday tradition in New England. "The truly distinguishing feature of the Thanksgiving feast, and the task that occupied housewives for days beforehand, was the variety of pies to be baked and served; for pies are the crowning glory of New England cuisine," Appelbaum declared.

Throughout the 19th century, many New England families started preparing pies a week or more in advance of the Thanksgiving holiday. Adult women

Traditional New England Mincemeat Pie

Fond childhood memories of family Thanksgiving celebrations served as a topic for a number of 19th-century American writers. The recollections of many people who grew up in New England center around the ceremonious preparation and consumption of pies. In the following excerpt from her 1881 book *Childlife, Old-time*, New Hampshire native Ellen Chapman Rollins recalls the many pleasurable sensations associated with mincemeat pie:

> A true Thanksgiving mince pie should be an inch thick, with a thin, flaky crust, tinted by its imprisoned juices, which threaten to break through like blood from overfull veins. Around its edge must be a slight crinkle made by the tines of a fork or castor-bottle cover; and in its top a hole here and there from the stroke of a knife to let the steam out. This steam, once known, can never be forgotten—the intermingled exhalation of beef and pork or suet, and apples and raisins and citron and sugar and spices and boiled cider, and, in profane families, of a dash of good brandy. When you press down upon its upper crust, there should gush up from the slashes a brown gravy, sparkling with tiny gobules of fat, and deliciously scenting the room. Fortunate they who have been permitted to relish, with a slice of cream cheese, and a mug of sweet cider, this healthful, bliss-giving pie!

typically oversaw the actual filling and baking of the pies, but other members of the household often helped out with related tasks, such as splitting and carrying firewood, peeling and slicing fruits and vegetables, shelling nuts, mincing beef, and chopping herbs and spices.

In some households, bakers would use the tines of a fork to prick special designs into the top crust of each pie. The designs might include harvest themes, depictions of the *Mayflower,* or the initials of a couple that was planning a Thanksgiving wedding. Until the mid-1800s, the pies were typically baked in brick ovens. During the second half of the 19th century, brick ovens gradually gave way to cast-iron stoves, which heated more evenly and were easier to use. Dozens of pies were usually baked ahead of time and stored in a cool pantry or underground cellar. Some of the pies were eaten at Thanksgiving dinner, some were given away to less fortunate members of the community, and some were allowed to freeze for later use.

Thanksgiving pies had a variety of possible fillings, from savory meats or vegetables to sweet fruits or custards. Although the dish is virtually unknown today, chicken pie practically defined the holiday meal in New England during parts of the 18th and 19th centuries. The influential magazine editor Sarah Josepha Hale, who convinced President Abraham Lincoln to make Thanksgiving a national holiday in 1863, promoted chicken pie in the pages of *Godey's Lady's Book:* "This pie, which is wholly formed of the choicest parts of fowls, enriched and seasoned with a profusion of butter and pepper, and covered with an excellent puff paste, is, like the celebrated pumpkin pie, an indispensable part of a good and true Yankee Thanksgiving."

Mincemeat is another type of pie that has enjoyed a long association with Thanksgiving. Many farm families chose to butcher animals in the fall, partly to avoid the expense of feeding livestock through the winter months, and partly to take advantage of the cold weather for storing meat. Mincemeat pie was typically made from scraps of meat—including the tongue, neck, and feet—mixed with a combination of other seasonal foods, such as apples and nuts. In the 18th century, the dish tended to be more savory and was usually served along with the main course. During the 19th century, though, sweet ingredients became a more prominent part of the dish. As a result, mincemeat pie increasingly began to be served toward the end of the meal, along with dessert.

Side dishes of winter vegetables, such as pumpkins, turnips, potatoes, and cabbage, remained part of the Thanksgiving meal during this era. A few new vegetable dishes joined the menu as well, including creamed onions and succotash (a mixture of dried corn and beans that was boiled until soft). Apple cider emerged as the main beverage of Thanksgiving during this period. Farmers in New England pressed cider from a combination of tart and sweet apples and allowed it to ferment into a sparkling alcoholic drink.

One of the only foods to be served raw at 19th-century Thanksgiving dinners was celery. First considered a luxury item, fresh celery stalks soon became a holiday tradition. In the early 1800s this crunchy treat was usually displayed on the dinner table in a special celery vase. In later years the stalks were typi-

The Turkey: The Undisputed Centerpiece of Thanksgiving Dinner

The turkey was first domesticated by the ancient Aztecs in Mexico. The large birds made their way to Europe with Spanish explorers in the 1500s, and later were introduced to the woodlands of eastern North America. By the time the Pilgrims arrived in New England, wild turkeys were plentiful. The early English colonists typically hunted them in the winter, when they could be tracked through the snow, so it is uncertain whether turkey was among the wild fowl served at the 1621 feast known as the First Thanksgiving. But turkey undoubtedly became an important food source in the American colonies.

By the early 19th century, turkey had claimed its place at the center of the table for the annual Thanksgiving feast, as well as a place in American culture as the main symbol of the holiday. Large roasted birds had been the centerpiece of European holiday celebrations for centuries, and turkey was the most festive meat that most American families of this era could afford. Wild turkeys had suffered a marked decline in New England due to over-hunting, however, so most families consumed domesticated birds that had been raised on their own farms.

As the United States grew increasingly urbanized during the 20th century, most Americans obtained fresh or frozen holiday turkeys from a supermarket. Most of these birds came from large-scale poultry-processing operations. The poultry industry developed new breeds, such as the Large White, that grew rapidly and provided plentiful white meat. In the meantime, industry marketing campaigns helped solidify turkey's position as a necessary part of Thanksgiving dinner. By the turn of the 21st century, over 90 percent of Americans ate turkey at the annual holiday meal, consuming more than 50 million of the birds every Thanksgiving.

Today, the majority of Thanksgiving turkeys are roasted in a gas or electric oven. But the late 20th century also saw a surge in turkey preparation using outdoor cooking methods, such as grilling, smoking, and deep frying. These methods tend to be especially popular in warm climates, where roasting a turkey indoors for several hours can make homes unbearably hot.

Beginning in the 1970s, some health and animal-rights activists protested against the consumption of turkey at Thanksgiving. Such organizations as People for the Ethical Treatment of Animals (PETA) have complained about inhumane conditions in industrial poultry-breeding operations and campaigned for turkey-free holiday meals. But these protests have had little impact on Thanksgiving eating habits in most American homes.

Three men carry home turkeys won at a raffle on November 22, 1912.

cally stuffed with cream cheese and placed on a relish tray, along with such goodies as pickles and olives. Some other novelties that tended to appear in New England homes only on Thanksgiving Day include lemons, oranges, figs, and dates.

*T*HANKSGIVING GROWS MORE REFINED

During the 19th century extended families gathered together to celebrate the holiday, thus establishing a tradition that has continued to the present day. As relatives arrived from nearby farms or distant cities, they were often recruited to help prepare the upcoming feast. In addition to family reunion, Thanksgiving also became a time of hospitality and charity. Many New England families gladly welcomed students, widows, elderly neighbors, or even strangers to join them for the festive meal. Others distributed turkeys, pies, or hearty baskets full of food to less fortunate members of the community (*see the Primary Sources section for an article on extending charity on Thanksgiving*). Another holiday custom involved sending food items to the local minister and his wife as a token of respect and esteem.

In order to accommodate a large number of guests, many families served Thanksgiving dinner on a large table placed in the parlor. When it became impossible to fit everyone around one table, the children were sometimes seated at a smaller table in an adjoining room (*see the Primary Sources section for a reminiscence on a modern "kids' table"*). The ladies of the house typically set the table with the family's best silver and china, then spread out all of the various foods for guests to serve themselves. The turkey generally arrived last and was placed before the head of the household for carving. Before the meal began, the family usually offered thanks for the fruits of the harvest, the presence of extended family and friends, and the blessings of the past year.

At the end of the feast came dessert, usually pumpkin pie or plum pudding. The latter dish was a rich, moist, cake-like combination of flour, suet, sugar, spices, raisins, and currants. These ingredients were placed into a pudding bag, tied up, and steamed in the oven. The introduction of even-heating cast-iron stoves in the late 1800s made cakes and other elaborate desserts possible. Ice cream also became available around this time as a special treat.

During the Victorian era, some American women adopted the French custom of serving meals in courses, rather than placing all of the food on the table at once. The widespread availability of manufactured ceramics, silverware, and linens also made table settings more refined and elegant during this time. More households came to own a variety of platters, bowls, and other service items that were intended for a specific purpose. For instance, many Thanksgiving tables featured a castor, or a decorative stand designed to hold condiments like oil, vinegar, salt, pepper, and mustard.

The Victorian emphasis on sophistication and elegance also introduced some fancier foods to the Thanksgiving menu in the late 1800s. An influential cookbook of the era, Fannie Farmer's 1896 *Boston Cooking-School Cooking*, reflected this refinement in taste by including recipes for such delicacies as oyster soup, salted almonds, Neapolitan ice cream, bonbons, and meringue. It also instructed readers how to turn cranberry jelly into decorative molded dishes.

*T*HANKSGIVING IN THE **20**TH CENTURY

Around the turn of the 20th century, many Americans gravitated back to the traditional Thanksgiving menu based on New England harvest foods. The

A family in Neffsville, Pennsylvania, says grace before Thanksgiving dinner in 1942.

forces of industrialization and immigration brought rapid changes to American society during this era. These disorienting changes sparked new appreciation for the stability and comfort of old-fashioned customs and recipes. Women's magazines and cookbooks from the early decades of the 20th century featured a fairly consistent selection of Thanksgiving foods. Over time, these dishes—including roast turkey, bread stuffing, cranberry sauce, mashed potatoes, and pumpkin pie—became accepted as *the* bill of fare for a proper American Thanksgiving dinner. A few traditional dishes also fell out of favor somewhat during this period, such as chicken pie, mincemeat pie, and plum pudding.

Improvements in transportation also made new types of food available across the United States. For instance, refrigerated railroad cars carried fresh produce to northern cities, regardless of the season. The nation's growing urban population could also purchase Thanksgiving turkeys that were plucked and ready to be stuffed and roasted, as well as canned holiday favorites like pumpkin and squash.

In addition, a variety of technological changes took place within American kitchens in the early 1900s. At the turn of the 20th century, most people preserved food in iceboxes and cooked it on stoves fueled by coal, oil, or wood. But the introduction of gas ranges in the 1910s, and electric ranges a short time later, gave cooks a source of steady, reliable heat and made cooking safer, easier, and faster. Likewise, the introduction of refrigerators and freezers in the late 1920s and 1930s enabled Americans to purchase greater quantities of food at once and store it for longer periods of time. A variety of smaller electrical appliances also appeared around this time—including mixers, toasters, skillets, and coffeemakers—that led to significant changes in people's cooking and eating habits.

During World War II, foods like sugar, wheat, coffee, meat, butter, and cheese were affected by rationing. Many of the nation's newspapers and magazines published special, patriotic Thanksgiving recipes that eliminated the use of rationed food items. But as ordinary citizens endured privation at home, the U.S. military made special efforts to ensure that all American servicemen received a traditional turkey dinner on Thanksgiving. Feasts were delivered to front lines of battle by any means necessary, including helicopter, jeep, boat, and mule. Gene Currivan, an American soldier who was stationed in France on Thanksgiving Day 1944, recalled in the *New York Times* how members of his squad were called out of their foxholes to greet a very special meal truck: "They lined up with their mess kits and one of the great moments of the year was at hand. Their eyes literally popped when they saw the generous portions and unexpected variety. There were large slabs of turkey, a mound of potatoes with savory gravy, carrots, peas, raisin bread, butter, cookies and candy. And each man got a cigar."

POST-WORLD WAR II CHANGES AFFECT THE FEAST

Rapid changes continued to take place in American society following World War II. Women joined the workforce in increasing numbers, for instance, which reduced the amount of time available to them for meal preparation. Large food-processing companies emerged to meet the growing need for affordable, convenient food products among American consumers. Instead of daily shopping trips to local markets filled with the fresh products of local farms, millions of people began making weekly trips to large supermarkets full of standardized canned, frozen, and packaged foods. Many cooks soon came to depend on these foods, which eliminated most seasonal and regional restrictions on food availability.

Many Thanksgiving favorites—from turkey and stuffing to pie crusts and fillings—became available as ready-to-cook, prepared food products. By the second half of the 20th century, it was possible to assemble an entire holiday meal from store-bought materials. A feast that once took days or weeks to prepare, and involved contributions from the entire family, could be readied by one person in a matter of hours. Many people appreciated this newfound freedom from the kitchen, but others missed the festive, communal aspect of preparing large, home-cooked meals.

As food products companies proliferated and introduced a wide variety of new items to American grocery stores, advertisers often tried to associate these products with the Thanksgiving holiday in an effort to generate sales. Magazine advertisements featured recipes for trendy new foods to add to the feast, including gelatin salads, cranberry cheesecake, and green bean casserole. These foods became regular components of the Thanksgiving meal for many families.

New time-saving kitchen appliances also proliferated in the second half of the 20th century. Microwave ovens made cooking faster and easier, food processors eliminated the need to chop and dice ingredients by hand, and meat thermometers reduced the uncertainty involved in roasting a turkey. Cleaning up after a big family meal also became simpler with the introduction of automatic dishwashers. Toward the end of the century, food magazines and television cooking shows introduced people to a multitude of new recipes, while the Internet helped accelerate the spread of food trends across the country. Not surprisingly, many of these new information sources devoted special attention to the Thanksgiving meal.

REGIONAL AND ETHNIC MENU VARIATIONS

As Thanksgiving celebrations spread westward and southward from New England during the 19th and early 20th centuries, a number of regional variations appeared on the holiday menu. Some traditional foods were not readily available outside of New England, forcing cooks to substitute local items. In Washington state, for example, stuffing often featured locally grown hazelnuts instead of the walnuts and chestnuts favored in the East. But many cooks out-

Barbecued Thanksgiving turkey has been a popular tradition in parts of the U.S. where the weather is warm on the holiday.

side of New England made adjustments to the traditional Thanksgiving menu in an effort to cater to their families' tastes. Residents of Texas, New Mexico, and Arizona preferred spicy southwestern flavors in various dishes, for instance, while people in Florida often enjoyed Key lime pie for dessert.

Some regional variations in Thanksgiving meals—such as the serving of sauerkraut in Baltimore, Maryland—remained highly localized. Other changes, however, became influential trends that spread across the country. A number of common dishes on the modern Thanksgiving menu originated in the South, for instance, as the holiday gained popularity in that region during the late 19th and early 20th centuries. Migrations of workers from South to North, as well as cookbooks published by well-known Southern chefs and recipes appearing in magazines like *Southern Living,* helped fuel this trend. Some contributions to the feast that can be traced to Southern influences include sweet potato casseroles, biscuits and gravy, macaroni and cheese, pecan pie, and ambrosia salad.

An unusual regional specialty that has gained some national attention as a Thanksgiving dish is turducken. Originating among Louisiana Cajuns, turducken consists of a turkey, which is stuffed with a duck, which is stuffed with a chicken. A different type of dressing is placed within and between the three birds: oyster dressing inside the chicken, spicy andouille sausage dressing between the chicken and duck, and traditional cornbread dressing between the duck and turkey. Although the complicated recipe for turducken has appeared in a number of cookbooks, many households obtain the regional dish from one of the Louisiana mail-order businesses that ship it preassembled and ready to cook (*see Recipes section for instructions from the U.S. Department of Agriculture on preparing turducken, as well as recipes for some other dishes mentioned in this essay*).

In the late 19th and early 20th centuries, Thanksgiving became a tool in efforts to introduce new immigrants to American history and culture. Many immigrants, eager to assimilate, adopted the traditional holiday menu of turkey and pumpkin pie during this period. In the second half of the 20th century, however, international cuisines—from Italian and Chinese to Mexican and Middle Eastern—saw an increase in popularity across the United States. As exotic flavors and dishes became more widely available and accepted, Americans of many ethnic and cultural backgrounds felt free to explore other culinary traditions at Thanksgiving.

Thanksgiving Today

In many American households today, the annual Thanksgiving meal consists of two parts: traditional foods associated with the holiday and nontraditional foods associated with the family's background, history, and tastes. "Today, an infinite number of menu variations reflect the complex tapestry of regional heritage, family traditions, ethnic background, and even social class," Curtin and Oliver wrote in *Giving Thanks*. More and more American families have created their own celebratory traditions, while also honoring the sentiment of the holiday by respecting shared traditions from the past. Turkey may be prepared using seasonings or cooking methods from a different culture, for instance, or it may serve as the main course in a meal that features a number of regional or ethnic specialties.

Thanksgiving Dinner in Space

Of all the places that Americans have gathered for a Thanksgiving meal, perhaps the most unusual location is out in space. U.S. astronauts Gerald Carr, Edward Gibson, and William Pogue celebrated the first Thanksgiving in space in 1973, when they were part of the third American crew to live in the orbiting space station Skylab. Since then, several crews of astronauts have observed the holiday in space while participating in various space shuttle missions and while living at the International Space Station.

The Thanksgiving meal provided by the National Aeronautics and Space Administration (NASA) is not as elaborate as the typical feast on Earth. Although the astronauts' menu includes many traditional holiday dishes, the foods are rehydrated and served in foil packages to make them easy to eat in a weightless environment.

Peggy Whitson, a science officer who lived on the International Space Station in 2002, recalled that year's holiday meal on NASA's web site: "After a challenging day of work, which included the preparations for and the conduct of a space walk with robotic arm support, we celebrated with smoked turkey in foil pouches, rehydrated mash potatoes (unfortunately sans gravy), and rehydrated green beans with mushrooms (better than it might sound). Blueberry-cherry cobbler ... served on a tortilla was a real dessert treat for the Station crew, since that was not included in our meal rotations. Celebrating this holiday in space ... was a very special experience, one that I will remember fondly in Thanksgivings to come."

Lasagna is one example of an ethnic dish that has become a popular part of the Thanksgiving meal for many American families. Lasagna first appeared in big-city Italian restaurants in the 1920s, and over the next 50 years it became a mainstay on countless dinner tables across the United States. In fact, the layered pasta dish became so widely accepted that many people began to think of it as an American food. From there it was only a short leap for lasagna to join the Thanksgiving menu.

Despite all the changes that have taken place through history, the Thanksgiving feast has retained its vital place in American culture for more than 300 years. Food remains at the center of the holiday tradition, but the exact components of the meal are less important than the fact that it is shared with friends and family.

Thanksgiving
Primary Sources

The Pilgrims and the First Thanksgiving

This painting of the *Mayflower*, and its small landing boat heading to shore,
was created by William Formby Halsall between 1900 and 1920.

The Mayflower Compact (1620)

After an arduous 66-day journey across the Atlantic Ocean, the Mayflower *and its 102 English passengers finally reached Cape Cod on November 11, 1620. Before going ashore, the colonists drew up and signed an agreement that formalized their intention to live together as a "civil Body Politick." This document, known as the Mayflower Compact, included provisions that allowed the colonists to elect leaders and to make and enforce laws. Some historians consider it to be the first instance of a democratic government being established in America.*

The original document was lost, but the earliest version printed, in Mourt's Relation *in 1622, included the signatures of each male head of household in Plymouth Colony. This transcript retains the spelling and punctuation of the document as it appeared in the source below.*

IN THE NAME OF GOD, AMEN. We, whose names are underwritten, the Loyal Subjects of our dread Sovereign Lord King *James,* by the Grace of God, of *Great Britain, France,* and *Ireland,* King, *Defender of the Faith,* &c. Having undertaken for the Glory of God, and Advancement of the Christian Faith, and the Honour of our King and Country, a Voyage to plant the first Colony in the northern Parts of *Virginia;* Do by these Presents, solemnly and mutually, in the Presence of God and one another, covenant and combine ourselves together into a civil Body Politick, for our better Ordering and Preservation, and Furtherance of the Ends aforesaid: And by Virtue hereof do enact, constitute, and frame, such just and equal Laws, Ordinances, Acts, Constitutions, and Officers, from time to time, as shall be thought most meet and convenient for the general Good of the Colony; unto which we promise all due Submission and Obedience. IN WITNESS whereof we have hereunto subscribed our names at *Cape-Cod* the eleventh of November, in the Reign of our Sovereign Lord King *James,* of *England, France,* and *Ireland,* the eighteenth, and of *Scotland,* the fifty-fourth, *Anno Domini;* 1620.

John Carver	William Brewster	John Alden
William Bradford	Isaac Allerton	Samuel Fuller
Edward Winslow	Miles Standish	Christopher Martin

James Chilton
John Craxton
John Billington
Moses Fletcher
John Goodman
Edward Tilly
John Tilly
Francis Cooke
Thomas Rogers
Thomas Tinker
John Rigdale

Edward Fuller
John Turner
Francis Eaton
John Allerton
Thomas English
Edward Doten
Edward Leister
Richard Gardiner
Digery Priest
Thomas Williams
Gilbert Winslow

Edmund Margeson
Peter Brown
Richard Bitteridge
George Soule
Richard Clark
William Mullins
William White
Richard Warren
John Howland
Stephen Hopkins

Source: Thorpe, Francis Newton, ed. *The Federal and State Constitutions, Colonial Charters, and Other Organic Laws of the States, Territories, and Colonies Now or Heretofore Forming the United States of America.* Compiled and edited under the Act of Congress of June 30, 1906. Washington, DC: Government Printing Office, 1909.

The Pilgrims' Peace Treaty with Massasoit (1621)

In March 1621 the Pilgrims made formal contact with the Native American peoples who lived in the area of Plymouth Colony. John Carver, the first governor of the colony, spent several days entertaining and engaging in diplomacy with Massasoit, the sachem or leader of the Wampanoag tribe. On March 22 the two men signed a peace treaty in which they agreed to come to each other's defense if they were attacked by the Narragansett Indians or other powerful rivals. Twenty-four years later, colonist William Bradford recounted the terms of the agreement with Massasoit in his book Of Plimoth Plantation.

I.   That neither he nor any of his, should injure or do hurt to any of their people.

II. That if any of his did any hurt to any of theirs, he should send the offender that they might punish him.

III. That if any thing were taken away from any of theirs, he should cause it to be restored; and they should do the like to his.

IV. That if any did unjustly war against him, they would aid him; and if any did war against them, he should aid them.

V.   That he should send to his neighbours confederates to certify them of this, that they might not wrong them, but might be likewise comprised in the conditions of peace.

VI. That when their men came to them, they should leave their bows and arrows behind them.

Source: Bradford, William. *Of Plymouth Plantation, 1620-1647.* Edited by Samuel Eliot Morison. New York: Knopf, 1970. Available online at Pilgrim Hall Museum, http://www.pilgrimhall. org/massa-tr.htm.

Edward Winslow's Account of the First Thanksgiving (1622)

The Pilgrims struggled through a harsh first winter in the New World, during which 46 people died from cold, hunger, and disease. By the end of the summer of 1621, however—thanks in part to the assistance of the local Wampanoag Indians—the Pilgrims had harvested plenty of food to last through the next winter. The colony's governor, William Bradford, suggested that they celebrate their good fortune with a feast.

The only information available to historians regarding the Pilgrims' 1621 feast comes from two surviving accounts of the event. One of these accounts was written by Edward Winslow, the colony's Indian ambassador, who mentioned the feast in a letter to a friend back in England. Winslow's letter was preserved in a collection of writings about the founding of Plymouth Colony called Mourt's Relation, *which was first published in London in 1622.*

In the text of the letter, which is excerpted below, Winslow recalls that Bradford sent four men out "fowling," or hunting the wild geese and ducks that were migrating through New England. He also notes that the Wampanoags' leader, Massasoit, and 90 of his men took part in the celebration.

Our harvest being gotten in, our governour sent foure men on fowling, that so we might after a speciall manner rejoyce together, after we had gathered the fruits of our labours; they foure in one day killed as much fowle, as with a little helpe beside, served the Company almost a weeke, at which time amongst other Recreations, we exercised our Armes, many of the Indians coming amongst us, and amongst the rest their greatest king Massasoyt, with some ninetie men, whom for three dayes we entertained and feasted, and they went out and killed five Deere, which they brought to the Plantation and bestowed on our Governour, and upon the Captaine [Miles Standish] and others. And although it be not always so plentifull, as it was at this time with us, yet by the goodness of God, we are so farre from want, that we often wish you partakers of our plentie.

Source: Winslow, Edward. Letter reprinted in *Mourt's Relation: A Journal of the Pilgrims at Plymouth 1622.* Edited by Dwight B. Heath. Boston: Applewood Books, 1963. Available online at Pilgrim Hall Museum, http://www.pilgrimhall.org/1stthnks.htm.

William Bradford's Account of the First Thanksgiving (1621)

Following a difficult first winter in America, the Pilgrims enjoyed a season of plenty in the fall of 1621. In addition to growing such crops as corn, squash, beans, barley, and peas, they also caught good quantities of fish and shellfish and hunted wild ducks, geese, turkeys, and deer. The governor of Plymouth Colony, William Bradford, suggested that the colonists hold a feast to celebrate their good fortune. He described the successful harvest in his journal, which was later published as a book called Of Plimoth Plantation, 1620-1647.

They begane now to gather in ye small harvest they had, and to fitte up their houses and dwellings against winter, being all well recovered in health & strength, and had all things in good plenty; For as some were thus imployed in affairs abroad, others were excersised in fishing, aboute codd, & bass, & other fish, of which yey [they] tooke good store, of which every family had their portion. All ye somer ther was no want. And now begane to come in store of foule, as winter approached, of which this place did abound when they came first (but afterward decreased by degrees). And besids water foule, ther was great store of wild Turkies, of which they tooke many, besids venison, &c. Besids, they had about a peck a meale a weeke to a person, or now since harvest, Indean corn to yt [that] proportion. Which made many afterwards write so largly of their plenty hear to their freinds in England, which were not fained [feigned], but true reports.

Source: Bradford, William. *Of Plymoth Plantation, 1620-1647.* Edited by Samuel Eliot Morison. New York: Knopf, 1970. Available online at Pilgrim Hall Museum, http://www.pilgrimhall. org/1stthnks.htm.

English Colonists Give Thanks
for Victory in King Philip's War (1676)

The Pilgrims initially established peaceful, cooperative relations with the Native American peoples who lived in the area of Plymouth Colony. The 1621 feast known as the "first Thanksgiving," which the Pilgrims shared with the local Wampanoag Indians, often serves as a symbol of this relationship. The situation changed dramatically in 1675, however, when a coalition of Native American tribes went to war against the rapidly expanding English colonies. The bloody, 14-month-long conflict, which became known as King Philip's War, marked the first chapter in a long history of conflict between European settlers and Native American peoples.

As King Philip's War neared an end in 1676, the governing council of Charlestown, Massachusetts, proclaimed June 29 as a day of thanksgiving. This holiday followed in the early tradition of proclaiming a solemn, holy day to express gratitude to God for a victory in battle or another instance of good fortune.

The Holy God having by a long and Continual Series of his Afflictive dispensations in and by the present Warr with the Heathen Natives of this land, written and brought to pass bitter things against his own Covenant people in this wilderness, yet so that we evidently discern that in the midst of his judgements he hath remembered mercy, having remembered his Footstool in the day of his sore displeasure against us for our sins, with many singular Intimations of his Fatherly Compassion, and regard; reserving many of our Towns from Desolation Threatened, and attempted by the Enemy, and giving us especially of late with many of our Confederates many signal Advantages against them, without such Disadvantage to ourselves as formerly we have been sensible of, if it be the Lord's mercy that we are not consumed, It certainly bespeaks our positive Thankfulness, when our Enemies are in any measure disappointed or destroyed; and fearing the Lord should take notice under so many Intimations of his returning mercy, we should be found an Insensible people, as not standing before Him with Thanksgiving, as well as lading him with our Complaints in the time of pressing Afflictions:

The Council has thought meet to appoint and set apart the 29th day of this instant June, as a day of Solemn Thanksgiving and praise to God for such his Goodness and Favour, many Particulars of which mercy might be Instanced, but we doubt not those who are sensible of God's Afflictions, have been as diligent to espy him returning to us; and that the Lord may behold us as a People offering Praise and thereby glorifying Him; the Council doth commend it to the Respective Ministers, Elders and people of this Jurisdiction; Solemnly and seriously to keep the same Beseeching that being perswaded by the mercies of God we may all, even this whole people offer up our bodies and soulds as a living and acceptable Service unto God by Jesus Christ.

Source: Governing Council of Charlestown, Massachusetts. "Thanksgiving Proclamation," June 20, 1676. Available online at The University of Oklahoma College of Law, Chronology of U.S. Historical Documents, http://www.law.ou.edu/ushistory/thanksgiv.shtml.

One of the Oldest Surviving
Printed Thanksgiving Proclamations (1723)

By the 1700s Thanksgiving Day had evolved into an annual holiday throughout the English colonies in the New World. Most colonial governors proclaimed a special day every fall to thank God for the year's blessings. One of the earliest surviving printed thanksgiving proclamations dates back to 1723, when Governor William Dummer of Massachusetts Bay Colony set aside November 28 for residents to celebrate the holiday.

By the HONOURABLE William Dummer Esq; Lieutenant GOVERNOUR and Commander in Chief of His Majesty's Province of the *Massachusetts-Bay* in *New-England*: A Proclamation for a General THANKSGIVING.

FORASMUCH as amidst the various & awful Rebukes of Heaven with which we are righteously aflicted, We are still under the highest and most indispensible Obligations of Gratitude for the many Instances of the divine Goodness in the course of the Year past, More especially, That it has pleased Almighty GOD to prolong the Life of our most gracious Sovereign Lord the KING, Their Royal Highnesses the Prince & Princess of Wales, and Their Illustrious Offspring, and to give an happy Increase to the Royal Family; To defeat the wicked and desperate Conspiracies against His Majesty's Sacred Person and rightful Government, and to Direct the Councils of the Nation to such Measures for the Suppressing & Punishing the same, as under GOD may prove the Means of their lasting Quiet & Security; So far to succeed the Administrations of His Majesty's Government in this Province, To continue our invaluable Privileges, To restore Health to us, To give us great Plenty of the Fruits of the Earth, to Defeat in some Measure the repeated Attempts of the Indian Enemy against us, and to defend so many of our frontier Plantations from their Rage & Fury, To guard our Sea-Coasts against the rapacious & bloody Pirates, and deliver many of them into the Hands of Justice; and above all that He continues to us the precious Benefits & Liberties of the Gospel:

I have therefore thought fit, by and with the Advice of his Majesty's Council, to Order & Appoint that Thursday the Twenty-eighth of November Currant be solemnly Observed as a Day of Publick THANKSGIVING throughout this Province, exhorting both Ministers and People in their respective Assemblies to offer up their unfeigned THANKS to almighty GOD for these and all other his unmerited Favours; And all Service Labour is forbidden on the said Day.

Given at the Council Chamber in Boston the Sixth Day November 1723. In the tenth Year of the Reign of Our Sovereign Lord GEORGE, by the Grace of GOD of Great Britain, France and Ireland, KING, Defender of the Faith, &c.

By Order ofthe Honourable the Lieutenant Governour, W. DUMMER by and with the Advice of the Council, Josiah Willard, Sec.

GOD Save the King.

Source: Dummer, William. "Thanksgiving Proclamation 1723." Available online at Pilgrim Hall Museum, http://www.pilgrimhall.org/GivingThanks3a.htm.

Colonial Governor Jonathan Belcher's
Proclamation of a General Fast (1735)

As Thanksgiving gradually became an annual holiday throughout New England in the 1700s, the English colonies in America also continued to observe public days of fasting, prayer, and humiliation. Some colonial governors proclaimed an annual day of fasting every spring, while others proclaimed special days of fasting in response to specific misfortunes. In the proclamation reproduced below, Governor Jonathan Belcher declares April 1, 1735, a day of fasting for the residents of Massachusetts Bay Colony, in an effort to regain God's favor during an epidemic.

By His EXCELLENCY JONATHAN BELCHER, Esq; Captain General and Governor in Chief in and over His Majesty's Province of the Massachusetts Bay in New England

A Proclamation for a general FAST.

UPON consideration of the holy anger of Almighty GOD evidently manifested in the various judgments inflicted on us (more especially in sending among us a mortal sickness, which has already greatly wasted our numbers, and threatens yet more terrible effects unless prevented by the merciful imposition of Providence), upon consideration likewise of our absolute dependance on the blessing of GOD for success in the interests and affairs of the spring and summer ensuing:

I have thought fit, with the advice of His Majesty's Council, to order and appoint Thursday the first day of April next to be observed as a day of solemn fasting and prayer throughout the Province, thereby exhorting both ourselves and people religiously to attend the duties of the said day by sincere and penitent confession of their manifold sins, whereby GOD has been provoked to visit this people with sore and grievous calamities, and by humble and earnest supplications to the GOD of all grace for averting the tokens of His righteous displeasure and conferring on us all needful favors: In particular, that He would long preserve the life of our sovereign lord the KING and our most gracious QUEEN, together with His Royal Highness the Prince of Wales, the Duke, and the other branches of the Royal Family; That He would grant His merciful influence and conduct to His Majesty's Councils for the continuance of the peace of his kingdoms and dominions, and for the restoring of peace to Europe, under His Majesty's wise mediation; That He would please to direct and bless the administration of the government of this Province; That He would give us a favorable seed time and in due season, a plentiful harvest; That He would prosper our trade and navigation and maintain the peace of our sea coasts and inland borders, and that He would compassionate [show compassion toward] our great distress under the wasting and mortal sickness by sanctifying this awful visitation and restoring to us the voice of health. And above all, that He would grant unto us the plentiful effusions of the HOLY SPIRIT, that the sense of His righteous displeasure against us may effect a general repentance and reformation throughout our whole land, and the kingdom of our Lord and Savior JESUS CHRIST may come and the whole earth be filled with His glory. And all servile labor and recreations are hereby forbidden on said day.

Given at the Council Chamber in Boston the twenty-sixth day of February, 1735, in the ninth year of the reign of Our Sovereign Lord GEORGE the Second, by the grace of GOD, of Great Britain, France, and Ireland, KING, Defender of the Faith, etc.

By His Excellency's Command, with the Advice of the Council,
J. Willard, Secretary J. BELCHER.

GOD save the KING.

Source: Belcher, Jonathan. "Proclamation for a General Fast," February 26, 1735. Available online at This Common Feast: The South Atlantic Thanksgiving Project, http://www. southatlanticcenter.org/tgiving/proclaim.html.

The Revolutionary Period

The Continental Congress issued this proclamation in thanksgiving
for the victory over British troops at Saratoga in 1777.
See the first document in this section for the transcription of the proclamation.

The Continental Congress Gives Thanks
during the Revolutionary War (1777)

During the Revolutionary War, the American colonies often proclaimed days of thanksgiving for victories in battle. On November 1, 1777, the Continental Congress proclaimed a day of thanksgiving to be held on December 18 in gratitude for the patriots' victory at Saratoga. This historic proclamation, written by Samuel Adams, was the first holiday to be designated by a national authority for all 13 American states. Rather than creating an annual holiday, however, it followed in the tradition of proclaiming special days of thanks for positive events.

IN CONGRESS
November 1, 1777

FORASMUCH as it is the indispensable Duty of all Men to adore the superintending Providence of Almighty God; to acknowledge with Gratitude their Obligation to him for Benefits received, and to implore such farther Blessings as they stand in Need of: And it having pleased him in his abundant Mercy, not only to continue to us the innumerable Bounties of his common Providence; but also to smile upon us in the Prosecution of a just and necessary War, for the Defense and Establishment of our unalienable Rights and Liberties; particularly in that he hath been pleased, in so great a Measure, to prosper the Means used for the Support of our Troops, and to crown our Arms with most signal success:

It is therefore recommended to the legislative or executive Powers of these UNITED STATES to set apart THURSDAY, the eighteenth Day of December next, for SOLEMN THANKSGIVING and PRAISE: That at one Time and with one Voice, the good People may express the grateful Feelings of their Hearts, and consecrate themselves to the Service of their Divine Benefactor; and that, together with their sincere Acknowledgments and Offerings, they may join the penitent Confession of their manifold Sins, whereby they had forfeited every Favor; and their humble and earnest Supplication that it may please GOD through the Merits of JESUS CHRIST, mercifully to forgive and blot them out of Remembrance; That it may please him graciously to afford his

Blessing on the Governments of these States respectively, and prosper the public Council of the whole: To inspire our Commanders, both by Land and Sea, and all under them, with that Wisdom and Fortitude which may render them fit Instruments, under the Providence of Almighty GOD, to secure for these United States, the greatest of all human Blessings, INDEPENDENCE and PEACE: That it may please him, to prosper the Trade and Manufactures of the People, and the Labor of the Husbandman, that our Land may yield its Increase: To take Schools and Seminaries of Education, so necessary for cultivating the Principles of true Liberty, Virtue and Piety, under his nurturing Hand; and to prosper the Means of Religion, for the promotion and enlargement of that Kingdom, which consisteth "in Righteousness, Peace and Joy in the Holy Ghost."

And it is further recommended, That servile Labor, and such Recreation, as, though at other Times innocent, may be unbecoming the Purpose of this Appointment, be omitted on so solemn an Occasion.

Source: Continental Congress. "Thanksgiving Proclamation," November 1, 1777. Available online at This Common Feast: The South Atlantic Thanksgiving Project, http://www. southatlanticcenter.org/tgiving/proclaim.html.

Arguments before Congress Regarding a National Thanksgiving Holiday (1789)

Shortly after the Constitution created the U.S. government, the first Congress of the United States considered adopting a proposal calling for a national Thanksgiving holiday. The effort to create such a holiday was led by Elias Boudinot of New Jersey, who had served as president of the Continental Congress during the Revolution. But the proposal met with stiff resistance from some members of the legislative body, especially Thomas Tucker of South Carolina. The following excerpt from the Annals of Congress *describes the arguments surrounding the issue that took place on September 25, 1789.*

Mr. BOUDINOT said, he could not think of letting the session pass over without offering an opportunity to all the citizens of the United States of joining with one voice, in returning to Almighty God their sincere thanks for the many blessings he had poured down upon them. With that view, therefore, he would move the following resolution:

> *Resolved,* That a joint committee of both Houses be directed to wait upon the President of the United States, to request that he would recommend to the people of the United States a day of public thanksgiving and prayer, to be observed by acknowledging, with grateful hearts, that many signal favors of Almighty God, especially by affording them an opportunity peaceably to establish a Constitution of government for their safety and happiness.

Mr. BURKE did not like this mimicking of European customs, where they make a mere mockery of thanksgivings. Two parties at war frequently sung *TE DEUM* for the same event, though to one it was a victory, and to the other a defeat.

Mr. BOUDINOT was sorry to hear arguments drawn from the abuse of a good thing against the use of it. He hoped no gentleman would make a serious opposition to a measure both prudent and just.

Mr. TUCKER thought the House had no business to interfere in a matter which did not concern them. Why should the President direct the people to do what, perhaps, they have no mind to do? They may not be inclined to return thanks for a Constitution until they have experienced that it promotes their safety and happiness. We do not yet know but they may have reason to be dissatisfied with the effects it has already produced; but whether this be so or not, it is a business with which Congress have nothing to do; it is a religious matter, and, as such, is proscribed to us. If a day of thanksgiving must take place, let it be done by the authority of the several States; they know best what reason their constituents have to be pleased with the establishment of this Constitution.

Mr. SHERMAN justified the practice of thanksgiving, on any signal event, not only as a laudable one in itself, but as warranted by a number of precedents in holy writ: for instance, the solemn thanksgivings and rejoicings which took place in the time of Solomon, after the building of the temple, was a case in point. This example, he thought, worthy of Christian imitation on the present occasion; and he would agree with the gentleman who moved the resolution.

Mr. BOUDINOT quoted further precedents from the practice of the late Congress; and hoped the motion would meet a ready acquiescence.

The question was now put on the resolution, and it was carried in the affirmative: and Messers. BOUDINOT, SHERMAN, and SYLVESTER were appointed a committee on the part of the House.

Source: *Annals of Congress*, House of Representatives, 1st Cong., 1st sess., September 25, 1789. Vol. I, pp. 949-50. Washington, DC: Gales and Seaton, 1834. Available online at the Library of Congress, American Memory Collection, http://memory.loc.gov/ammem/amlaw/lwac.html.

George Washington's
Thanksgiving Proclamation for the United States (1789)

Shortly after taking office under the U.S. Constitution, President George Washington issued the first Thanksgiving proclamation for the new nation, setting aside November 26, 1789, as a national holiday. In an interesting historical footnote, Washington's original, handwritten proclamation was lost for more than a century. The document finally resurfaced in 1921, when an expert from the manuscripts division of the Library of Congress discovered it among the sale items at an auction in New York City and purchased it for the National Archives at a cost of $300.

By the President of the United States of America, a Proclamation

Whereas it is the duty of all Nations to acknowledge the providence of Almighty God, to obey his will, to be grateful for his benefits, and humbly to implore his protection and favor—and whereas both Houses of Congress have by their joint Committee requested me to recommend to the People of the United States a day of public thanksgiving and prayer to be observed by acknowledging with grateful hearts the many signal favors of Almighty God especially by affording them an opportunity peaceably to establish a form of government for their safety and happiness.

Now therefore I do recommend and assign Thursday the 26th day of November next to be devoted by the People of these States to the service of that great and glorious Being, who is the beneficent Author of all the good that was, that is, or that will be—That we may then all unite in rendering unto him our sincere and humble thanks—for his kind care and protection of the People of this Country previous to their becoming a Nation—for the signal and manifold mercies, and the favorable interpositions of his Providence which we experienced in the course and conclusion of the late war—for the great degree of tranquillity, union, and plenty, which we have since enjoyed—for the peaceable and rational manner, in which we have been enabled to establish constitutions of government for our safety and happiness, and particularly the national One now lately instituted—for the civil and religious liberty with which we are blessed; and the means we have of acquiring and diffusing useful knowledge; and in general for all the great and various favors which he hath been pleased to confer upon us.

And also that we may then unite in most humbly offering our prayers and supplications to the great Lord and Ruler of Nations and beseech him to pardon our national and other transgressions—to enable us all, whether in public or private stations, to perform our several and relative duties properly and punctually—to render our national government a blessing to all the people, by constantly being a Government of wise, just, and constitutional laws, discreetly and faithfully executed and obeyed—to protect and guide all Sovereigns and Nations (especially such as have shewn kindness unto us) and to bless them with good government, peace, and concord—To promote the knowledge and practice of true religion and virtue, and the encrease of science among them and us—and generally to grant unto all Mankind such a degree of temporal prosperity as he alone knows to be best.

Given under my hand at the City of New York the third day of October in the year of our Lord 1789.

Go. WASHINGTON

Source: Washington, George. "Thanksgiving Proclamation," October 3, 1789. Available online at the Library of Congress, American Memory Collection, http://memory.loc.gov/ammem/gwhtml/gwhome.html.

Thomas Jefferson Explains His Opposition to a National Thanksgiving Holiday (1802)

Although George Washington proclaimed an annual Thanksgiving Day throughout his presidency, some of his successors objected to the idea of making it a federal holiday. Thomas Jefferson, the third president of the United States, refused to proclaim a national Thanksgiving Day because he felt that it violated the constitutional separation of church and state. He explained his decision in an 1802 letter to a group of Baptists in Danbury, Connecticut.

To messers. Nehemiah Dodge, Ephraim Robbins, & Stephen S. Nelson, a committee of the Danbury Baptist association in the state of Connecticut.

Gentlemen

The affectionate sentiments of esteem and approbation which you are so good as to express towards me, on behalf of the Danbury Baptist association, give me the highest satisfaction. My duties dictate a faithful and zealous pursuit of the interests of my constituents, & in proportion as they are persuaded of my fidelity to those duties, the discharge of them becomes more & more pleasing.

Believing with you that religion is a matter which lies solely between Man & his God, that he owes account to none other for his faith or his worship, that the legitimate powers of government reach actions only, & not opinions, I contemplate with sovereign reverence that act of the whole American people which declared that their legislature should "make no law respecting an establishment of religion, or prohibiting the free exercise thereof," thus building a wall of separation between Church & State. Adhering to this expression of the supreme will of the nation in behalf of the rights of conscience, I shall see with sincere satisfaction the progress of those sentiments which tend to restore to man all his natural rights, convinced he has no natural right in opposition to his social duties.

I reciprocate your kind prayers for the protection & blessing of the common father and creator of man, and tender you for yourselves & your religious association, assurances of my high respect & esteem.

Th Jefferson
Jan. 1. 1802.

Source: Jefferson, Thomas. "Letter to the Danbury Baptists," January 1, 1802. *Library of Congress Information Bulletin*, Vol. 57, No. 6, June 1998. Available online at Library of Congress, http://www.loc.gov/ loc/lcib/9806/danpre.html.

America Embraces the Pilgrims

A view of Plymouth Rock, the supposed landing spot of the Pilgrims.

Daniel Webster
Honors the Pilgrims in a Famous Speech (1820)

After receding to the background of U.S. history during the 18th and early 19th centuries, the Pilgrims began claiming a place in the popular imagination in 1820. On December 22 of that year, the famous orator Daniel Webster presented a moving tribute to them at a bicentennial celebration of their arrival in Plymouth, Massachusetts. Webster's speech, excerpted below, helped elevate the Pilgrims to iconic status as "forefathers of the nation" in the eyes of many Americans. In honoring the English colonists, however, Webster also condemns the indigenous peoples of America as "barbarians" and "savages." These sorts of deeply prejudiced views of Native Americans were commonplace at that time.

We have come to this Rock, to record here our homage for our Pilgrim Fathers; our sympathy in their sufferings; our gratitude for their labors; our admiration of their virtues; our veneration for their piety; and our attachment to those principles of civil and religious liberty, which they encountered the dangers of the ocean, the storms of heaven, the violence of savages, disease, exile, and famine, to enjoy and to establish. And we would leave here, also, for the generations which are rising up rapidly to fill our places, some proof that we have endeavored to transmit the great inheritance unimpaired; that in our estimate of public principles and private virtue, in our veneration of religion and piety, in our devotion to civil and religious liberty, in our regard for whatever advances human knowledge or improves human happiness, we are not altogether unworthy of our origin.

There is a local feeling connected with this occasion, too strong to be resisted; a sort of *genius of the place,* which inspires and awes us. We feel that we are on the spot where the first scene of our history was laid; where the hearths and altars of New England were first placed; where Christianity, and civilization, and letters made their first lodgement, in a vast extent of country, covered with a wilderness, and peopled by roving barbarians. We are here, at the season of the year at which the event took place. The imagination irresistibly and rapidly draws around us the principal features and the leading characters in the original scene. We cast our eyes abroad on the ocean, and we see where the little bark, with the interesting group upon its deck, made its slow progress to the shore. We look around us, and behold the hills and promontories where the anxious eyes of our fathers first saw the places of habitation and of rest. We feel the cold which benumbed, and listen to the winds which pierced them. Beneath us is the Rock, on which New England received the feet of the Pilgrims. We seem even to behold them, as they struggle with the elements, and, with toilsome efforts, gain the shore. We listen to the chiefs in council; we see the unexampled exhibition of female fortitude and resignation; we hear the whisperings of youthful impatience, and we see, what a painter of our own has also represented by his pencil, chilled and shivering childhood, houseless, but for a mother's arms, couchless, but for a mother's breast, till our own blood almost freezes....

The hours of this day are rapidly flying, and this occasion will soon be passed. Neither we nor our children can expect to behold its return. They are in the distant regions of futurity, they exist only in the all-creating power of God, who shall stand here a hundred years hence, to trace, through us, their descent from the Pilgrims, and to survey, as we have now surveyed, the progress of their country, during the lapse of a century. We would anticipate their concurrence with us in our sentiments of deep regard for our common ancestors. We would anticipate and partake the pleasure with which they will then recount the steps of New England's advancement. On the morning of that day, although it will not disturb us in our repose, the voice of acclamation and gratitude, commencing on the Rock of Plymouth, shall be transmitted through millions of the sons of the Pilgrims, till it lose itself in the murmurs of the Pacific seas.

We would leave for the consideration of those who shall then occupy our places, some proof that we hold the blessings transmitted from our fathers in just estimation; some proof of our attachment to the cause of good government, and of civil and religious liberty; some proof of a sincere and ardent desire to promote every thing which may enlarge the understandings and improve the hearts of men. And when, from the long distance of a hundred years, they shall look back upon us, they shall know, at least, that we possessed affections, which, running backward and warming with gratitude for what our ancestors have done for our happiness, run forward also to our posterity, and meet them with cordial salutation, ere yet they have arrived on the shore of being.

Advance, then, ye future generations! We would hail you, as you rise in your long succession, to fill the places which we now fill, and to taste the blessings of existence where we are passing, and soon shall have passed, our own human duration. We bid you welcome to this pleasant land of the fathers. We bid you welcome to the healthful skies and the verdant fields of New England. We greet your accession to the great inheritance which we have enjoyed. We welcome you to the blessings of good government and religious liberty. We welcome you to the treasures of science and the delights of learning. We welcome you to the transcendent sweets of domestic life, to the happiness of kindred, and parents, and children. We welcome you to the immeasurable blessings of rational existence, the immortal hope of Christianity, and the light of everlasting truth!

Source: Webster, Daniel. "First Settlement of New England." Speech delivered in Plymouth, Massachusetts, December 22, 1820. In *The Great Speeches and Orations of Daniel Webster with an Essay on Daniel Webster as a Master of English Style* by Edwin P. Whipple. Boston: Little, Brown, & Co., 1889.

"The Landing of the Pilgrim Fathers in New England" a Poem by Felicia Dorothea Hemans (1826)

The story of the Pilgrims and the founding of Plymouth Colony began to claim an important place in American popular culture during the early 1800s. The following poem by Felicia Dorothea Hemans, first published in 1826, presents the Pilgrims as strong and courageous people who overcame all sorts of dangers in order to establish a lasting tradition of religious freedom in America.

The breaking waves dash'd high
On a stern and rock-bound coast,
And the woods against a stormy sky
Their giant branches toss'd;

And the heavy night hung dark,
The hills and waters o'er,
When a band of exiles moor'd their bark
On the wild New England shore.

Not as the conqueror comes,
They, the true-hearted, came;
Not with the roll of the stirring drums,
And the trumpet that sings of fame;

Not as the flying come,
In silence and in fear;—
They shook the depths of the desert gloom
With their hymns of lofty cheer.

Amidst the storm they sang,
And the stars heard and the sea:
And the sounding aisles of the dim woods rang
To the anthem of the free!

The ocean eagle soar'd
From his nest by the white wave's foam
And the rocking pines of the forest roar'd—
This was their welcome home!

There were men with hoary hair
Amidst that pilgrim band:—
Why had they come to wither there,
Away from their childhood's land?

There was woman's fearless eye,
Lit by her deep love's truth;
There was manhood's brow serenely high,
And the fiery heart of youth.

What sought they thus afar?
Bright jewels of the mine?
The wealth of seas, the spoils of war?—
They sought a faith's pure shrine!

Ay, call it holy ground,
The soil where first they trode.
They have left unstained, what there they found—
Freedom to worship God.

Source: Hemans, Felicia Dorothea. "The Landing of the Pilgrim Fathers in New England." In *The League of the Alps, The Siege of Valencia, The Vespers of Palermo, and Other Poems.* Boston: Hilliard, Gray, Little, and Wilkins, 1826. Available online at Representative Poetry Online, Department of English, University of Toronto, http://rpo.library.utoronto.ca/poem/937.html.

A Historian Makes Reference to the "First Thanksgiving" (1841)

Throughout the eighteenth and early nineteenth centuries, the story of the Pilgrims and their 1621 harvest celebration was largely forgotten and did not play a role in popular celebrations of Thanksgiving. This situation began to change in 1841, when historian Alexander Young published a collection of writings by the founders of Plymouth Colony called Chronicles of the Pilgrim Forefathers. *This work contains colonist Edward Winslow's account of the Pilgrims' 1621 harvest celebration.*

In an explanatory footnote, Young refers to the event Winslow describes as the "first Thanksgiving" and speculates that the Pilgrims' feast included turkey. Historians have since determined that this marked the earliest scholarly reference to any event as the "first Thanksgiving." As it turned out, Young's interpretation forged a lasting connection between the Pilgrims' feast and New England's Thanksgiving holiday tradition. The document below includes excerpts from the preface to Young's book, as well as the influential footnote from Chapter XV.

Preface.

This volume will be found to contain an authentic History of the Pilgrim Fathers who planted the Colony of Plymouth, from their origin in John Robinson's congregation in 1602, to his death in 1625, written by themselves. Some account of the nature of these Chronicles, and of the circumstances which led to their compilation in this form, may not be unacceptable to the reader....

[Young describes how he discovered a copy of Governor William Bradford's history of Plymouth Colony, which most historians had believed to be lost. He goes on to describe the various documents contained in his own book.]

The next document is Bradford's and Winslow's Journal of the first settlement of the Colony, containing a minute diary of events from the arrival of the *Mayflower* at Cape Cod, November 9, 1620, to the return of the *Fortune*, December 11, 1621. This document joins on to the former, making a continuous narrative. It was printed in London in 1622, with a Preface signed by G. Mourt, and has since been usually cited as *Mourt's Relation*. It will be seen from the notes on pages 113 and 115 of this volume, that Mourt was probably George Morton, the father of Nathaniel, the Secretary, then resident in England, that he had no hand in writing the Journal, but that it was actually written by Bradford and Winslow, a circumstance which gives to it new value and interest, and confers on it the highest authority....

The value of these contemporaneous documents cannot be overstated. They are the earliest chronicles of New England. We have here the first book of our history, written by the actors themselves. We should esteem it a fortunate circumstance, a peculiar privilege, that we thus have the whole story of the origin of this earliest of our northern colonies in the very words of the first planters. In authority and importance nothing can exceed them; and I feel that I have been engaged in a useful as well as interesting labor in collecting together and illustrating these scattered memorials of the Fathers. The notes will be found to be copious and various, touching upon all points, and in all cases referring to authorities from which the statements may be verified, and fuller information be obtained. Considering myself as engaged in erecting another monument to the memory of the Pilgrims, I have spared neither labor nor expense in endeavoring to render the work accurate and complete. If the reader shall derive from its perusal the same satisfaction which I have found in its compilation, I shall feel myself abundantly remunerated for this labor of love.

Regarding these documents as the only authentic chronicles of those times, I have considered all deviations from them in subsequent writers as errors, and when they have fallen under my notice, I have not scrupled to point them out. In this I have no other object in view than historical accuracy; and accordingly for whatever errors I may have fallen into, I shall hold myself equally obnoxious to criticism....

Chapter XV.

[Young reprints the text of the famous December 1621 letter from Edward Winslow to a friend in England, which describes a feast shared by the Pilgrims and the local Wampanoag people. The following sentence, taken from Winslow's letter, includes Young's footnotes.]

Our harvest being gotten in, our governor[2] sent four men on fowling, that so we might, after a special manner, rejoice together after we had gathered the fruits of our labors.[3]

[2] Bradford

[3] This was the first Thanksgiving, the harvest festival of New England. On this occasion they no doubt feasted on the wild turkey as well as venison.

Source: Young, Alexander. *Chronicles of the Pilgrim Fathers of the Colony of Plymouth, from 1602 to 1625.* Boston: C.C. Little, & J. Brown, 1841.

New England Thanksgivings

HOME TO THANKSGIVING.

Currier & Ives created this print, titled *Home to Thanksgiving,* around 1867.

Harriet Beecher Stowe Recalls
a Traditional New England Thanksgiving (1820s)

Harriet Beecher Stowe is probably best known as the author of Uncle Tom's Cabin, *an 1852 novel that vividly portrayed the horrors of slavery and thus increased the tensions between North and South that led to the Civil War. After that conflict ended, Stowe published what is widely considered to be her next most-important work, a reminiscence about small-town life in New England during the early 19th century called* Oldtown Folks. *In the following excerpt from the chapter "How We Kept Thanksgiving at Oldtown," Stowe recalls the excitement that surrounded the holiday in New England during the 1820s.*

On the whole, about this time in our life we were a reasonably happy set of children. The Thanksgiving festival of that year is particularly impressed on my mind as a white day.

Are there any of my readers who do not know what Thanksgiving day is to a child? Then let them go back with me, and recall the image of it as we kept it at Oldtown....

When the apples were all gathered and the cider was all made, and the yellow pumpkins were rolled in from many a hill in billows of gold, and the corn was husked, and the labors of the season were done, and the warm, late days of Indian Summer came in, dreamy and calm and still, with just frost enough to crisp the ground of a morning, but with warm trances of benignant, sunny hours at noon, there came over the community a sort of genial repose of spirit,—a sense of something accomplished, and of a new golden mark made in advance on the calendar of life,—and the deacon began to say to the minister, of a Sunday, "I suppose it's about time for the Thanksgiving proclamation."

Rural dress-makers about this time were extremely busy in making up festival garments, for everybody's new dress, if she was to have one at all, must appear on Thanksgiving day....

For as much as a week beforehand, "we children" were employed in chopping mince for pies to a most wearisome fineness, and in pounding cinnamon, allspice, and cloves in a great lignum-vitae mortar; and the sound of this pounding and chopping re-echoed through all the rafters of the old house with a hearty and vigorous cheer, most refreshing to our spirits....

At other times of the year we sometimes murmured at these labors, but those that were supposed to usher in the great Thanksgiving festival were always entered into with enthusiasm. There were signs of richness all around us,— stoning of raisins, cutting of citron, slicing of candied orange-peel. Yet all these were only dawnings and intimations of what was coming during the week of real preparation, after the Governor's proclamation had been read.

The glories of that proclamation! We knew beforehand the Sunday it was to be read, and walked to church with alacrity, filled with gorgeous and vague expectations.

The cheering anticipation sustained us through what seemed to us the long waste of the sermon and prayers; and when at last the auspicious moment approached,—when the last quaver of the last hymn had died out,—the whole house rippled with a general movement of complacency, and a satisfied smile of pleased expectation might be seen gleaming on the faces of all the young people, like a ray of sunshine through a garden of flowers.

Thanksgiving was now dawning! We children poked one another, and fairly giggled with unreproved delight as we listened to the crackle of the slowly unfolding document. That great sheet of paper impressed us as something supernatural, by reason of its mighty size, and by the broad seal of the State affixed thereto; and when the minister read therefrom, "By his Excellency, the Governor of the Commonwealth of Massachusetts, a Proclamation," our mirth was with difficulty repressed by admonitory glances from our sympathetic elders. Then, after a solemn enumeration of the benefits which the Commonwealth had that year received at the hands of Divine Providence, came at the last naming of the eventful day, and, at the end of all, the imposing heraldic words, "God save the Commonwealth of Massachusetts." And then, as the congregation broke up and dispersed, all went their several ways with schemes of mirth and feasting in their heads.

And now came on the week in earnest....

The making of pies at this period assumed vast proportions that verged upon the sublime. Pies were made by forties and fifties and hundreds, and made of everything on the earth and under the earth....

Fancy the heat and vigor of the great pan-formation, when Aunt Lois and Aunt Keziah, and my mother and grandmother, all in ecstasies of creative inspiration, ran, bustled, and hurried,—mixing, rolling, tasting, consulting,—alternately setting us children to work when anything could be made of us, and then chasing us all out of the kitchen when our misinformed childhood ventured to take too many liberties with the sacred mysteries. Then out we would all fly at the kitchen door, like sparks from a blacksmith's window....

Well, at last, when all the chopping and pounding and baking and brewing, preparatory to the festival, were gone through with, the eventful day dawned. All the tribes of the Badger family were to come back home to the old house, with all the relations of every degree, to eat the Thanksgiving dinner. And it was understood that in the evening the minister and his lady would look in upon us, together with some of the select aristocracy of Oldtown.

Great as the preparations were for the dinner, everything was so contrived that not a soul in the house should be kept from the morning service of Thanksgiving in the church, and from listening to the Thanksgiving sermon, in which the minister was expected to express his views freely concerning the politics of the country, and the state of things in society generally, in a somewhat more secular vein of thought than was deemed exactly appropriate to the Lord's day. But it is to be confessed, that, when the good man got carried away by the enthusiasm of his subject to extend these exercises beyond a certain length, anxious glances, exchanged between good wives, sometimes indicated a weakness of the flesh, having a tender reference to the turkeys and chickens and chicken pies, which might possibly be over-doing in the ovens at home....

But who shall do justice to the dinner, and describe the turkey, and chickens, and chicken pies, with all that endless variety of vegetables which the American soil and climate have contributed to the table, and which . . . were all piled together in jovial abundance upon the smoking board?

When sermons and prayers were all over, we children rushed home to see the great feast of the year spread.

What chitterings and chatterings there were all over the house, as all the aunties and uncles and cousins came pouring in, taking off their things, looking at one another's bonnets and dresses, and mingling their comments on the morning sermon with various opinions on the new millinery outfits, and with bits of home news, and kindly neighborhood gossip....

But who shall do justice to the dinner, and describe the turkey, and chickens, and chicken pies, with all that endless variety of vegetables which the American soil and climate have contributed to the table, and which, without regard to the French doctrine of courses, were all piled together in jovial abundance upon the smoking board? There was much carving and laughing and talking and eating, and all showed that cheerful ability to despatch the provisions which was the ruling spirit of the hour. After the meat came the plum-puddings, and then the endless array of pies, till human nature was actually bewildered and overpowered by the tempting variety; and even we children turned from the profusion offered to us, and wondered what was the matter that we could eat no more....

And now, the dinner being cleared away, we youngsters, already excited to a tumult of laughter, tumbled into the best room, under the supervision of Uncle Bill, to relieve ourselves with a game of "blind-man's-buff," while the elderly women washed up the dishes and got the house in order, and the menfolks went out to the barn to look at the cattle, and walked over the farm and talked of the crops.

In the evening the house was all open and lighted with the best of tallow candles, which Aunt Lois herself had made with especial care for this illumination. It was understood that we were to have a dance, and black Caesar, full of turkey and pumpkin pie, and giggling in the very jollity of his heart, had that afternoon rosined his bow, and tuned his fiddle, and practised jigs and Virginia reels, in a way that made us children think him a perfect Orpheus....

As nine o'clock struck, the whole scene dissolved and melted; for what well-regulated village would think of carrying festivities beyond that hour?

And so ended our Thanksgiving at Oldtown.

Source: Stowe, Harriet Beecher. "Chapter XXVII — How We Kept Thanksgiving at Oldtown." *Oldtown Folks.* Boston: Fields, Osgood, 1869.

"Come, Ye Thankful People, Come,"
a Hymn by Henry Alford (1844)

"Come, Ye Thankful People, Come" is a hymn often sung in Christian churches at Thanksgiving. The noted English hymnologist Henry Alford wrote the words in 1844. George J. Elvey, organist for St. George's Chapel in Windsor, England, composed the music in 1858, and the tune was set to Alford's words three years later. The first verse of the hymn refers to "harvest home," an annual harvest festival observed in England from the Middle Ages. The later verses use the cultivation and harvest of crops as a metaphor for spiritual growth and God's final judgment.

Come, ye thankful people, come, raise the song of harvest home;
All is safely gathered in, ere the winter storms begin.
God our Maker doth provide for our wants to be supplied;
Come to God's own temple, come, raise the song of harvest home.

All the world is God's own field, fruit unto His praise to yield;
Wheat and tares [destructive weeds] together sown unto joy or sorrow grown.
First the blade and then the ear, then the full corn shall appear;
Lord of harvest, grant that we wholesome grain and pure may be.

For the Lord our God shall come, and shall take His harvest home;
From His field shall in that day all offenses purge away,
Giving angels charge at last in the fire the tares to cast;
But the fruitful ears to store in His garner [granary] evermore.

Even so, Lord, quickly come, bring Thy final harvest home;
Gather Thou Thy people in, free from sorrow, free from sin,
There, forever purified, in Thy garner to abide;
Come, with all Thine angels come, raise the glorious harvest home.

Source: Alford, Henry. "Come, Ye Thankful People, Come." In *It's Time for Thanksgiving*, by Elizabeth Hough Sechrist and Janette Woolsey. 1957. Reprint. Detroit: Omnigraphics, 1999. Available online at http://www.cyberhymnal.org/htm/c/o/comeytpc.htm.

"Over the River and Through the Wood," a Poem by Lydia Maria Child (1845)

"Over the River and Through the Wood" is one of the most familiar and beloved songs of the holiday season. It captures the excitement and joy that many people—especially children—feel while traveling homeward for a Thanksgiving feast. The lyrics come from a 19th-century poem by Lydia Maria Child, which describes a traditional New England winter holiday celebration. It was originally published as "A New-England Boy's Song about Thanksgiving Day" in an 1845 volume of poetry called Flowers for Children. *In her later career, Child wrote popular advice books for women and girls, edited a children's magazine, and became a prominent member of the movement to abolish slavery in the United States.*

Over the river and through the wood
To Grandmother's house we go.
The horse knows the way
To carry the sleigh
Through white and drifted snow.

Over the river and through the wood
Oh, how the wind does blow!
It stings the toes
And bites the nose,
As over the ground we go.

Over the river and through the wood
To have a first-rate play.
Hear the bells ring,
Ting-a-ling-ling!
Hurrah for Thanksgiving Day!

Over the river and through the wood,
Trot fast, my dapple gray!
Spring over the ground
Like a hunting hound,
For this is Thanksgiving Day.

Over the river and through the wood,
And straight through the barnyard gate.

We seem to go
Extremely slow—
It is so hard to wait!

Over the river and through the wood—
Now Grandmother's cap I spy!
Hurrah for fun!
Is the pudding done?
Hurrah for the pumpkin pie!

Source: Child, Lydia Maria. "The New-England Boy's Song about Thanksgiving Day." *Flowers for Children*. Vol. 2. New York: C. S. Francis, 1845. Available online at Representative Poetry Online, University of Toronto Libraries, http://rpo.library.utoronto.ca/poem/473.html.

"An Old-Fashioned Thanksgiving,"
a Story by Louisa May Alcott (1881)

Louisa May Alcott, author of the beloved novel Little Women, *also penned a humorous and heartfelt short story about a New England farm family's Thanksgiving celebration. "An Old-Fashioned Thanksgiving" was first published in November 1881, but the story is set in the 1820s. It describes what happens in the Bassett household when the parents are called away by an emergency on the eve of Thanksgiving, and the two teenaged daughters attempt to prepare the annual holiday feast.*

SIXTY YEARS AGO, up among the New Hampshire hills, lived Farmer Bassett, with a houseful of sturdy sons and daughters growing up about him. They were poor in money, but rich in land and love, for the wide acres of wood, corn, and pasture land fed, warmed, and clothed the flock, while mutual patience, affection, and courage made the old farmhouse a very happy home.

November had come; the crops were in, and barn, buttery, and bin were overflowing with the harvest that rewarded the summer's hard work. The big kitchen was a jolly place just now, for in the great fireplace roared a cheerful fire; on the walls hung garlands of dried apples, onions, and corn; up aloft from the beams shone crook-necked squashes, juicy hams, and dried venison—for in those days deer still haunted the deep forests, and hunters flourished. Savory smells were in the air; on the crane hung steaming kettles, and down among the red embers copper saucepans simmered, all suggestive of some approaching feast.

A white-headed baby lay in the old blue cradle that had rocked six other babies, now and then lifting his head to look out, like a round, full moon, then subsided to kick and crow contentedly, and suck the rosy apple he had no teeth to bite. Two small boys sat on the wooden settle shelling corn for popping, and picking out the biggest nuts from the goodly store their own hands had gathered in October. Four young girls stood at the long dresser, busily chopping meat, pounding spice, and slicing apples; and the tongues of Tilly, Prue, Roxy, and Rhody went as fast as their hands. Farmer Bassett, and Eph, the oldest boy, were "chorin' 'round" outside, for Thanksgiving was at hand, and all must be in order for that time-honored day.

To and fro, from table to hearth, bustled buxom Mrs. Bassett, flushed and floury, but busy and blithe as the queen bee of this busy little hive should be.

"I do like to begin seasonable and have things to my mind. Thanksgivin' dinners can't be drove, and it does take a sight of victuals to fill all these hungry stomicks," said the good woman, as she gave a vigorous stir to the great kettle of cider applesauce, and cast a glance of housewifely pride at the fine array of pies set forth on the buttery shelves.

"Only one more day and then it will be the time to eat. I didn't take but one bowl of hasty pudding this morning, so I shall have plenty of room when the nice things come," confided Seth to Sol, as he cracked a large hazelnut as easily as a squirrel.

"No need of my starvin' beforehand. I always have room enough, and I'd like to have Thanksgiving every day," answered Solomon, gloating like a young ogre over the little pig that lay near by, ready for roasting.

"Sakes alive, I don't, boys! It's a marcy it don't come but once a year. I should be worn to a thread paper with all this extra work atop of my winter weavin' and spinnin'," laughed their mother, as she plunged her plump arms into the long bread trough and began to knead the dough as if a famine were at hand.

Tilly, the oldest girl, a red-cheeked, black-eyed lass of fourteen, was grinding briskly at the mortar, for spices were costly, and not a grain must be wasted. Prue kept time with the chopper, and the twins sliced away at the apples till their little brown arms ached, for all knew how to work, and did so now with a will.

"I think it's real fun to have Thanksgiving at home. I'm sorry Gran'ma is sick, so we can't go there as usual, but I like to mess 'round here, don't you, girls?" asked Tilly, pausing to take a sniff at the spicy pestle.

"It will be kind of lonesome with only our own folks." "I like to see all the cousins and aunts, and have games, and sing," cried the twins, who were regular little romps, and could run, swim, coast, and shout as well as their brothers.

"I don't care a mite for all that. It will be so nice to eat dinner together, warm and comfortable at home," said quiet Prue, who loved her own cozy nooks like a cat.

"Come, girls, fly 'round and get your chores done, so we can clear away for dinner jest as soon as I clap my bread into the oven," called Mrs. Bassett presently, as she rounded off the last loaf of brown bread which was to feed the hungry mouths that seldom tasted any other.

"Here's a man comin' up the hill lively!" "Guess it's Gad Hopkins. Pa told him to bring a dezzen [dozen] oranges, if they warn't too high!" shouted Sol and Seth, running to the door, while the girls smacked their lips at the thought of this rare treat, and Baby threw his apple overboard, as if getting ready for a new cargo.

But all were doomed to disappointment, for it was not Gad, with the much-desired fruit. It was a stranger, who threw himself off his horse and hurried up to Mr. Bassett in the yard, with some brief message that made the farmer drop his ax and look so sober that his wife guessed at once some bad news had come; and crying, "Mother's wuss [worse]! I know she is!" Out ran the good woman, forgetful of the flour on her arms and the oven waiting for its most important batch.

The man said old Mr. Chadwick, down to Keene, stopped him as he passed, and told him to tell Mrs. Bassett her mother was failin' fast, and she'd better come today. He knew no more, and having delivered his errand he rode away, saying it looked like snow and he must be jogging, or he wouldn't get home till night.

"We must go right off, Eldad. Hitch up, and I'll be ready in less'n no time," said Mrs. Bassett, wasting not a minute in tears and lamentations, but pulling off her apron as she went in, with her head in a sad jumble of bread, anxiety, turkey, sorrow, haste, and cider applesauce.

A few words told the story, and the children left their work to help her get ready, mingling their grief for "Gran'ma" with regrets for the lost dinner.

"I'm dreadful sorry, dears, but it can't be helped. I couldn't cook nor eat no way now, and if that blessed woman gets better sudden, as she has before, we'll have cause for thanksgivin', and I'll give you a dinner you won't forget in a hurry," said Mrs. Bassett, as she tied on her brown silk pumpkin-hood, with a sob for the good old mother who had made it for her.

Not a child complained after that, but ran about helpfully, bringing moccasins, heating the footstone, and getting ready for a long drive, because Gran'ma lived twenty miles away, and there were no railroads in those parts to whisk people to and fro like magic. By the time the old yellow sleigh was at the door, the bread was in the oven, and Mrs. Bassett was waiting, with her camlet cloak on, and the baby done up like a small bale of blankets.

"Now, Eph, you must look after the cattle like a man and keep up the fires, for there's a storm brewin', and neither the children nor dumb critters must suffer," said Mr. Bassett, as he turned up the collar of his rough coat and put on his blue mittens, while the old mare shook her bells as if she preferred a trip to Keene to hauling wood all day.

"Tilly, put extry comfortables on the beds to-night, the wind is so searchin' up chamber. Have the baked beans and Injun-puddin' for dinner, and whatever you do, don't let the boys get at the mince-pies, or you'll have them down sick. I shall come back the minute I can leave Mother. Pa will come to-morrer anyway, so keep snug and be good. I depend on you, my darter; use your jedgment, and don't let nothin' happen while Mother's away."

"Yes'm, yes'm—good-bye, good-bye!" called the children, as Mrs. Bassett was packed into the sleigh and driven away, leaving a stream of directions behind her.

Eph, the sixteen-year-old boy, immediately put on his biggest boots, assumed a sober, responsible manner and surveyed his little responsibilities with a paternal air, drolly like his father's. Tilly tied on her mother's bunch of keys, rolled up the sleeves of her homespun gown, and began to order about the younger girls. They soon forgot poor Granny, and found it great fun to keep house all alone, for Mother seldom left home, but ruled her family in the good old-fashioned way. There were no servants, for the little daughters were Mrs. Bassett's only maids, and the stout boys helped their father, all working happily together with no wages but love; learning in the best manner the use of the heads and hands with which they were to make their own way in the world.

*T*HE BIG KITCHEN WAS A JOLLY PLACE JUST NOW, FOR IN THE GREAT FIREPLACE ROARED A CHEERFUL FIRE; ON THE WALLS HUNG GARLANDS OF DRIED APPLES, ONIONS, AND CORN; UP ALOFT FROM THE BEAMS SHONE CROOK-NECKED SQUASHES, JUICY HAMS, AND DRIED VENISON.

The few flakes that caused the farmer to predict bad weather soon increased to a regular snowstorm, with gusts of wind, for up among the hills winter came early and lingered long. But the children were busy, gay, and warm indoors, and never minded the rising gale nor the whirling white storm outside....

When the moon-faced clock behind the door struck nine, Tilly tucked up the children under the "extry comfortables," and having kissed them all around, as Mother did, crept into her own nest, never minding the little drifts of snow that sifted in upon her coverlet between the shingles of the roof, nor the storm that raged without.

As if he felt the need of unusual vigilance, old Bose lay down on the mat before the door, and pussy had the warm hearth all to herself. If any late wanderer had looked in at midnight, he would have seen the fire blazing up again, and in the cheerful glow the old cat blinking her yellow eyes, as she sat bolt upright beside the spinning wheel, like some sort of household goblin, guarding the children while they slept.

When they woke, like early birds, it still snowed, but up the little Bassetts jumped, broke the ice in their jugs, and went down with cheeks glowing like winter apples, after a brisk scrub and scramble into their clothes. Eph was off to the barn, and Tilly soon had a great kettle of mush ready, which, with milk warm from the cows made a wholesome breakfast for the seven hearty children.

"Now about dinner," said the young housekeeper, as the pewter spoons stopped clattering, and the earthen bowls stood empty.

"Ma said, have what we liked, but she didn't expect us to have a real Thanksgiving dinner, because she won't be here to cook it, and we don't know how," began Prue, doubtfully.

"I can roast a turkey and make a pudding as well as anybody, I guess. The pies are all ready, and if we can't boil vegetables and so on, we don't deserve any dinner," cried Tilly, burning to distinguish herself, and bound to enjoy to the utmost her brief authority.

"Yes, yes!" cried all the boys, "let's have a dinner anyway; Ma won't care, and the good victuals will spoil if they ain't eaten right up."

"Pa is coming tonight, so we won't have dinner till late; that will be real genteel and give us plenty of time," added Tilly, suddenly realizing the novelty of the task she had undertaken.

"Did you ever roast a turkey?" asked Roxy, with an air of deep interest.

"Should you darst [dare] to try?" said Rhody, in an awe-stricken tone.

"You will see what I can do. Ma said I was to use my judgment about things, and I'm going to. All you children have got to do is to keep out of the way, and let Prue and me work. Eph, I wish you'd put a fire in the best room, so the little ones can play in there. We shall want the settin-room for the table, and I won't have them pickin' round when we get things fixed," commanded Tilly, bound to make her short reign a brilliant one.

"I don't know about that. Ma didn't tell us to," began cautious Eph who felt that this invasion of the sacred best parlor was a daring step.

"Don't we always do it Sundays and Thanksgivings? Wouldn't Ma wish the children kept safe and warm anyhow? Can I get up a nice dinner with four rascals under my feet all the time? Come, now, if you want roast turkey and onions, plum-puddin' and mince-pie, you'll have to do as I tell you, and be lively about it."

Tilly spoke with such spirit, and her suggestion was so irresistible, that Eph gave in, and, laughing good-naturedly, tramped away to heat up the best room, devoutly hoping that nothing serious would happen to punish such audacity.

The young folks delightedly trooped away to destroy the order of that prim apartment with housekeeping under the black horsehair sofa, "horseback-riders" on the arms of the best rocking chair, and an Indian war dance all over the well-waxed furniture. Eph, finding the society of peaceful sheep and cows more to his mind than that of two excited sisters, lingered over his chores in the barn as long as possible, and left the girls in peace.

Now Tilly and Prue were in their glory, and as soon as the breakfast things were out of the way, they prepared for a grand cooking time. They were handy girls, though they had never heard of a cooking school, never touched a piano, and knew nothing of embroidery beyond the samplers which hung framed in the parlor; one ornamented with a pink mourner under a blue weeping willow, the other with this pleasing verse, each word being done in a different color, which gave the effect of a distracted rainbow:

This sampler neat was worked by me,
In my twelfth year, Prudence B.

> *I*F ANY LATE WANDERER HAD LOOKED IN AT MIDNIGHT, HE WOULD HAVE SEEN THE FIRE BLAZING UP AGAIN, AND IN THE CHEERFUL GLOW THE OLD CAT BLINKING HER YELLOW EYES, AS SHE SAT BOLT UPRIGHT BESIDE THE SPINNING WHEEL, LIKE SOME SORT OF HOUSEHOLD GOBLIN, GUARDING THE CHILDREN WHILE THEY SLEPT.

Both rolled up their sleeves, put on their largest aprons, and got out all the spoons, dishes, pots, and pans they could find, "so as to have everything handy," Prue said.

"Now, sister, we'll have dinner at five; Pa will be here by that time, if he is coming tonight, and be so surprised to find us all ready, for he won't have had any very nice victuals if Gran'ma is so sick," said Tilly, importantly. "I shall give the children a piece at noon" (Tilly meant luncheon); "doughnuts and cheese, with apple pie and cider, will please 'em. There's beans for Eph; he likes cold pork, so we won't stop to warm it up, for there's lots to do, and I don't mind saying to you I'm dreadful dubersome about the turkey."

"It's all ready but the stuffing, and roasting is as easy as can be. I can baste first-rate. Ma always likes to have me, I'm so patient and stiddy, she says," answered Prue, for the responsibility of this great undertaking did not rest upon her, so she took a cheerful view of things.

"I know, but it's the stuffin' that troubles me," said Tilly, rubbing her round elbows as she eyed the immense fowl laid out on a platter before her. "I don't know how much I want, nor what sort of yarbs [herbs] to put in, and he's so awful big, I'm kind of afraid of him."

"I ain't! I fed him all summer, and he never gobbled at me. I feel real mean to be thinking of gobbling him, poor old chap," laughed Prue, patting her departed pet with an air of mingled affection and appetite.

"Well, I'll get the puddin' off my mind fust, for it ought to bile [boil] all day. Put the big kettle on, and see that the spit is clean, while I get ready."

Prue obediently tugged away at the crane, with its black hooks, from which hung the iron teakettle and three-legged pot; then she settled the long spit in the grooves made for it in the tall andirons, and put the dripping pan underneath, for in those days meat was roasted as it should be, not baked in ovens.

Meantime Tilly attacked the plum pudding. She felt pretty sure of coming out right, here, for she had seen her mother do it so many times, it looked very easy. So in went suet and fruit; all sorts of spice, to be sure she got the right ones, and brandy instead of wine. But she forgot both sugar and salt, and tied it in the cloth so tightly that it had no room to swell, so it would come out as heavy as lead and as hard as a cannonball, if the bag did not burst and spoil it all. Happily unconscious of these mistakes, Tilly popped it into the pot, and proudly watched it bobbing about before she put the cover on and left it to its fate.

"I can't remember what flavorin' Ma puts in," she said, when she had got her bread well soaked for stuffing. "Sage and onions and applesauce go with goose, but I can't feel sure of anything but pepper and salt for a turkey."

"Ma puts in some kind of mint, I know, but I forget whether it is spearmint, peppermint, or pennyroyal," answered Prue, in a tone of doubt, but trying to show her knowledge of "yarbs," or, at least, of their names.

"Seems to me it's sweet marjoram or summer savory. I guess we'll put both in, and then we are sure to be right. The best is up garret; you run and get some, while I mash the bread," commanded Tilly, diving into the mess.

Away trotted Prue, but in her haste she got catnip and wormwood, for the garret was darkish, and Prue's little nose was so full of the smell of the onions she had been peeling, that everything smelt of them. Eager to be of use, she pounded up the herbs and scattered the mixture with a liberal hand into the bowl.

"It doesn't smell just right, but I suppose it will when it is cooked," said Tilly, as she filled the empty stomach, that seemed aching for food, and sewed it up with the blue yarn, which happened to be handy. She forgot to tie down his legs and wings, but she set him by till his hour came, well satisfied with her work.

"Shall we roast the little pig, too? I think he'd look nice with a necklace of sausages, as Ma fixed him at Christmas," asked Prue, elated with their success.

"I couldn't do it. I loved that little pig, and cried when he was killed. I should feel as if I was roasting the baby," answered Tilly, glancing toward the buttery where piggy hung, looking so pink and pretty it certainly did seem cruel to eat him.

It took a long time to get all the vegetables ready, for, as the cellar was full, the girls thought they would have every sort. Eph helped, and by noon all was ready for cooking, and the cranberry sauce, a good deal scorched, was cooking in the lean-to....

[The younger children go out sledding, while Tilly and Prue set the table for dinner. They are distracted from this task when the children run inside screaming about a bear in the yard. The bear turns out to be family friend Gad Hopkins, who has come to deliver the dozen oranges. He wore a fur wrap over his head to fool the children and nearly ended up being shot by the Bassett's eldest son, Eph. When the joke is revealed, Gad merrily throws the oranges to the children in the kitchen.]

"My sakes alive—the turkey is all burnt one side, and the kettles have biled over so the pies I put to warm are all ashes!" scolded Tilly, as the flurry subsided and she remembered her dinner.

"Well, I can't help it. I couldn't think of victuals when I expected to be eaten alive myself, could I?" pleaded poor Prue, who had tumbled into the cradle when the rain of oranges began.

Tilly laughed, and all the rest joined in, so goodhumor was restored, and the spirits of the younger ones were revived by sucks from the one orange which passed from hand to hand with great rapidity while the older girls dished up the dinner. They were just struggling to get the pudding out of the cloth when Roxy called out: "Here's Pa!"

"There's folks with him," added Rhody.

"Lots of 'em! I see two big sleighs chock full," shouted Seth, peering through the dusk.

"It looks like a semintary [cemetery]. Guess Gran'ma's dead and come up to be buried here," said Sol, in a solemn tone. This startling suggestion made Tilly, Prue, and Eph hasten to look out, full of dismay at such an ending of their festival.

"If that is a funeral, the mourners are uncommonly jolly," said Eph, dryly, as merry voices and loud laughter broke the white silence without.

"I see Aunt Cinthy, and Cousin Hetty—and there's Mose and Amos. I do declare, Pa's bringin' 'em all home to have some fun here," cried Prue, as she recognized one familiar face after another.

"Oh, my patience! Ain't I glad I got dinner, and don't I hope it will turn out good!" exclaimed Tilly, while the twins pranced with delight, and the small boys roared:

"Hooray for Pa! Hooray for Thanksgivin'!"

The cheer was answered heartily, and in came Father, Mother, Baby, aunts, and cousins, all in great spirits; and all much surprised to find such a festive welcome awaiting them.

"Ain't Gran'ma dead at all?" asked Sol, in the midst of the kissing and hand-shaking.

"Bless your heart, no! It was all a mistake of old Mr. Chadwick's. He's as deaf as an adder, and when Mrs. Brooks told him Mother was mendin' fast, and she wanted me to come down today, certain sure, he got the message all wrong, and give it to the fust person passin' in such a way as to scare me 'most to death, and send us down in a hurry. Mother was sittin' up as chirk as you please, and dreadful sorry you didn't all come."

"So, to keep the house quiet for her, and give you a taste of the fun, your Pa fetched us all up to spend the evenin', and we are goin' to have a jolly time on't, to jedge by the looks of things," said Aunt Cinthy, briskly finishing the tale when Mrs. Bassett paused for want of breath.

THEN TILLY SET OUT THE LIGHT STAND WITH THE BIG BIBLE ON IT, AND A CANDLE ON EACH SIDE, AND ALL SAT QUIETLY IN THE FIRELIGHT, SMILING AS THEY LISTENED WITH HAPPY HEARTS TO THE SWEET OLD WORDS THAT FIT ALL TIMES AND SEASONS SO BEAUTIFULLY.

"What in the world put it into your head we was comin', and set you to gittin' up such a supper?" asked Mr. Bassett, looking about him, well pleased and much surprised at the plentiful table.

Tilly modestly began to tell, but the others broke in and sang her praises in a sort of chorus, in which bears, pigs, pies, and oranges were oddly mixed. Great satisfaction was expressed by all, and Tilly and Prue were so elated by the commendation of Ma and the aunts, that they set forth their dinner, sure everything was perfect.

But when the eating began, which it did the moment wraps were off; then their pride got a fall; for the first person who tasted the stuffing (it was big Cousin Mose, and that made it harder to bear) nearly choked over the bitter morsel.

"Tilly Bassett, whatever made you put wormwood and catnip in your stuffin'?" demanded Ma, trying not to be severe, for all the rest were laughing, and Tilly looked ready to cry.

"I did it," said Prue, nobly taking all the blame, which caused Pa to kiss her on the spot, and declare that it didn't do a mite of harm, for the turkey was all right.

"I never see onions cooked better. All the vegetables is well done, and the dinner a credit to you, my dears," declared Aunt Cinthy, with her mouth full of the fragrant vegetable she praised.

The pudding was an utter failure in spite of the blazing brandy in which it lay—as hard and heavy as one of the stone balls on Squire Dunkin's great gate. It was speedily whisked out of sight, and all fell upon the pies, which were perfect. But Tilly and Prue were much depressed, and didn't recover their spirits till dinner was over and the evening fun well under way.

"Blind-man's bluff," "Hunt the slipper," "Come, Philander," and other lively games soon set everyone bubbling over with jollity, and when Eph struck up "Money Musk" on his fiddle, old and young fell into their places for a dance. All down the long kitchen they stood, Mr. and Mrs. Bassett at the top, the twins at the bottom, and then away they went, heeling and toeing, cutting pigeon-wings, and taking their steps in a way that would convulse modern children with their new-fangled romps called dancing. Mose and Tilly covered themselves with glory by the vigor with which they kept it up, till fat Aunt Cinthy fell into a chair, breathlessly declaring that a very little of such exercise was enough for a woman of her "heft."

Apples and cider, chat and singing, finished the evening, and after a grand kissing all round, the guests drove away in the clear moonlight which came out to cheer their long drive.

When the jingle of the last bell had died away, Mr. Bassett said soberly, as they stood together on the hearth:

"Children, we have special cause to be thankful that the sorrow we expected was changed into joy, so we'll read a chapter 'fore we go to bed, and give thanks where thanks is due."

Then Tilly set out the light stand with the big Bible on it, and a candle on each side, and all sat quietly in the firelight, smiling as they listened with happy hearts to the sweet old words that fit all times and seasons so beautifully.

When the good-nights were over, and the children in bed, Prue put her arm round Tilly and whispered tenderly, for she felt her shake, and was sure she was crying:

"Don't mind about the old stuffin' and puddin', deary—nobody cared, and Ma said we really did do surprisin' well for such young girls."

The laughter Tilly was trying to smother broke out then, and was so infectious, Prue could not help joining her, even before she knew the cause of the merriment.

"I was mad about the mistakes, but don't care enough to cry. I'm laughing to think how Gad fooled Eph and I found him out. I thought Mose and Amos would have died over it, when I told them, it was so funny," explained Tilly, when she got her breath.

"I was so scared that when the first orange hit me, I thought it was a bullet, and scrabbled into the cradle as fast as I could. It was real mean to frighten the little ones so," laughed Prue, as Tilly gave a growl.

Here a smart rap on the wall of the next room caused a sudden lull in the fun, and Mrs. Bassett's voice was heard, saying warningly, "Girls, go to sleep immediate, or you'll wake the baby."

"Yes'm," answered two meek voices, and after a few irrepressible giggles, silence reigned, broken only by an occasional snore from the boys, or the soft scurry of mice in the buttery, taking their part in this old-fashioned Thanksgiving.

Source: Alcott, Louisa May. "An Old-Fashioned Thanksgiving." *St. Nicholas Magazine*, November 1881. Reprinted in *An Old-Fashioned Thanksgiving and Other Stories* by Louisa May Alcott. New York: Penguin, 1995.

"We Gather Together," A Thanksgiving Hymn (1894)

"We Gather Together" is a hymn that is closely associated with Thanksgiving. For the first half of the 20th century, it was commonly sung by children in schools as well as by worshippers in churches across the country. But few people realize that this short hymn has a long and complicated history that began in 16th-century Europe.

The melody used for "We Gather Together" started out as a European folk song, and it had various lyrics associated with it through the years. It turned into a hymn about overcoming religious oppression in 1597, when a group of Dutch Protestants defeated the Spanish Catholics who had long occupied their town and sang to celebrate their religious freedom. The first printed version of the song appeared in a book of patriotic songs called Nederlandtsche Gedenckclanck, which was published in Holland in 1626.

The Dutch-language version of "We Gather Together" traveled to the New World with early Dutch settlers. It was first translated into English in 1894 by Theodore Baker, an American scholar who heard it while studying in Germany. The song began appearing in American hymnals in 1903, and its popularity increased during both World Wars.

We gather together to ask the Lord's blessing;
He chastens and hastens His will to make known.
The wicked oppressing now cease from distressing.
Sing praises to His Name; He forgets not His own.

Beside us to guide us, our God with us joining,
Ordaining, maintaining His kingdom divine;
So from the beginning the fight we were winning;
Thou, Lord, were at our side, all glory be Thine!

We all do extol Thee, Thou Leader triumphant,
And pray that Thou still our Defender will be.
Let Thy congregation escape tribulation;
Thy Name be ever praised! O Lord, make us free!

Source: "We Gather Together," 1597. First published as "Wilt heden nu treden" in the Dutch songbook *Nederlandtsche Gedenckclanck*, collected by Adrianus Valerius, Haarlem, Holland: 1626. Translated into English by Theodore Baker, 1894. Available online at http://www.cyberhymnal.org/htm/w/e/wegattog.htm.

"The Pumpkin," a Poem by John Greenleaf Whittier (1898)

The 19th-century American poet John Greenleaf Whittier wrote a number of folksy, sentimental poems about life in the New England countryside. One of his best-known works is "The Pumpkin," which sings the praises of the versatile vegetable that plays an important role in traditional Thanksgiving celebrations.

Oh, greenly and fair in the lands of the sun,
The vines of the gourd and the rich melon run,
And the rock and the tree and the cottage enfold,
With broad leaves all greenness and blossoms all gold,
Like that which o'er Nineveh's prophet once grew,
While he waited to know that his warning was true,
And longed for the storm-cloud, and listened in vain
For the rush of the whirlwind and red fire-rain.

On the banks of the Xenil the dark Spanish maiden
Comes up with the fruit of the tangled vine laden;
And the Creole of Cuba laughs out to behold
Through orange-leaves shining the broad spheres of gold;
Yet with dearer delight from his home in the North,
On the fields of his harvest the Yankee looks forth,
Where crook-necks are coiling and yellow fruit shines,
And the sun of September melts down on his vines.

Ah! on Thanksgiving day, when from East and from West,
From North and from South come the pilgrim and guest,
When the gray-haired New Englander sees round his board
The old broken links of affection restored,
When the care-wearied man seeks his mother once more,
And the worn matron smiles where the girl smiled before,
What moistens the lip and what brightens the eye?
What calls back the past, like the rich Pumpkin pie?

Oh, fruit loved of boyhood! the old days recalling,
When wood-grapes were purpling and brown nuts were falling!
When wild, ugly faces we carved in its skin,
Glaring out through the dark with a candle within!

When we laughed round the corn-heap, with hearts all in tune,
Our chair a broad pumpkin,—our lantern the moon,
Telling tales of the fairy who travelled like steam,
In a pumpkin-shell coach, with two rats for her team!

Then thanks for thy present! none sweeter or better
E'er smoked from an oven or circled a platter!
Fairer hands never wrought at a pastry more fine,
Brighter eyes never watched o'er its baking, than thine!
And the prayer, which my mouth is too full to express,
Swells my heart that thy shadow may never be less,
That the days of thy lot may be lengthened below,
And the fame of thy worth like a pumpkin-vine grow,
And thy life be as sweet, and its last sunset sky
Golden-tinted and fair as thy own pumpkin pie!

Source: Whittier, John Greenleaf. "The Pumpkin." In *The Poetical Works of John Greenleaf Whittier*, edited by W. Garrett Horder. London: Henry Frowde, 1898. Available online at http://www.potw.org/archive/potw209.html.

"Thanksgiving at the Polls,"
a Story by Edward Everett Hale (1899)

The short story "Thanksgiving at the Polls," by the Boston-born author, minister, and social reformer Edward Everett Hale, offers an alternately amusing and affecting account of a highly unusual 19th-century holiday celebration. The city of Boston is preparing to hold elections and has placed polling booths—small cabins with basic supplies like a stove, a table, and a few chairs—around the city. Struggling newspaperman Frederick Dane takes over an empty polling booth near his office and turns it into a cozy shelter for himself and a motley crew of recent immigrants. The charitable season of Thanksgiving makes an overwhelming bounty of food available to the group. When Dane and his friends decide to share their good fortune with hungry people throughout the city, their efforts produce surprising results.

Part 1

Frederick Dane was on his way towards what he called his home. His home, alas, was but an indifferent attic in one of the southern suburbs of Boston. He had been walking; but he was now standing still, at the well-known corner of Massachusetts and Columbus Avenues. As often happens, Frederick Dane had an opportunity to wait at this corner a quarter of an hour. As he looked around him on the silent houses, he could not but observe the polling-booth, which a watchful city government had placed in the street, a few days before, in preparation for the election which was to take place three weeks afterward. Dane is of an inquiring temper, and seeing that the polling-booth had a door and the door had a keyhole, he tried in the keyhole a steel key which he had picked up in Dock Square the day before. Almost to his surprise, the key governed the lock at once, and he found himself able to walk in.

He left the door wide open, and the gaslight streaming in revealed to him the aspect of the cells arranged for Australian voting. The rails were all in their places, and the election might take place the very next day. It instantly occurred to Dane that he might save the five cents which otherwise he would have given to his masters of the street railway, and be the next morning three miles nearer his work, if he spent the night in the polling-cabin. He looked around for a minute or two, and found some large rolls of street posters, which had been left there by some disappointed canvasser the year before, and which had accompanied one cell of the cabin in its travels. Dane is a prompt man,

RIDGEMONT PUBLIC LIBRARY
MT. VICTORY, OHIO

133

and, in a minute more, he had locked the door behind him, had struck a wax taper which he had in his cigar-box, had rolled the paper roll out on the floor, to serve as a pillow. In five minutes more, covered with his heavy coat, he lay on the floor, sleeping as soundly as he had slept the year before, when he found himself on the lee side of an iceberg under Peary's command.

This is perhaps unnecessary detail, by way of saying that this is the beginning of the arrangement which a city, not very intelligent, will make in the next century for unsettled people, whose own houses are not agreeable to them. There exist in Boston at this moment three or four hundred of the polling-booths,—nice little houses, enough better than most of the peasantry of most of Europe ever lived in. They are, alas, generally packed up in lavender and laid away for ten months of the year. But in the twentieth century we shall send them down to the shores of islands and other places where people like to spend the summer, and we shall utilize them, not for the few hours of an election only, but all the year round. This will not then be called "Nationalism," it will be called "Democracy;" and that is a very good name when it is applied to a very good thing.

Dane was an old soldier and an old seaman. He was not troubled by disagreeable dreams, and in the morning, when the street-cars began to travel, he was awaked a little after sunrise, by their clatter on the corner. He felt well satisfied with the success of his experiment, and began on a forecast, which the reader shall follow for a few weeks, which he thought, and thought rightly, would tend to his own convenience, possibly to that of his friends.

Dane telegraphed down to the office that he should be detained an hour that morning, went out to his home of the day before at Ashmont, paid his landlady her scot, brought in with him his little possessions in a valise to the office, and did not appear at his new home until after nightfall.

He was then able to establish himself on the basis which proved convenient afterwards, and which it is worth while to explain to a world which is not too well housed. The city had provided three or four chairs there, a stove, and two tables. Dane had little literature, but, as he was in the literary line himself, he did not care for this so much; men who write books are not commonly eager to read books which are worse than their own. At a nine-cent window of a neighboring tinman's he was able to buy himself the few little necessities which he wanted for housekeeping. And not to detain the reader too long upon merely fleshly arrangements, in the course of a couple of hours of Tuesday evening and Wednesday evening, he had fitted up his convenient if not pretty bower with all that man requires. It was easy to buy a mince pie or a cream cake, or a bit of boiled ham or roast chicken, according as payday was near or distant. One is glad to have a tablecloth. But if one have a large poster warning people, a year before, that they should vote the Prohibition ticket, one's conscience is not wounded if this poster, ink down, takes the place which a tablecloth would have taken under other circumstances. If there is not much crockery to use, there is but little to wash. And, in short, as well trained a man of the world as Dane had made himself thoroughly comfortable in his new quarters before the week was over.

Part 2

At the beginning Frederick's views were purely personal, or, as the preachers say, selfish. Here was an empty house, three miles nearer his work than his hired attic was, and he had taken possession. But conscience always asserts itself, and it was not long before he felt that he ought to extend the benefits of this new discovery of his somewhat further. It really was a satisfaction to what the pulpits call a "felt want" when as he came through Massachusetts Avenue on Thursday evening, he met a boy and a girl, neither of them more than ten years old, crying on the sidewalk. Dane is sympathetic and fond of children. He stopped the little brats, and satisfied himself that neither had had any supper. He could not understand a word of the language in which they spoke, nor could they understand him. But kindness needs little spoken language; and accordingly Frederick led them along to his cabin, and after waiting, as he always did, a minute or two, to be sure that no one was in sight, he unlocked the door, and brought in his little companions.

It was clear enough that the children were such waifs and strays that nothing surprised them, and they readily accepted the modest hospitalities of the position. Like all masculine housekeepers, Frederick had provided three times as much food as he needed for his own physical wants, so that it was not difficult to make these children happy with the pieces of mince pie and lemon pie and cream cake and eclairs which were left from his unknown festivals of the day before. Poor little things, they were both cold and tired, and, before half an hour was over, they were snugly asleep on and under a pile of Prohibition posters....

[The next day, Frederick Dane convinces the children, Ezra and Sarah, to take him to the place they lived before they joined him in the polling booth.

There, on a rooftop in the North End of Boston, they find Oleg and Vladimir, two Jewish men who recently arrived from Russia on the same boat as the children. Dane invites them to join their party at the polling booth, and the men gladly accept. Within a week, the group expands to include ten happy compatriots, and the children enroll in the local school.]

AT THE BEGINNING FREDERICK'S VIEWS WERE PURELY PERSONAL, OR, AS THE PREACHERS SAY, SELFISH. HERE WAS AN EMPTY HOUSE, . . . AND HE HAD TAKEN POSSESSION. BUT CONSCIENCE ALWAYS ASSERTS ITSELF, AND IT WAS NOT LONG BEFORE HE FELT THAT HE OUGHT TO EXTEND THE BENEFITS OF THIS NEW DISCOVERY OF HIS SOMEWHAT FURTHER.

Dane and his settlement were well aware that after this election they would all have to move out from their comfortable quarters. But, while they were in, they determined to prepare for a fit Thanksgiving to God, and the country which makes provision so generous for those in need. It is not every country, indeed, which provides four hundred empty houses, every autumn, for the convenience of any unlodged night-editor with a skeleton key, who comes along.

He explained to his companions that a great festival was near. They heard this with joy. He explained that no work would be done that day,—not in any cigar-shop or sweating-room. This also pleased them. He then, at some length, explained the necessity of the sacrifice of turkeys on the occasion. He told briefly how Josselyn and the fathers shot them as they passed through the sky. But he explained that now we shoot them, as one makes money, not directly but indirectly. We shoot our turkeys, say, at shooting-galleries. All this proved intelligible, and Frederick had no fear for turkeys.

As for Sarah and Ezra, he found that at Ezra's boys' club and at Sarah's girls' club, and each of her Sabbath-school classes and Sunday-school classes, and at each of his, it had been explained that on the day before Thanksgiving they must come with baskets to places named, and carry home a Thanksgiving dinner.

These announcements were hailed with satisfaction by all to whom Dane addressed them. Everything in the country was as strange to them as it would have been to an old friend of mine, an inhabitant of the planet Mars. And they accepted the custom of this holiday among the rest. Oddly enough, it proved that one or two of them were first-rate shots, and, by attendance at different shooting-galleries, they brought in more than a turkey apiece, as

Governor Bradford's men did in 1621. Many of them were at work in large factories, where it was the custom of the house to give a roasted turkey and a pan of cranberry sauce to each person who had been on the pay-list for three months. One or two of them were errand men in the market, and it was the practice of the wholesale dealers there, who at this season become to a certain extent retailers, to encourage these errand men by presenting to each of them a turkey, which was promised in advance. As for Dane himself, the proprietors of his journal always presented a turkey to each man on their staff. And in looking forward to his Thanksgiving at the polls, he had expected to provide a twenty-two pound gobbler which a friend in Vermont was keeping for him.

It may readily be imagined, then, that, when the day before Thanksgiving came, he was more oppressed by an embarrassment of riches than by any difficulty on the debtor side of his account. He had twelve people to feed, himself included. There were the two children, their eight friends, and a young Frenchman from Paris who, like all persons of that nationality who are six months in this country, had found many enemies here. Dane had invited him to dinner. He had arranged that there should be plates or saucers enough for each person to have two. And now there was to be a chicken-pie from Obed Shalom, some mince pies and Marlborough pies from the Union for Christian Work, a turkey at each end of the board; and he found he should have left over, after the largest computation for the appetites of the visitors, twenty-three pies of different structure, five dishes of cranberry sauce, three or four boxes of raisins, two or three drums of figs, two roasted geese and eleven turkeys. He counted all the turkeys as roasted, because he had the promise of the keeper of the Montgomery House that he would roast for him all the birds that were brought in to him before nine o'clock on Thanksgiving morning.

Part 6

Having stated all this on a list carefully written, first in the English language and second in the language of the Hebrews, Frederick called his fellow-lodgers together earlier than usual on the evening before Thanksgiving Day. He explained to them, in the patois which they used together, that it would be indecent for them to carry this supply of food farther than next Monday for their own purposes. He told them that the occasion was one of exuberant thanksgiving to the God of heaven. He showed them that they all had great reason for thanksgiving. And, in short, he made three heads of a discourse which might have been expanded by the most eloquent preacher in Boston the next day, and would have well covered the twenty-five minutes which the regulation would have required for a sermon. He then said that, as they had been favored with much more than they could use for their own appetites, they must look up those who were not so well off as themselves.

He was well pleased by finding that he was understood, and what he said was received with applause in the various forms in which Southern Russia applauds on such occasions. As for the two children, their eyes were wide open, and their mouths, and they looked their wonder.

Frederick then proposed that two of their number should volunteer to open a rival establishment at the polling-booth at the corner of Gates Street and Burgoyne Street, and that the company should on the next day invite guests enough to make another table of twelve. He proposed that the same course should be taken at the corner of Shapleigh and Bowditch Streets, and yet again at the booth which is at the corner of Curtis Avenue and Quincy Street. And he said that, as time would press upon them, they had better arrange to carry a part at least of the stores to these places that evening. To this there was a general assent. The company sat down to a hasty tea, administered much as the Israelites took their last meal in Egypt; for every man had on his long frieze coat and his heavy boots, and they were eager for the active work of Thanksgiving. For each the stewards packed two turkeys in a basket, filled in as far as they could with other stores, and Frederick headed his procession.

It was then that he was to learn, for the first time, that he was not the only person in Boston.

It was then that he found out that the revelation made to one man is frequently made to many.

He found out that he was as wise as the next fellow, but was no wiser; was as good as the next fellow, but was no better; and that, in short, he had no special patent upon his own undertaking....

[Dane and his friends begin visiting nearby polling booths, with the intention of setting up additional facilities to house and feed needy people. In each booth they enter, however, they find an established group, similar to their own. The first booth is occupied by Native Americans, the second by French Canadians, and the third by Italians. When Dane and his friends arrive, each of these groups is trying to find a way to share the bountiful food they have collected for Thanksgiving. A few members of each group join Dane's procession, which soon discovers a group of Boston policemen using a fourth polling booth as an off-hours clubhouse.]

No one ever knew who made the great suggestion, but it is probable that it was one of these officials, well acquainted with the charter of the city of Boston and with its constitution and by-laws, who offered the proposal which was adopted. In the jealousy of the fierce democracy of Boston in the year 1820, when the present city charter was made, it reserved for itself permission to open Faneuil Hall at any time for a public meeting. It proves now that whenever fifty citizens unite to ask for the use of the hall for such a meeting, it must be given to them. At the time of which we are reading the mayor had to preside at every such meeting. At the "Cops'" club it was highly determined that the names of fifty citizens should at once be obtained, and that the Cradle of Liberty should be secured for the general Thanksgiving.

It was wisely resolved that no public notice should be given of this in the journals. It was well known that that many-eyed Argus called the press is very apt not to interfere with that which is none of its business.

Part 7

And thus it happened that, when Thanksgiving Day came, the worthy janitor of Faneuil Hall sent down his assistant to open it, and that the assistant, who meant to dine at home, found a good-natured friend from the country who took the keys and lighted the gas in his place. Before the sun had set, Frederick Dane and Antonio Fero and Michael Chevalier and the Honorable Mr. Walk-in-the-Water and Eben Kartschoff arrived with an

> [THE] TABLES WERE SET WITH TURKEYS, WITH GEESE, WITH VENISON, WITH MALLARDS AND PLOVER, WITH QUAIL AND PARTRIDGES, WITH CRANBERRY AND SQUASH, AND WITH DISHES OF RUSSIA AND ITALY AND GREECE AND BOHEMIA.

express-wagon driven by a stepson of P. Nolan. There is no difficulty at Faneuil Hall in bringing out a few trestles and as many boards as one wants for tables, for Faneuil Hall is a place given to hospitality. And so, before six o'clock, the hour assigned for the extemporized dinner, the tables were set with turkeys, with geese, with venison, with mallards and plover, with quail and partridges, with cranberry and squash, and with dishes of Russia and Italy and Greece and Bohemia, such as have no names. The Greeks brought fruits, the Indians brought venison, the Italians brought red wine, the French brought walnuts and chestnuts, and the good God sent a blessing. Almost every man found up either a wife or a sweetheart or a daughter or a niece to come with him, and the feast went on to the small hours of Friday. The Mayor came down on time, and being an accomplished man, addressed them in English, in Latin, in Greek, in Hebrew, and in Tuscan. And it is to be hoped that they understood him.

But no record has ever been made of the feast in any account-book on this side the line. Yet there are those who have seen it, or something like it, with the eye of faith. And when, a hundred years hence, some antiquary reads this story in a number of the "Omaha Intelligencer," which has escaped the detrition of the thirty-six thousand days and nights, he will say,—

"Why, this was the beginning of what we do now! Only these people seem to have taken care of strangers only one month in the twelve. Why did they not welcome all strangers in like manner, until they had made them feel at home? These people, once a year, seem to have fed the hungry. Would it not have been simpler for them to provide that no man should ever be hungry? These people certainly thanked God to some purpose once a year; how happy is the nation which has learned to thank Him always!"

Source: Hale, Edward Everett. "Thanksgiving at the Polls: A Thanksgiving Story." In *The Brick Moon and Other Stories*. Boston: Little, Brown, 1899. Available online at http://www.gutenberg.org/etext/1633.

"The Lost Turkey," a Story by Sarah Orne Jewett (1902)

Sarah Orne Jewett grew up in South Berwick, Maine, a fishing village near the New Hampshire border. Throughout her childhood in the 1850s, she accompanied her father—a country doctor—on his rounds to visit patients on rural farms. These experiences formed the basis for her later stories about country life in New England. The story below first appeared in the magazine Youth's Companion *in 1902. Jewett paints a sentimental portrait of a poor widow who struggles to provide her son with a proper Thanksgiving dinner.*

There were only two persons in the kitchen, a woman and a boy, who had spread his school-books on the table by the window, and set a determined elbow on either side of his slate like buttresses for failing energy. The arithmetic was wide open above the slate at an early page of fractions.

The boy's mother, a sad-looking, pretty woman, was busy getting supper, but she hovered near the table and cast many a loving glance at her son's distress. She had been a quick scholar herself, and such sums were as easy as plain knitting. One often hears of the sorrows of hens that have hatched ducks, but Mrs. Sarah Jones knew the more painful solicitudes of the duck—the swimming bird who must see her feathered darling balked and landlocked upon the shore.

"I thought they looked easy, Johnny," she ventured, timidly. "If I didn't know 'twas best for you to puzzle 'em out alone I'd—"

"If I can only do this one!" said Johnny, in a dreamy tone, as he figured away with new hopefulness. "There, you see here, mother!" and he held up his slate.

"Yes, you've got it!" she cried, joyfully, as her eager eye found its way through a queer maze of stumbling figures. "Yes, that's all right. Now you've got the right idea, you won't have so much trouble again." She looked the prouder because he could not see her as she stood over him. Johnny had shown first-rate pluck and courage, and had been pleasant, too, as she reminded her affectionate heart, all through this great emergency.

"Now you won't find the rest of them so hard," she said, as she turned away and stooped down to open the oven door.

"How good my supper's goin' to taste!" exclaimed the boy. "Fred Hollis says they're goin' to have a lot of folks from out West at his house to spend Thanksgiving."

Mrs. Jones sighed, and a quick flush of color came into her face; the boy thought she had burned her hand at the oven.

"No, I ain't hurt," she said, seeing his troubled face. "No, I was only thinking o' your Thanksgiving day. I am afraid I ain't goin' to have anything nice to give you. I hoped to have some kind of a treat, Johnny, but having to pay for shingling the house has taken every mite o' money I had, and I'm owin' four dollars yet. We've got to do with what there is in the house."

"Ain't we goin' to have any turkey?" inquired Johnny, ruefully.

"No, nor any chicken, either. I ain't got 'em, and I can't go in debt to buy. If I begin to get in debt I can't ever get out again. But I'll make you a nice, good cake," she urged, by way of consolation as she saw his disappointed face. "There's lots of people that don't have turkeys."

Johnny could not bring himself to smile or treat so grave a subject lightly. "Cake alone ain't enough for dinner!" he said to himself, bitterly. The news of their poverty was harder to bear at this hungry moment than if it were after supper, instead of before it.

"Why don't we keep turkeys ourselves, mother?" Johnny demanded. "Lots of folks do, and then we could have one whenever we wanted it."

"We did keep them, you know, but something has ailed the chicks of late years. I heard to-day that even your grandfather would have to buy, and I've known him to raise a flock of sixty. Your Grandma Jones was luckier than anybody, and always got the highest prices."

There was a silence. Johnny was now plunged in deep reflection, and his face almost for the first time took on a serious, manly look. "Mother," he said, "what is it makes us feel so poor? Is it because my father died?"

"Yes, dear," said Sarah Jones.

She stood still in the middle of the floor, looking at him, and her eyes were filled with tears. The boy's clothes were faded and outgrown; she could see a great patch on the elbow next her, and his stockings below his short trousers were darned half-way down the leg. Johnny's face was bright and handsome, but she could hardly bear his honest, questioning look.

"Your grandpa and grandma don't like me, dear. They didn't want your father to marry when he did, and he went right against their wishes. 'Twas chiefly because your Grandfather Jones and my father had quarreled, and there was a lawsuit between them. I see now 'twas hard for the old folks; 'twas like having an enemy come among 'em. When your father died they came and offered to take you and bring you up, and I refused 'em. I said I could get along. But they pressed it too far when my heart was 'most broken, anyway, losing o' your father, and I said things I wish now I hadn't said and reproached 'em as I shouldn't now. So that's why we don't speak together, and why you're so poor. If they had you I don't know but they'd give you every single thing you want. They'd lost their only son; I should have had patience with them," she continued, reproaching herself, and standing before Johnny.

The boy's face did not change; he looked away, and then he took his pencil again and made some marks on his slate as if he were going on with his figuring. His grandfather had the same slow, set way of behaving, and the mother's heart knew a sudden pain. Johnny was nothing but a boy; she ought not to have told him.

"I'd rather live with you," he said, presently, with great effort. "I belong to you and father most, don't I? I don't care if there ain't a turkey just this once," and the mother took a step nearer, and kissed him quite unexpectedly.

"Come, put away your books now; I want the table for supper," she said to him, trying to speak as if there were nothing the matter.

❦

It was, as everybody said, real Thanksgiving weather. There was not quite snow enough for sleighing, but the sky was already gray with the promise of more. The mountains on the far horizon looked blue and cold, and the nearer hills were black and dismal, as if even the thick fur of pine-trees that covered them could hardly keep the world from freezing.

Old Mr. Jones was one of the last to untie his horse and start toward home. It was three miles from the village to his farm, and he had spent nearly the whole afternoon in Barton's store; there had been some business to do with men whom he met there, and an inner pocket was filled with money that had been paid him for some pine timber.

> "YOUR GRANDPA AND GRANDMA DON'T LIKE ME, DEAR. THEY DIDN'T WANT YOUR FATHER TO MARRY WHEN HE DID, AND HE WENT RIGHT AGAINST THEIR WISHES. . . . SO THAT'S WHY WE DON'T SPEAK TOGETHER, AND WHY YOU'RE SO POOR."

He was a very stern-looking person as he sat in the old armchair by the stove. One could believe that he was possessed of authority as well as wealth, and that he had kept his mind upon a grudge for years together. The loss of his son had seemed harder to him than it might have seemed to most men; he had almost resented it. Whatever cheerfulness had been his in early life was all gone now, and his wife, a timid, affectionate woman, who feared and obeyed him in all things, believed as he did, that they were unjustly treated in the matter of happiness. Each year found them better off in this world's goods, and poorer in the power of using things to make either themselves or other people happy.

The good old doctor had come into the store late in the afternoon to wait for the mail-carrier, who was due at five o'clock.

"How's your wife getting on?" he asked, kindly, and was told that she was still ailing, but no worse than common.

"You need a younger woman there to help her, Henry," said the doctor. "She needs somebody there while you are away at work. I thought the other day that she was drooping from being so much alone, and from brooding over the past," he added, in a low voice. "I want to have a talk with you some of these days. You know I mean your good as much as hers. Why don't you let bygones be bygones?"

"You can't make believe if the right feelings aren't there," said Henry Jones. "If you are alluding to my family, I can only say that that woman my son married has expressed her feelings once for all. She probably feels the same way now."

"Now, Henry," said the doctor, pleasantly, "you know that we went to school together and have always been friendly. I've seen you through a good many troubles, and before I die I want to see you through this biggest one. That's a nice boy growing up, and he's got a good mother. You never showed her any great kindness, and yet you wanted to rob her of all she had to live for. She turned on you that day just as any creature will that fights for her young. You took the wrong way to do the right thing, and only got your pay for it. You must put your pride in your pocket and go and tell her you're sorry and want her to come right home and bring Johnny and spend the winter. You've got a better teacher in your district this year than there is in theirs."

The old man shook his head. "You don't understand nothin' at all about it," he began, dolefully. "I don't see what I can do. I wish there was peace amongst us, but—" And at this point the doctor moved impatiently away.

"I had to buy a turkey for Thanksgivin' this year," he heard the old farmer complaining to a fresh arrival. The store was full of neighbors now, who had seen the mail-carrier arrive. "Yes, I had to buy a turkey, first time I ever done such a thing, and there's nobody but wife and me to set down to it. Seems hard; yes, but 'tis one o' them Vermont turkeys, and a very handsome one, too; I don't know's 'twill equal those we've been accustomed to."

The doctor sighed as he looked over his shoulder and saw Henry Jones's stolid face, and saw him lift the great turkey with evident pride because it was the best and largest to be bought that year; the doctor could not help wondering what Johnny and his mother would feast upon.

There was a good deal of cheerfulness in the store—jokes and laughter and humorous questioning of newcomers. The busy storekeeper and postmaster was not averse to taking his part in these mild festivities of Thanksgiving eve.

As Mr. Jones approached to take his evening mail of the weekly newspaper and a circular or two he found another small budget [paper] pressed into his hand.

"You're goin' right by, an' I'm goin' to close early. I expect you'll be willin' to leave it. 'Tis for your grandson, Johnny. He'll want his little paper to read to-morrow. It's one the doctor sends him," said the storekeeper, boldly. "You just give a call as you go by, an' they'll come right out."

If Henry Jones had heard the roar of laughter in the store a moment after he had shut the door behind him, that copy of the paper might have been dropped at once and lain under the fresh-fallen snow until spring. A certain pride and stiffness of demeanor stood the old man in good stead, but he was very angry indeed as he put the great turkey into his wagon and the mail-matter beside it. He drove away up the road in grim fury. Perhaps he should meet some one to whom he could depute the unwelcome errand. But the doctor's words could not be put out of mind, and his own conscience became more and more disturbed. It was beginning to snow hard, and the young horse was in a hurry to get home. The turkey soon joggled and bumped from its safe place under the seat to the very back of the farm wagon, while the newspaper, which had been in the corner, blew forward out of sight and got under the buffalo-robe.

Just as the reluctant messenger came to a cold-looking little house by the roadside Johnny himself came out to shut the gate, which was blowing in the wind. He was bareheaded, and as warm as a furry squirrel with his good supper of bread and butter and milk and gingerbread, but he looked very small and thin as his grandfather caught sight of him. For years the two had never been so near together,—Johnny and his mother sat far back in the church,—and there was now an unexpected twinge in the old man's heart, while Johnny was dumb with astonishment at this unexpected appearance.

> [JOHNNY'S] FACE SHONE WITH JOY AS HE DUMPED THE GREAT BIRD ON THE KITCHEN FLOOR AND BADE HIS MOTHER LOOK. "'TWAS MY GRANDPA OUT THERE, AND HE SAID HE'D BROUGHT SOMETHING FOR MY FOLKS. NOW, SIR, AIN'T WE GOIN' TO HAVE A TURKEY FOR THANKSGIVIN'!"

"That you, John?" said the old farmer, in a businesslike tone, but with no unkindness; his heart was beating ridiculously fast. "There's something there in the wagon for your folks. The postmaster was in a hurry to get it to you," he added. But the horse would not stand, and he did not look back again at the boy. Johnny reached up, and seeing nothing but the great turkey, made a manful effort to master the weight of it and get it over the tailboard, and then went triumphantly through the swinging gate as his grandfather, perfectly unconscious of such an involuntary benefaction, passed rattling up the road trying to hold the colt as best he might.

As for Johnny, his face shone with joy as he dumped the great bird on the kitchen floor and bade his mother look.

"'Twas my grandpa out there, and he said he'd brought something for my folks. Now, sir, ain't we goin' to have a turkey for Thanksgivin'!"

Whereupon, to Johnny's despair and complete surprise, his mother sat down in the little rocking-chair and began to cry.

"I certain sure put it into the wagon, well under the seat," said old Mr. Jones to his wife, who had come out through the long shed to the barn to hold the lantern. "I certain sure put it in with my own hands; as nice a gobbler as we ever raised ourselves."

"Did you pass anybody on the road, or leave the horse so they could have stolen anything out?" asked Mrs. Jones, looking very cold and deeply troubled. "Why, I've got the stuffing all made a'ready. I counted on your bringin' it, and on getting it all prepared to roast to-morrow. I have to divide up my work; I can't do as I used to," she mourned, adding her mite of trouble to their general feeling of despair. "There, I don't care much whether we have a turkey or not. We don't seem to have as much to be thankful for as some folks."

The lantern-light shone on her face, and Mr. Jones saw how old and pitiful she looked, and by contrast he thought of the little boy's cheerful chirp and hearty "Thank you!" as he took the paper. Whether it was what the doctor had said, or whether it was the natural workings of a slow conscience, there was a queer disturbance in his mind. He could not manage to tell his wife about stopping to leave the mail.

"I guess I'll drive back," he said, doubtfully. But the snow was falling like a blizzard, faster and faster, as he looked out of the door. "I certain would if I had anybody to go with me, but this colt is dreadful restless. I couldn't get out and leave him to pick the turkey up if I saw it laying right in the road. I guess we've got to let it go and trust to Providence. The road's rough enough, but I can't see how that turkey jolted out, either!" he grumbled. "I feel too lame to go afoot."

"There, I thought when you let Asa go off to-day, 'stead of to-morrow, you'd be liable to need him; you ain't so young as you used to be, Henry," said his wife. "I'll have ye a good cup o' tea, and we won't mind about the turkey more than we can help."

They passed a solemn evening together, and the great snow-storm raged about their warm house. Many times the old man reproached his own want of spirit in not going back along the road.

<hr>

In the morning, very early, there was a loud knocking at the kitchen door. When Mrs. Jones opened it she found a boy standing there with a happy, eager face.

"Are you my grandma?" demanded Johnny. "Mother sent her best respects, and we thank you very much for the turkey, and she hopes you and my grandpa will stop, going home from meeting, and eat dinner. She'd be real glad to have you."

"What's all this?" demanded Mr. Henry Jones, who had heard the message with astonished ears, and stood in the doorway behind his wife, with his spectacles on his forehead like a lighthouse. "Where'd you get your turkey, sir? I'd like to know!"

"Why, right out of your wagon," said Johnny. "That one you brought last night. It's the handsomest one mother ever had in the house; she cried like everything about it." The child's voice faltered, he was so excited with his errand, and so spent with his eager journey through the deep snow.

"Come right in, dear!" cried the grandmother, grateful enough for the sight of him. And when Henry Jones saw her lead him to the fire, and then with a sob take the little fellow right into her arms and hug him, and begin to cry, too, he turned away and looked out of the window. The boy was their very own.

"There, give him some warm breakfast before he goes back; he must have started early," said the grandfather. "I'll put the colt in and take him back myself. She must have meant what she said, to start him up here like that, soon as day broke!"

When Johnny's mother saw the old man and the little boy plowing along in the old sleigh, and saw how they were talking and even laughing together, she thanked Heaven for this sudden blessing. "I wa'n't going to be slow about taking the next step, when an old man like him had taken the first one," she said to herself.

As for the lost turkey, it was already in the oven at that moment; but the true Thanksgiving feast that year was the feast of happiness in all their hearts.

"O my!" exclaimed Johnny early that afternoon, as he leaned back in his chair. "Grandma, aren't you glad this turkey didn't wander in the wet grass and die when it was a chick?"

Source: Jewett, Sarah Orne. "The Lost Turkey." *Youth's Companion*, November 27, 1902. Available online at Jewett Texts, http://www.public.coe.edu/~theller/soj/unc/turkey.htm.

Thanksgiving Spreads beyond New England

This lithograph, titled *American Progress*, was produced by George A. Crofutt around 1873, after an 1872 painting of the same title by John Gast. The woman, symbolizing America, leads settlers across the frontier.

Remembering Loved Ones Back Home at Thanksgiving during the California Gold Rush (1849)

As New Englanders moved westward to settle the American frontier, they carried the Thanksgiving holiday with them. Franklin Agustus Buck set sail for California in January 1849, as soon as he heard about the first gold strikes in the West. He chronicled his experiences in a series of letters to his sister back home in Maine, which were published years later as A Yankee Trader in the Gold Rush. *In this excerpt from a letter dated November 25, 1849, Buck describes the climate, scenery, and business opportunities of his new home. He also expresses a strong desire to see his family at Thanksgiving.*

I am in possession of a letter dated in August from you and also received one from Uncle Richard, dated Sept.15th, but nothing from the rest of the family. I am glad to know that you are all alive and well and hope you will continue so for some years, at least until I come home which I intend doing at some future time—when, the Lord only knows. I have not come 20,000 miles to turn around and go right back again like some persons who have been here and gotten homesick. I prophesy that they will be sick to come back here again when they hear of the prosperity of this great and growing country. I finished your letter from San Francisco, as you will see if you ever get it.

Shortly after, I returned to this place on the steamer *Senator.* It really seemed like travelling again to sit on a sofa in her splendid saloon. If it had not been for the entire absence of ladies, the smoking in the saloon (this suited me, of course), and the *monte tables*, I could have imagined myself going down east from Boston. It was her first trip and she started the echoes for the first time on the Sacramento with a regular steamboat's bell and whistle. Great was the astonishment of the Indians as they stared at us from the bank.

Upon our arrival at Sacramento City we were greeted with the firing of cannon and the cheers of the inhabitants. She now runs regularly three times a week, through by day light, fare $25, meals $2. She must coin money.

Today is Sunday. Gloomy November, probably, with you, but here the weather is splendid, not cold enough to need a fire. Although this is the winter or rainy season it has rained about 15 days out of this month so far. When it rains it is gloomy enough and muddy enough, but as soon as it clears off the mud dries up mighty quickly.

> THE SIERRA NEVADA MOUNTAINS LOOK MAGNIFICENT FROM HERE, COVERED WITH SNOW, BUT DOWN IN THE VALLEY SNOW SELDOM FALLS. PEOPLE ARE PLANTING GARDENS. THE TREES ARE EVERGREEN AND THE GRASS SO LONG PARCHED UP IT IS JUST SPRINGING UP GREEN AGAIN.

The Sierra Nevada mountains look magnificent from here, covered with snow, but down in the valley snow seldom falls. People are planting gardens. The trees are evergreen and the grass so long parched up it is just springing up green again.

So much for the climate. I want to tell you about our domestic arrangements. We have fitted up the upper part of our store: clothed it with sheeting, carpeted it with Chinese mats, furnished it with chairs and tables and live in luxury for this country. The heaviest bill was for the cook-stove, $100 was the lowest cent we could get one for and a common one at that. Mrs. Lindley does the cooking and we furnish the material and eat it. The Captain lugs all the wood and water up stairs. We have a parlor and kitchen and begin to live like rational beings again. It costs us about $10 a week and you can't board at any place less than $20. In the evening we have a social game of whist and spend our time very agreeably. Lindley is a lawyer and his wife a New Haven girl and a lady in every sense of the word.

Captain Cole has sent the brig down to S.F. and if the rains stop the hauling to the mines and trade is dull, he may go to the Sandwich Islands with her. The rain does not stop the place from going ahead. Two large hotels are being erected and a city hospital. The city contains over 800 framed buildings, besides the tents. In the *election* last held, over 1800 votes were thrown. This will give you some idea of this "right smart place."

Trade has fallen off some since the rainy weather but week before last we sold out of our little store $1500 worth of goods. All cash trade in one day. Tell Joseph to beat that. We make a percentage here, too. The flour that I bought in San Francisco for $18 per sack (200 lbs) we sold for $44 and are all out. Flour is a little cheaper now. We sold at the top of the market and for once were *lucky*, for great quantities are arriving from Chile. It is now worth $35 here and $2 a lb in the mines. It costs 75¢ a pound to transport goods from here to the mines and our merchant from Weaver Creek, 50 miles from here, whose team we loaded, paid $1000 for having one load hauled. This is on account of the muddy roads.

So much for California. It has gotten to be an old story to me. The first [gold] dust that I received, $2800, on our selling two houses in San Francisco, made my eyes sparkle and my heart beat rather quickly as I spooned it into a two quart pail. But now, I receive it and weigh it out with as little feeling as I would so much sand.

I should like to be at home on Thanksgiving Day. I suppose you have had or will have one about this time. (Bake me a turnover!) Be sure and write me all about it. I look forward with great pleasure to spending a Thanksgiving with all the family once more in my life. We shall be different persons from what we were on the last we spent together, but our affections will remain the same. I know mine will. Talk to me about a man's forgetting old times and losing his interest in his home and friends—it is all humbug. The farther I am removed from you and the longer I stay, mine increases. My remembrances of home and my youth are dear to me. We were blest, Mary, with the best of parents and a happy home. Probably they were the happiest years of our lives—those that we spent at home. How much wiser a person gets to be by going abroad and mixing with the ups and downs of this world—in these truths which he never can realize until he leaves home.

Source: Buck, Franklin Agustus. "Letter from Sacramento," November 25, 1849, pp. 55, 57. *A Yankee Trader in the Gold Rush; The Letters of Franklin A. Buck, Compiled by Katherine A. White*. Boston: Houghton Mifflin Company, 1930. Available online at Library of Congress, American Memory Collection, http://memory.loc.gov/ammem/cbhtml/cbhome.html.

Longing for a New England Thanksgiving
Onboard a Ship in the South Seas (1857)

In the following excerpt from her book Incidents on Land and Water, *Mass-achusetts-born Mrs. D. B. Bates recalls an episode from her arduous 1850 sea voyage to California. After her ship is destroyed by fire, Mrs. Bates finds herself stuck in a remote port in the Falkland Islands in November of that year. Although she observes the local colonies of penguins and albatrosses with great interest, she also longs to return home for a traditional New England Thanksgiving celebration.*

The feathered tribes are very numerous on these islands of Southern hemisphere. Of penguins, there are four kinds—the king penguin, the macaroni, the jackass, and the rookery. The first of these is much larger than a goose; the other three are smaller, differing in appearance in several particulars. They all walk upright, with their legs projecting from their bodies in the same direction with their tails. When fifty or more of them are seen in file, they appear, at a distance, like a company of soldiers. They carry their heads high, with their wings drooping like two arms. The breast-feathers are delicately white, with a line of black running across the crops. Seen at a distance, they have the appearance of little men, with a white bosom, black neckerchief, and short breeches. Their gait on land, however, is very awkward—rather more so than that of a sailor just returned from a long voyage.

When tamed, the penguin becomes quite tractable. A lady at the isle had domesticated and made quite a pet of a king penguin, which she, however, proposed to relinquish for the sum of thirty dollars. She had taught him to sit at table with her. A sip of coffee he seemed to enjoy with much gusto; and if, perchance, she attempted to raise the cup to her lips before first presenting his majesty with a draught, he would, quick as thought, with a blow from one of his "hands," dash the cup to the floor. He followed her about the house as a child follows its mother; and she assured us he was a great deal of company for her when alone.

Another sea-fowl peculiar to the islands is the upland-goose, which is about the size of our domestic goose. Their plumage is rich and glossy: that of the gander is dazzlingly white. The down is equal to that of the swan. The teal are also found here, and far surpassing in beauty those of this country. Their bills and feet are blue; their wings of a golden green. The ducks are similar to those found in the United States; but the manner of going a-ducking very dissimilar,—no lying in wait half a day before getting a good shot. You might take your gun and shoot them down, and dozens will come to ascertain the cause of the report.

Previous to our arrival, three other vessels had put into the harbor in distress, and had been condemned. The crews of these vessels were constantly out gunning. I would see them often returning over the hills, laden with those beautiful white geese, looking like so many swans. A Dutch captain, whose vessel had been condemned, was very contentedly pursuing the "even tenor of his way," bringing in the game, while "mine frow" [his wife] was as industriously manufacturing feather beds. Never having heard them say anything about getting away, I presume they are yet at the old vocation.

A moral philosopher and naturalist would be highly interested in contemplating, for days, the operations of a South Sea rookery, observing the order and regularity with which everything is conducted. When a sufficient number of penguins, albatross, etc., are assembled on shore, they proceed to the execution of the grand object for which they left their native element. First, they trace a well-defined parallelogram, of requisite extent to accommodate the whole fraternity,—perhaps from one to four or five acres. One side runs parallel with the water's edge, and is left open for egress and regress. They then commence picking up the stones, and depositing them outside the lines; thus creating quite a little wall on three sides. Within this wall they form a pathway, several feet in width, which would not suffer, in regard to smoothness, compared with any fashionable promenade in our city parks. This path is for the sentinels to patrol at night. They next lay out the whole in little squares, formed by narrow paths which cross each other at right angles. At each intersection of these paths, an albatross constructs her nest; while in the centre of each square is a penguin's nest.

> *A* LADY AT THE ISLE HAD DOMESTICATED AND MADE QUITE A PET OF A KING PENGUIN, WHICH SHE, HOWEVER, PROPOSED TO RELINQUISH FOR THE SUM OF THIRTY DOLLARS. SHE HAD TAUGHT HIM TO SIT AT TABLE WITH HER. A SIP OF COFFEE HE SEEMED TO ENJOY WITH MUCH GUSTO.

Although the penguin and albatross profess such sincere attachment for one another, they not only form their nests in a different manner, but the penguin will rob her friend's nest, whenever an opportunity presents; being ambitious, I suppose, to produce a large family. The penguin's nest is formed by an excavation in the earth; while that of the albatross if formed by throwing up a mound of earth, eight or ten inches high; on the summit of which she can scrutinize the proceedings of her nearest neighbors and best friends.

The camp of the rookery is in continual motion; penguins passing through the different paths, on their return from aquatic excursions, eager to caress their mates after a temporary absence; while the latter are passing out in quest of refreshment and recreation. At the same time, the air is almost darkened by an innumerable number of albatross hovering over the rookery, continually lighting, and meeting their companions; while others are rising, and shaping their course for the sea. To see these creatures of the ocean so faithfully discharge the duties assigned them by the great Creator; to witness their affectionate re-unions, their numerous acts of tenderness and courtesy to each other, the reflection naturally arises, that, if there was only as much harmony and genuine affection between wedded pairs of the human family, the connubial state would then indeed be "all that we dream of heaven."

We had remained at the islands about a month, when the ship *Humayoon*, from Dundee, (McKenzie, master,) bound to Valparaiso, laden with coal, tar, and liquors, put into port to procure water and beef. The captain formed an acquaintance with my husband, and, after learning the particulars of our situation, very kindly offered us a passage to Valparaiso; from whence we could, in all probability, arrive home sooner than by remaining where we were. After having procured the necessaries required, I expected the captain would at once proceed on his voyage; but, being perfectly independent, as he was sole owner of the fine ship and cargo, he protracted his stay at the settlement day after day, thereby gratifying the mirth-loving portion of the community by assembling them at different times on ship-board, to join in the merry dance. He had on board several musical instruments, which he was taking out to dispose of; and, being possessed of extraordinary musical talents, the people were perfectly delighted and entranced with specimens of his skill. He had a perfect passion for Scotch airs, which, all conceded, never before sounded half so enlivening. But pleasures, however transporting, unhappily cannot last. No chain, be it of gold, or pearl, or flowers, can bind the stubborn wings of Time, and bid him loiter on his way. On the morning of the 25th of November, he weighed anchor, and turned her bows towards the entrance.

I cast a last, sad, lingering look at the old *Nonantum*, and bade adieu to kind friends, whom, probably, I should never meet again on the journey of life, although they would be often remembered. During my sojourn at the islands, although I found kind friends, I passed many a gloomy hour. As the season approached which, from time immemorial, in dear old New England, has been observed as a day of thanksgiving and prayer,—a day, of all others, when severed families assemble under the paternal roof, to meet once again the loved friends of their youth, to tread again the paths hallowed by childhood's earliest recollection,—the anniversary of such a day, while in this remote region, crowded my memory with reminiscences of the past, pleasurable, from the associations which they recalled, and painful, from the position which I then occupied.

Source: Bates, Mrs. D. B. "Chapter V. A South Sea Rookery," pp. 39-45. *Incidents on Land and Water, or Four Years on the Pacific Coast. Being a Narrative of the Burning of the Ships Nonantum, Humayoon and Fanchon, Together with Many Startling and Interesting Adventures on Sea and Land.* Boston: J. French and Company, 1857. Available online at Library of Congress, American Memory Collection, http://memory.loc.gov/ammem/cbhtml/cbhome.html.

An Orphaned Girl Recalls the Excitement of Thanksgiving in California (1850s)

Thanksgiving observances spread westward during the first half of the 19th century, eventually reaching California. Many new arrivals to the area reveled in the opportunity to celebrate the holiday. In the reminiscence below, Eliza Donner Houghton shares her fond childhood memories of dressing up for a Thanksgiving feast in Sonoma, California, during the 1850s.

Houghton was one of 46 surviving members of the Donner Party—a group of emigrants from Springfield, Illinois, who traveled westward by wagon train in 1846. Before reaching California, the Donner Party left the established wagon trail and attempted to find a shortcut. Unfortunately, the unproven route cost them a great deal of time and left them stranded on the east side of the Sierra Nevada at the onset of a harsh winter. Nearly half of the group perished from exposure or starvation, including Houghton's parents, before the survivors were rescued five months later. Houghton and her sisters were raised and educated by family members in California. She eventually published her life story in a book called The Expedition of the Donner Party and Its Tragic Fate.

My educational advantages in Sonoma closed with my half term at St. Mary's Hall, grandma believing that I had gone to school long enough to be able to finish my studies without teachers.

Georgia was more fortunate. When Miss Hutchinson opened "The Young Ladies' Seminary" in the Fall, grandma decided to lend it a helping hand by sending her a term as a day scholar. My delighted sister was soon in touch with a crowd of other little girls, and brought home many of their bright sayings for my edification.

One evening she rushed into the house bubbling over with excitement and joyously proclaimed: "Oh, Eliza, Miss Hutchinson is going to give a great dinner to her pupils on Thanksgiving Day; and I am to go, and you also, as her guest."

Grandma was pleased that I was invited, and declared that she would send a liberal donation of milk and cheese as a mark of appreciation. I caught much of Georgia's spirit of delight, for I had a vivid recollection of the grand dinner given in commemoration of our very first legally appointed Thanksgiving Day in California; I had only to close my eyes, and in thought would reappear the longest and most bountifully spread table I had ever seen. Turkey, chicken, and wild duck, at the ends; a whole roasted pig in the centre, and more than enough delicious accompaniments to cover the spaces between. Then the grown folk dining first, and the flock of hungry children coming later; the speaking, laughing, and clapping of hands, with which the old home customs were introduced in the new land.

There, I wore a dark calico dress and sunbonnet, both made by poor Mrs. McCutchen of the Donner Party, who had to take in sewing for a livelihood; but to the Seminary, I should wear grandpa's gift, a costly alpaca, changeable in the sunlight to soft mingling bluish and greenish colors of the peacock. Its wide skirt reached to my shoetops, and the gathers to its full waist were gauged to a sharp peak in front. A wide open V from the shoulder down to the peak displayed an embroidered white Swiss chemisette. The sleeves, small at the wrist, were trimmed with folds of the material and a quilling of white lace at the hand.

On the all-important morning, grandma was anxious that I should look well; and after she had looped my braids with bows of blue ribbon and fastened my dress, she brought forth my dainty bonnet, her own gift. Deft fingers had shirred the pale-blue silk over a frame which had been cut down from ladies' size, arranged an exquisite spray of Maréchal Niel rosebuds and foliage on the outside, and quilled a soft white ruching around the face, which emphasized the Frenchy style and finish so pleasing to grandma.

Did I look old fashioned? Yes, for grandma said, "Thou art like a picture I saw somewhere long ago." Then she continued brightly, "Here are thy mits, and thy little embroidered handkerchief folded in a square. Carry it carefully so it won't get mussed before the company see it, and come not back late for milking."

The Seminary playground was so noisy with chatter and screams of joy, that it was impossible to remember all the games we played; and later the dining-room and its offerings were so surprising and so beautifully decorated that the sight nearly deprived me of my appetite.

Source: Houghton, Eliza Poor Donner. "Chapter XXIX—Thanksgiving Day in California," pp. 260-62. *The Expedition of the Donner Party and Its Tragic Fate.* Chicago: A. C. McClurg and Co., 1911. Available online at the Library of Congress, http://memory.loc.gov/ammem/cbhtml/cbhome.html.

A Thanksgiving Comedy of Errors
on the Nebraska Frontier (1873)

In the recollection below, George Strester describes his family's disastrous attempt at farming on the Nebraska frontier in the 1870s, which culminates in an unforgettable Thanksgiving dinner. Strester told the story 60 years later as part of the Federal Writers' Project; it appears in the Library of Congress in the American Life Histories Collection.

My father was a Methodist preacher and at one time was assigned to take charge of a small church at Indianola, Nebraska, when that country was being settled, our family arriving only one or two years later than the first pioneers, or about 1873.

There were mostly very poor people who came to try to make a living farming in that dry arid country, and father saw at the start that his followers would not be able to pay the preacher enough for him and family to live on, so he took to farming as a side line, and located a homestead a mile south of the general store and post office of Indianola. Here he built a two-room house made of sod out in ribbons three inches thick by twelve in width. The floor was the bare ground with the grass shaved off and tamped to make it firm to walk on. The doors were of boards cleated together and hung with leather hinges.

It was a happy day for all when father and I moved the cook stove from the covered wagon into our new home. We didn't have any table but my pa was quite a genius; he went right to work and made one. He drove four stakes in the ground—all the proper height—and layed the front end gate of the wagon box on top of the stakes and when mother spread the cloth on, you wouldn't know but what it was a beautiful table.

There were about five acres of land that had been plowed before by some settler who had abandoned the place before we came. Father hitched the oxen to the plow and stirred up this patch of earth. He planted part of it to garden vegetables for family use, and the balance to onions and sorghum cane, about one half to each. The onions and sorghum were to sell to buy other necessities.

Then I drove the oxen on the breaking plow and turned over about two acres of sod land. This was planted to corn. Father would travel down every third furrow with an ax and at every stop, strike the ax through the sod and I went along with a bucket of corn and dropped four kernels in each hole made by the ax, and stomped it shut with my heel, until the field was all planted.

The season was favorable and we raised a wonderful crop of everything. My brother and I did the most of the work. Father tended to his pastoral duties, and worked with us at his spare time. We built a cellar in the back yard with a dirt roof in which to store our winter supply of vegetables, also a building in which to store the onions. We were all well and happy, plenty of vegetables stored in the cellar, corn for the oxen and cow, which were already fat, from gorging on the buffalo grass. Corn meal for mush and johnny cake, which we ground as needed with a mortar and pestle. The cow gave a bucket of milk at a time, so we had plenty of milk to drink, cream for our mush and butter for our johnny cake.

Mother was an expert at making butter. We also had two dozen hens that were brought along in a crate tied on the back of the wagon. They seemed to be trying to see which could lay the most eggs. There was a great pile of buffalo chips at one side of the house that us kids had gathered and piled there for winter fuel. We seemed to be enjoying the height of prosperity when alas, several things happened to mar our happiness.

One day father opened the onion house to see how they were keeping, and found they had heated and were starting to rot. Father didn't say any cuss words, just "well, well, that's too bad."

He said something had to be done quick if we saved any of the onions. So we all went to work with a will, and in about a week we had the job done, and we had saved about one half of them, but there were rotten onions scattered far and near. The chickens pecked at them and it made their eggs taste like rotten onions, and the cow ate them and spoiled the milk and butter. So we didn't have cream for our mush or butter for our johnny cake. And father didn't say any cuss words just, "well, well, that's too bad."

So he says we'll harvest our cane, get it into sorghum, then we can have molasses on our johnny cake and that won't be so bad. He set my brother and I stripping the leaves off the cane with sticks while he loaded some onions on the wagon and started out to find a market for them, and get some barrels to put the molasses in. The store keeper at Indianola didn't want any onions so father decided to go down the river to Arapahoe. He traded his load for 12 long boards and two small barrels.

When father got home my brother and I had the cane all stripped and the seed tassels out from the tops, and father helped out the stalks which had to be kept from touching the ground and piled them on some leaves or seed tassels to keep them clean. Then we loaded them on the wagon and started for a sorghum mill which was one days drive over prairie where there was no road.

About noon we came to a dead carcas. The oxen stopped, smelled it, started to bellow an paw dirt, then bolted, and, one being a little faster runner than the other, they ran in a circle, and the cane being very slippery, it all lost off the wagon before father could get the oxen stopped. Father didn't say a cuss word, just says, "well, well, isn't that too bad." He brought the team and wagon to about the center of the scattered cane, unyoked the oxen and turned them loose to grass, while we went to work loading our cane. This took until dark when we made a dry camp for the night. We arrived at the mill at noon the next day. We made a bargain with the man who owned the mill to make the molasses for half if father would drive our oxen on the sweep to grind the cane and we boys would feed the stalks between the rollers. The owner of the mill was to do the boiling of the juice. We finished the next day and the following morning loaded our two little barrels of molasses, and started for home. We hadn't traveled far, when I noticed the bottom of the wagon box was nearly covered with molasses. Both barrels had sprung a leak. Father didn't cuss, he just said, "well, well, that sure is too bad." Then he urged the oxen to the top of their speed (which was about three miles per hour) in an effort to get home before all the sorghum leaked out, and when we arrived we emptied one barrel into the other and had just enough to fill one barrel which we set over a washtub to catch the drip. Mother put a wash boiler of water over the fire to heat, soaked the empty barrel with hot water until it was tight again, then poured in the molasses from the other barrel together with what had leaked into the tub. Father had a spigot but

WE CHILDREN ALL SHED A FEW TEARS WHEN [OUR COW] OLD BROCH WAS KILLED, FOR SHE WAS A FAMILY PET, BUT WE HAD TO HAVE SOMETHING TO EAT. THAT WAS THE DAY BEFORE THANKSGIVING, AND THE NEXT DAY MOTHER PLANNED A REAL THANKSGIVING FEAST——A LARGE ROAST OF MEAT WITH POTATOES AND CARROTS.

no sugar to bore a hole for it near the bottom of the barrel. So he put a rag around it and drove it in the bung hole, then all hands rolled it down into the vegetable cellar and set it in one corner by the door where it would be handy to get at, and father says, "Now we will be sure of that much of our sorghum." But he was wrong again, for in coming out after placing the barrel, the door was left open and my baby sister found her way down there and turned the spigot handle and before any of us knew it, all the sorghum in that part of the barrel above the bung hole had run out on the cellar floor and under the pile of vegetables stored there. They had to be taken out and the molasses scrubbed off and laid in the sun to dry and the cellar had to be dug about two or three inches deeper to get rid of the molasses that had soaked into the dirt floor.

Now everything was ready, and we put the vegetables back in the cellar but daddy didn't want to run any more chances of loosing the rest of the sorghum, so he got a large demijohn that he used to haul water from the river for home use, that he didn't use for that purpose any longer, and we had recently dug a well. He said "We'll fill that and set it in the corner of the bedroom where it will be easy to watch." There was just enough to fill it, and it was set in the corner by father and mother's bed and father said "It surely will be safe there, and we still have enough left for winter use." But alas, daddy was wrong again, for one night not long after, there was an explosion like the firing of a gun or the bursting of a bomb. Of course everybody jumped out of bed, to land half way to their ankles in sorghum molasses. The demijohn was in thousand or more pieces and molasses was all over everything in the house, even dripping from the ceiling. Our clothes, bedding and hair was smeared and poor father's beard was matted with it. But father didn't say any cuss words, he simply said "well, well, this surely is too bad." We didn't go back to bed that night, and we went to house cleaning, which lasted for several days before we got rid of the last of the molasses. Father said "well I am glad that is all over, and that is the last of the molasses." But dear old dad was wrong again, for some of the horrible stuff had gone through the cracks in the floor, and soon began to mould and smell, so we had to move things out of the room, take the floor up, dig the dirt out that the molasses had soaked into, scrub all the boards and replace them before the molasses deal was finally finished.

Mother decided if we did not eat the eggs on account of the rotten onion flavor, we would have to eat the hens, so she cooked a nice fat one, and made corn dumplings with it, but nobody could stomach the rotten onion taste that it had. So there was the milk, butter, eggs, and chicken dinners "gone with the wind." Father said we'll have to have something beside vegetables to eat, so he decided to butcher the cow. She had gone dry anyway (probably because of eating so many onions) and was nice and fat and would make prime beef and enough to last all winter.

We children all shed a few tears when Old Broch was killed, for she was a family pet, but we had to have something to eat. That was the day before Thanksgiving, and the next day mother planned a real Thanksgiving feast—a large roast of meat with potatoes and carrots laid around it. Something we had not had for years. But there was a peculiar odor that filled the house while it was cooking. Mother said she might have spilled something on the stove which in burning, caused the stench.

The table was set and the roast brought on and how delicious it looked, and father, after giving thanks for the prosperous year and the many blessings that we had enjoyed, carved the roast, placing a liberal helping of meat, carrots and spuds on each plate. Mother took a bite and looked at father; he took a taste and looked at us kids. I took a mouthful and my stomach heaved, and horrors of horrors, there was that familiar taste of rotten onions. So our dinner was entirely spoiled and all we had to eat was johnny cake straight with nothing to put on it or go with it. Still father did not say any cuss words and though sorely tried, was still able to say "well, well, that surely is too bad."

Well we took the remains of Old Broch and buried them out in the field, and my little sisters laid flowers on her grave. Father decided then and there to quit farming, and although this all happened over 60 years ago, to this day I just can't say that I'm very crazy about sorghum or onions.

Source: Strester, George. "A Preacher Tries Farming." In *American Life Histories: Manuscripts from the Federal Writers' Project, 1936-1940.* Available online at the Library of Congress, http://memory.loc.gov/ammem/wpaintro/wpahome.html.

The Civil War and
Creation of the National Holiday

A sheet music cover for "The President's Hymn," composed by J. W. Turner in celebration of President Abraham Lincoln's national Thanksgiving Proclamation of 1863.

Sarah Josepha Hale
Campaigns for a National Thanksgiving Holiday (1858)

Although Thanksgiving observances had spread beyond New England by the 1850s, celebrations of the holiday were not well-coordinated among the various states. Sarah Josepha Hale, the editor of the leading women's magazine of the day, launched a campaign to make Thanksgiving a legal holiday throughout the United States, which would be celebrated annually on a uniform date. She promoted Thanksgiving in the pages of her magazine, Godey's Lady's Book, *through editorials, recipes, and sentimental stories about family gatherings. In the 1858 column below, titled "Our National Thanksgiving," Hale argues that an annual day of gratitude would promote national harmony and unity.*

> All the blessings of the fields,
> All the stores the garden yields,
> All the plenty summer pours,
> Autumn's rich, o'erflowing stores,
> Peace, prosperity and health,
> Private bliss and public wealth,
> Knowledge with its gladdening streams,
> Pure religion's holier beams—
> Lord, for these our souls shall raise
> Grateful vows and solemn praise.

We are most happy to agree with the large majority of the governors of the different States—as shown in their unanimity of action for several past years, and which, we hope, will this year be adopted by all—that THE LAST THURSDAY IN NOVEMBER shall be the DAY OF NATIONAL THANKSGIVING for the American people. Let this day, from this time forth, as long as our Banner of Stars floats on the breeze, be the grand THANKSGIVING HOLIDAY of our nation, when the noise and tumult of worldliness may be exchanged for the laugh of happy children, the glad greetings of family reunion, and the humble gratitude of the Christian heart. This truly American Festival falls, this year on the *twenty-fifth day of this month.*

Let us consecrate the day to benevolence of action, by sending good gifts to the poor, and doing those deeds of charity that will, for one day, make every American home the place of plenty and of rejoicing. These seasons of refreshing are of inestimable advantage to the popular heart; and, if rightly managed, will greatly aid and strengthen public harmony of feeling. Let the people of all the States and Territories sit down together to the "feast of fat things," and drink, in the sweet draught of joy and gratitude to the Divine giver of all our blessings, the pledge of renewed love to the Union, and to each other; and of peace and good-will to all men. *Then the last Thursday in November will soon become the day of* AMERICAN THANKSGIVING throughout the world.

Source: Hale, Sarah Josepha. "Editor's Table: Our National Thanksgiving." *Godey's Lady's Book,* November, 1858. Available online at http://womenshistory.about.com/od/thanksgiving/a/hale_thanksday.htm.

Jefferson Davis Proclaims
Thanksgiving for the Confederacy (1861)

Following years of disagreements with the North over such issues as slavery and states' rights, the South seceded from the Union in 1861 to start the American Civil War. Both sides proclaimed special days of thanksgiving during the war years to express their gratitude for successes in battle. President Jefferson Davis also issued the first national Thanksgiving proclamation for the Confederate States of America in 1861. In his statement, which appears below, Davis asks citizens of the Confederacy to pray for victory and the restoration of peace.

A THANKSGIVING PROCLAMATION, 1861

WHEREAS, it hath pleased Almighty God, the Sovereign Disposer of events, to protect and defend us hitherto in our conflicts with our enemies as to be unto them a shield.

And whereas, with grateful thanks we recognize His hand and acknowledge that not unto us, but unto Him, belongeth the victory, and in humble dependence upon His almighty strength, and trusting in the justness of our purpose, we appeal to Him that He may set at naught the efforts of our enemies, and humble them to confusion and shame.

Now therefore, I, Jefferson Davis, President of the Confederate States, in view of impending conflict, do hereby set apart Friday, the 15th day of November, as a day of national humiliation and prayer, and do hereby invite the reverend clergy and the people of these Confederate States to repair on that day to their homes and usual places of public worship, and to implore blessing of Almighty God upon our people, that he may give us victory over our enemies, preserve our homes and altars from pollution, and secure to us the restoration of peace and prosperity.

Given under hand and seal of the Confederate States at Richmond, this the 31st day of October, year of our Lord, one thousand eight hundred and sixty one.

By the President, JEFFERSON DAVIS

Source: Davis, Jefferson. *Thanksgiving Proclamation for the Confederate States of America*, October 31, 1861. Available online at South Atlantic Thanksgiving Project, http://www.south atlanticcenter.org/tgiving/proclaim.html.

A Confederate Thanksgiving Sermon (1862)

Before the Civil War, many people in the South had rejected Thanksgiving because of its origins in New England and its association with the abolitionist movement. During the conflict, however, the Confederate states embraced the holiday with patriotic zeal. On September 18, 1862, President Jefferson Davis issued a national Thanksgiving proclamation for the Confederacy following the southern victory in the Battle of Bull Run. Many southern preachers—like Bishop Stephen Elliott of Savannah, Georgia, who is quoted below—used the occasion to give fiery sermons about the righteousness of the Confederate cause.

> PROVERBS, CH. XXIV, vv. 17-18. "Rejoice not when thine enemy falleth, and let not thine heart be glad when he stumbleth: Lest the Lord see it, and it displease him and he turn away his wrath from him."

We have been gathered together to-day by a proclamation of our President, to return thanks to Almighty God for a series of brilliant victories won by our gallant soldiers over the invaders of our soil. Most fervently do we thank Him for his presence with us upon those fields of terrible conflict, for the skill of our commanding generals, for the heroism of our officers of every grade, for the valor and self-sacrifice of our soldiers, for the glorious results which have followed upon the success of our arms. Most devoutly do we praise and bless His holy name, this day, for the deliverance of our country from the polluting tread of the enemy and for the punishment which he has seen fit to inflict upon those who vainly boasted that they would devour us. We give all the glory to Him, while we cannot forget the living heroes whose inspired courage led them triumphant over fields of desperate carnage, nor the martyred dead who have poured out the gushing tide of their young and noble life-blood for the sacred cause which carried them to the battle field. But battles, at last, even with all the dazzling halo which surrounds them, are but fields of slaughter, unless made illustrious by the principles which they involved or by the spirit which animated and ruled over them. The meeting of barbaric hordes upon the fields of blood, of which history is full, where men fought with the instinct and ferocity of beasts, simply for hatred's sake or the love of war, is disgusting to the noble mind, and carries with it no idea save that of brutality. We could not thank God for victories such as those, and therefore in keeping this Holy Festival, our thankfulness must rest more upon the cause for which he has called us to arms, upon the spirit which has accompanied it, and upon the guardianship which he has established over us, than upon the mere triumphs of the battle field.

We do not place our cause upon the highest level until we grasp the idea that God has made us the guardians and champions of a people whom he is preparing for his own purposes, and against whom the whole world is banded. The most solemn relation upon earth is that between parent and child, because in it immortal souls are committed to the training of man not only for time but for eternity. There is no measure to its sublimity, for it stretches upwards to the throne of God and links us with immortality. We tremble when we meditate upon it and cry for Divine help when we weigh its responsibilities. What shall we think, then, of the relation which subsists between a dominant race, professing to believe in God and to acknowledge Christ, and a subject race, brought from their distant homes and placed under its charge for culture, for elevation, and for salvation, and while so placed contributing by its labor to the welfare and comfort of the world. What a trust from God! What reliance has he placed upon our faithfulness and our integrity! What a sure confidence does it give us in his protection and favor! His divine arrangements are placed in our keeping. Will he not preserve them? His divine purposes seem to be intermingled with our success. Will he not be careful to give us that success, and just in the way that he shall see to be best for us? His purposes are yea and amen in Christ Jesus and cannot be overturned by man. It places our warfare above any estimate which unspiritual minds can make of it. While many other motives are urging us to the battle field, and we rush forward to defend our liberties, our homes, our altars, God is super-adding this other motive—the secret of His own will—is making it to produce within us, unconsciously perhaps to ourselves, a power which is irresistible. Our conscience in this war is thus made right towards God and towards man; our heart is filled with His fear and His love; our arm is nerved with almost super-human strength, and we have reason to thank him, not only for what he has done for us, but for what he has restrained us from doing for ourselves and others from doing for us. This noble cause has made him our guide and our overruling governor, and we are moving forward, as I firmly believe, as truly under his direction, as did the people of Israel when he led them with a pillar of cloud by day and of fire by night.

Next to the cause in which we are engaged, we have to thank God for the spirit of our people and of our armies. Such a contest as this which we are waging could never have been carried on successfully without such an entire devotion as pervades the States of this Confederacy. Although shut in from the rest of the world, and deprived of all our accustomed luxuries, and many, even, of our comforts; although cut off from intercourse with those we love in foreign lands, many of whom are near and dear to us; although forbidden even to know what is going on in science, or literature, or art; although stripped of all legitimate commerce and trade; although, in some of the professions, debarred from all business and all means of profit: although left with the ruling product of the country incapable of sale, save when a speculative demand within our own borders may arise for it, there is yet heard no murmuring, no complaint, no disaffection, but all are willing to bear and to suffer for the cause's sake. God has given us a willing mind, and we cheer each other on in faith and trustfulness. And not only to the sterner sex has God given this enduring temper, but the attitude of woman is sublime. Bearing all the sacrifices of which I have just spoken, she is moreover called upon to suffer in her affections, to be wounded and smitten where she feels deepest and most enduringly. Man goes to the battle field, but woman sends him there, even though her heart strings tremble while she gives the farewell kiss and the farewell blessing. Man is supported by the necessity of movement, by the excitement of action, by the hope of honor, by the glory of conquest. Woman remains at home to suffer, to bear the cruel torture of suspense, to tremble when the battle has been fought and the news of the slaughter is flashing over the electric wire, to know that defeat will cover her with dishonor and her little ones with ruin, to learn that the husband she doted upon, the son whom she cherished in her bosom and upon whom she never let the wind blow too rudely, the brother with whom she sported through all her happy days of childhood, the lover to whom her early vows were plighted, has died upon some distant battle field and lies there a mangled corpse, unknown and uncared for, never to be seen again even in death Oh! those fearful lists of the wounded and the dead! How careless we pass them over, unless our own loved ones happened to be linked with them in military association, and yet each name in that roll of slaughter carries a fatal pang to some

> WE HAVE BEEN GATHERED TOGETHER TO-DAY BY A PROCLAMATION OF OUR PRESIDENT, TO RETURN THANKS TO ALMIGHTY GOD FOR A SERIES OF BRILLIANT VICTORIES WON BY OUR GALLANT SOLDIERS OVER THE INVADERS OF OUR SOIL. MOST FERVENTLY DO WE THANK HIM FOR HIS PRESENCE WITH US UPON THOSE FIELDS OF TERRIBLE CONFLICT.

woman's heart—some noble, devoted woman's heart. But she bears it all and bows submissive to the stroke. "He died for the cause. He perished for his country. I would not have it otherwise, but I should like to have given the dying boy my blessing, the expiring husband my last kiss of affection, the bleeding lover the comfort of knowing that I kneeled beside him." This is the daily language of woman throughout the Confederacy, and whence could such a spirit come but from God, and what is worthy to produce it but some cause which lies beyond any mere human estimate. And when we turn to our armies, truly these victories are the victories of the privates. God forbid that I should take one atom of honor or of praise from those who led our hosts upon those days of glory—from the accomplished and skilful [Robert E.] Lee—the admirable Crichton of our armies—from the God-fearing and indomitable [Thomas "Stonewall"] Jackson, upon whose prayer-bedewed banner victory seems to wait—from the intrepid [Jeb] Stuart, whose cavalry charges imitate those of Murat, from that great host of generals who swarm around our country's flag as Napoleon's Marshals did around the Imperial Eagle, but nevertheless our victories are the victories of the privates. It is the enthusiastic dash of their onsets, the fearless bravery with which they rush even to the cannon's mouth, the utter recklessness of life, if so be that its sacrifice may only lead to victory, the heartfelt impression that the cause is the cause of every man, and that success is a necessity. What intense honor do I feel for the private soldier! The officers may have motives other than the cause, the private soldier can have none. He knows that his valor must pass unnoticed, save in the narrow circle of his company; that his sacrifice can bring no honor to his name, no reputation to his family: that if he survives he lives only to enter upon new dangers with the same hopelessness of distinction; that if he dies, he will receive nothing but an unmarked grave, and yet is he proud to do his duty and to maintain his part in the destructive conflict. His comrades fall around him thick and fast, but with a sigh and tear he closes his ranks and presses on to a like destiny. Truly the first monument which our Confederacy rears, when our independence shall have been won, should be a lofty shaft, pure and spotless, bearing this inscription: "TO THE UNKNOWN AND UNRECORDED DEAD."

Thanksgiving for Victory.

O Almighty God, the Sovereign Commander of all the world, in whose hand is power and might, which none is able to withstand; we bless and magnify Thy great and glorious name for these happy victories, the whole glory whereof we do ascribe to Thee, who art the only giver of victory. And we beseech Thee give us grace to improve these great mercies to Thy glory, the advancement of Thy Gospel, the honor of our country, and as much as in us lieth to the good of all mankind. And we beseech Thee, give us such a sense of these great mercies as may engage us to a true thankfulness, such as may appear in our lives by an humble, holy and obedient walking before Thee all our days; through Jesus Christ our Lord; to whom with Thee and the Holy Spirit, as for all Thy mercies, so in particular for this victory and deliverance, be all glory and honor, world without end— Amen.

Thanksgiving for Peace and Deliverance from our Enemies.

O, Almighty God, who art a strong tower of defence unto Thy servants against the face of their enemies, we yield Thee praise and thanksgiving for our deliverance from those great apparent dangers wherewith we were compassed. We acknowledge it Thy goodness that we were not delivered over as a prey unto them; beseeching Thee still to continue such Thy mercies towards us, that all the world may know that Thou art our Saviour and mighty deliverer; through Jesus Christ our Lord—Amen.

Source: Elliott, Stephen. "Extract from a Sermon Preached by Bishop Elliott, on the 18th of September, Containing a Tribute to the Privates of the Confederate Army." Savannah: [s.n.], 1862. Available online at Documenting the South, University of North Carolina at Chapel Hill, http://docsouth.unc.edu/imls/elliotts1/elliott.html.

Sarah Josepha Hale Asks President Abraham Lincoln to Create a National Thanksgiving Holiday (1863)

As part of her 15-year campaign to make Thanksgiving a national holiday, magazine editor Sarah Josepha Hale promoted the cause in hundreds of letters to prominent people across the country—from politicians and religious leaders to writers and other opinion makers. In 1863, during the dark days of the Civil War, one letter finally succeeded in convincing President Abraham Lincoln to adopt her recommendation. Less than a week after he received the following letter from Hale, Lincoln declared that the last Thursday of November should be set aside each year as a national day of Thanksgiving. (See also Hale's editorial.)

From Sarah J. Hale to Abraham Lincoln, September 28, 1863

Private
Philadelphia, Sept. 28th 1863.

Sir.—

Permit me, as Editress of the "Lady's Book," to request a few minutes of your precious time, while laying before you a subject of deep interest to myself and—as I trust—even to the President of our Republic, of some importance. This subject is to have the <u>day of our annual Thanksgiving made a National and fixed Union Festival.</u>

You may have observed that, for some years past, there has been an increasing interest felt in our land to have the Thanksgiving held on the same day, in all the States; it now needs National recognition and authoritive <u>fixation</u>, only, to become permanently, an American custom and institution.

Enclosed are three papers (being printed these are easily read) which will make the idea and its progress clear and show also the popularity of the plan.

For the last fifteen years I have set forth this idea in the "Lady's Book," and placed the papers before the Governors of all the States and Territories—also I have sent these to our Ministers abroad, and our Missionaries to the heathen—and commanders in the Navy. From the recipients I have received, uniformly the most kind approval. Two of these letters, one from Governor (now General) [Nathaniel P.] Banks and one from Governor [Edwin D.] Morgan are enclosed; both gentlemen as you will see, have nobly aided to bring about the desired Thanksgiving Union.

But I find there are obstacles not possible to be overcome without legislative aid—that each State should, by statute, make it obligatory on the Governor to appoint the last Thursday of November, annually, as Thanksgiving Day;—or, as this way would require years to be realized, it has occurred to me that a proclamation from the President of the United States would be the best, surest and most fitting method of National appointment.

I have written to my friend, Hon. Wm. H. Seward, and requested him to confer with President Lincoln on this subject. As the President of the United States has the power of appointments for the District of Columbia and the Territories; also for the Army and Navy and all American citizens abroad who claim protection from the U. S. Flag—could he not, with right as well as duty, issue his proclamation for a Day of National Thanksgiving for all the above classes of persons? And would it not be fitting and patriotic for him to appeal to the Governors of all the States, inviting and commending these to unite in issuing proclamations for the last Thursday in November as the Day of Thanksgiving for the people of each State? Thus the great Union Festival of America would be established.

Now the purpose of this letter is to entreat President Lincoln to put forth his Proclamation, appointing the last Thursday in November (which falls this year on the 26th) as the National Thanksgiving for all those classes of people who are under the National Government particularly, and commending this Union Thanksgiving to each State Executive: thus, by the noble example and action of the President of the United States, the permanency and unity of our Great American Festival of Thanksgiving would be forever secured.

An immediate proclamation would be necessary, so as to reach all the States in season for State appointments, also to anticipate the early appointments by Governors.

Excuse the liberty I have taken

With profound respect
Yrs truly
Sarah Josepha Hale,
Editress of the "Lady's Book"

Source: Hale, Sarah Josepha. "Letter to Abraham Lincoln," September 28, 1863. Transcribed and annotated by the Lincoln Studies Center, Knox College, Galesburg, Illinois. From the Abraham Lincoln Papers at the Library of Congress, 1863. Available online at http://memory.loc.gov/ammem/alhtml/malhome.html.

Abraham Lincoln Proclaims a
National Thanksgiving Holiday (1863)

On October 3, 1863, following the Union victory in the Battle of Gettysburg, President Abraham Lincoln declared that the last Thursday of November should be set aside each year as a national day of Thanksgiving. Lincoln's proclamation, which is reproduced below, emphasizes the president's wish that the holiday be celebrated by all Americans, whether they lived in the North or the South, in gratitude for the country's many blessings. Since every U.S. president from 1863 onward has followed Lincoln's precedent, this document is generally considered to have created the American Thanksgiving holiday.

BY THE PRESIDENT OF THE UNITED STATES OF AMERICA:
A PROCLAMATION

The year that is drawing toward its close has been filled with the blessings of fruitful fields and healthful skies. To these bounties, which are so constantly enjoyed that we are prone to forget the source from which they come, others have been added, which are of so extraordinary a nature that they cannot fail to penetrate and soften the heart which is habitually insensible to the ever-watchful providence of Almighty God.

In the midst of a civil war of unequalled magnitude and severity, which has sometimes seemed to foreign states to invite and provoke their aggressions, peace has been preserved with all nations, order has been maintained, the laws have been respected and obeyed, and harmony has prevailed everywhere, except in the theatre of military conflict; while that theatre has been greatly contracted by the advancing armies and navies of the Union.

Needful diversions of wealth and of strength from the fields of peaceful industry to the national defence have not arrested the plough, the shuttle, or the ship; the axe has enlarged the borders of our settlements, and the mines, as well of iron and coal as of the precious metals, have yielded even more abundantly than heretofore. Population has steadily increased, notwithstanding the waste that has been made in the camp, the siege, and the battle-field, and the country, rejoicing in the consciousness of augmented strength and vigor, is permitted to expect continuance of years with large increase of freedom.

No human counsel hath devised, nor hath any mortal hand worked out these great things. They are the gracious gifts of the Most High God, who, while dealing with us in anger for our sins, hath nevertheless remembered mercy.

It has seemed to me fit and proper that they should be solemnly, reverently, and gratefully acknowledged as with one heart and one voice by the whole American people. I do, therefore, invite my fellow-citizens in every part of the United States, and also those who are at sea and those who are sojourning in foreign lands, to set apart and observe the last Thursday of November next as a Day of Thanksgiving and Praise to our beneficent Father who dwelleth in the heavens. And I recommend to them that, while offering up the ascriptions justly due to Him for such singular deliverances and blessings, they do also, with humble penitence for our national perverseness and disobedience, commend to His tender care all those who have become widows, orphans, mourners, or sufferers, in the lamentable civil strife in which we are unavoidably engaged, and fervently implore the interposition of the Almighty hand to heal the wounds of the nation, and to restore it, as soon as may be consistent with the Divine purposes, to the full enjoyment of peace, harmony, tranquillity, and union.

In testimony whereof, I have hereunto set my hand, and caused the seal of the United States to be affixed.

Done at the city of Washington, this third day of October, in the year of our Lord one thousand eight hundred and sixty-three, and of the Independence of the United States the eighty-eighth.

ABRAHAM LINCOLN.
By the President:

WILLIAM H. SEWARD, *Secretary of State.*

Source: Lincoln, Abraham. *Thanksgiving Proclamation*, October 3, 1863. Available online at the Library of Congress, American Memory Collection, http://memory.loc.gov/ammem/amlaw/lawhome.html

A Thanksgiving Hymn
Written for President Abraham Lincoln (1863)

In 1863, the same year that President Abraham Lincoln created the national Thanksgiving holiday, William Augustus Muhlenberg (lyrics) and Joseph W. Turner (music) composed this hymn in his honor. "The President's Hymn" encourages Americans to give thanks to God for the bounty of the harvest and the many blessings they enjoy. Since it was written during the Civil War, the hymn also asks Americans to pray for the restoration of the Union and for peace and freedom to prevail throughout the land.

The President's Hymn

Give thanks, all ye people, give thanks to the Lord,
Alleluias of freedom with joyful accord:
Let the East and the West, North and South roll along,
Sea, mountain and prairie, One thanksgiving song.

<u>Chorus:</u>
Give thanks, all ye people, give thanks to the Lord,
Alleluias of freedom, with joyful accord.

For the sunshine and rainfall, enriching again
Our acres in myriads, with treasures of grain;
For the earth still unloading her manifold wealth,
For the Skies beaming vigor, the Winds breathing health.

For the nation's wide table, o'erflowingly spread,
Where the many have feasted, and all have been fed,
With no bondage, their God-given rights to enthral,
But Liberty guarded by Justice for all.

In the realms of the Anvil, the Loom and the Plow,
Whose the mines and the fields to Him gratefully bow;
His the flocks and the herds; sing ye hillsides and vales;
On His Ocean domains chant His Name with the gales.

Of commerce and traffic, ye princes behold
Your riches from Him whose the silver and gold;
Happier children of labor, true lords of the soil,
Bless the great Master-Workman, who blesseth your toil.

Brave men of our forces, Lifeguard of our coasts,
To your Leader be loyal, Jehovah of Hosts:
Glow the Stripes and the Stars aye with victory bright,
Reflecting His glory; He crowneth the Right.

Nor shall ye through our borders, ye stricken of heart,
Only wailing your dead, in the joy have no part;
God's solace be yours, and for you there shall flow
All that honor and sympathy's gifts can bestow.

In the Domes of Messiah, ye worshipping throngs,
Solemn litanies mingle with jubilant songs;
The Ruler of Nations beseeching to spare,
And our Empire still keep the Elect of His care.

Our guilt and transgressions remember no more;
Peace, Lord! righteous Peace, of Thy gift we implore;
And the Banner of Union, restored by Thy hand,
Be the Banner of Freedom o'er All in the Land.

Source: Muhlenberg, William Augustus. "The President's Hymn." Music by Joseph W. Turner. Boston: Oliver Ditson & Co., 1863. Sheet Music from the Alfred Whital Stern Collection of Lincolniana. Held in the Rare Book and Special Collections Division, Library of Congress. Available online at http://memory.loc.gov/ammem/scsmhtml/scsmhome.html.

Thanksgiving in the Early 20th Century

This photo shows the townspeople of Peterborough, New Hampshire, performing a Thanksgiving pageant in 1910.

Origins of the Macy's Thanksgiving Day Parade (1920s)

In their 2004 book Macy's Thanksgiving Day Parade, *Robert M. Grippo and Christopher Hoskins chronicle the origins and development of the beloved holiday tradition in words and historic photographs. The excerpt below, taken from Chapter 1, describes innovations and highlights of the parades that took place in the 1920s. Grippo and Hoskins recall how "Macy's brought fantasy to life" by introducing giant character balloons and Santa's sleigh to the streets of New York City.*

In 1924, R. H. Macy and Company, already part of the fabric of New York City, introduced two institutions: the first Seventh Avenue addition to the existing Broadway store in Herald Square (creating what became known as "the World's Largest Department Store") and the Macy's Christmas Parade. Yes, what we know now as Macy's Thanksgiving Day Parade started out as a Christmas pageant. R. H. Macy and Company was a company of immigrants, who were thankful for the opportunities that America and New York City gave them. They decided to give thanks and celebrate their good fortune with a tradition rooted in the festivals of their homelands: parades. Macy's employees incorporated their own traditions with what newspapers called an "Americanized modern slant." The press billed the event as "a surprise New York will never forget."

Preceding the 1925 parade, Macy's sponsored an amateur photograph contest with $500 in prizes to be awarded. Judges included staff from major New York newspapers—some of which are now just a memory, including the *New York Herald Tribune.* One judge, noted puppeteer and theatrical designer Tony Sarg, was also responsible for Macy's holiday windows and for staging the parade.

By 1926, some 300 Macy's employees were involved in staging the event, which was scheduled between 1:00 p.m. and 4:00 p.m. so that spectators could go to their houses of worship as decreed by Pres. Calvin Coolidge.

With the fourth annual Macy's Christmas Parade ready for its march, Macy's president, Jesse L. Strauss, announced at a luncheon on Tuesday, November

Reprinted with permission from *Macy's Thanksgiving Day Parade* by Robert M. Grippo and Christopher Hoskins. Available from Arcadia Publishing, www.arcadiapublishing.com.

22, 1927, that the event would be "bigger and better than ever." His statement could not have been more prophetic, for that year marked the first appearance of what would become the parade's superstars and goodwill ambassadors: the giant character balloons.

Again, Tony Sarg had designed the parade and Christmas windows. According to press coverage, Sarg "spoke wistfully, of sixty-foot dinosaurs and twenty-five foot dachshunds which will be in the line of march." The parade was to start "after a fence has been torn down to permit its egress from a vacant lot where it is to form at 110th St." Starting time was set at 1:00 p.m. The lion's share of the press coverage was devoted to the premiere of the giant balloons. The press noted, "Following the police vanguard of the pageant was a human behemoth," a balloon 21 feet tall. Much was made of the fact that this human greeted spectators at second-story windows along the route. Because of its height, the balloon had to be lowered so it could "crawl" under the elevated train line at 66th Street and Broadway.

[THE MACY'S] PARADE BECAME A CHERISHED EVENT UNIQUE TO NEW YORK CITY. NEW YORKERS TOOK THE EVENT TO HEART, AND FOR A COUPLE OF HOURS ON THANKSGIVING DAY, EVEN THE MOST CYNICAL BECAME BELIEVERS IN FANTASY.

The show-stopping figure of the parade was the 60-foot dinosaur, which was escorted by a tribe of cavemen. The 25-foot dachshund (not a balloon, but a papier mache costume needing two people to bring it to life) was accompanied by turkeys, chickens, and ducks of heroic size. Although the balloons were the main attraction, the crowd also enjoyed nine floats, featuring, among others, Robinson Crusoe, Little Red Riding Hood and the Wolf, a yule log drawn by woodsmen, and a puppet show animated by "twelve of the prettiest girls employed at Macy's," according to the press. Providing music were bands of the 71st Regiment, the 103rd Infantry, and the 22nd Engineers.

The 1928 parade commenced at 2:30 p.m. Led by the 71st Regiment band, clowns, doing what came naturally, clowned around balloons in the shape of a 40-foot-long blue elephant, a 60-foot-long tiger, and a 50-foot hummingbird. Macy's brought fantasy to life. At the end of the parade, Tony Sarg directed the release of five inflatables that were timed with slow leaks to stay aloft for approximately a week. Macy's issued a reward of $100 each for their return. Escorted by snowmen, Santa Claus rode into Herald Square on a housetop float, its chimney loaded with toys. As an estimated 100,000 children watched, enraptured, jolly St. Nick climbed the Macy's marquee to direct the unveiling of the Christmas windows, which were entitled "The Exploits of Columbus" and featured animated marionettes.

All was in readiness for the parade to get under way at 1:00 p.m. on Thursday, November 28, 1929. By that time, Macy's was choosing famous cartoon characters to become giant balloons. The main attractions were larger-than-life inflatables of the Katzenjammer family, characters from a famous comic strip of that era that featured the mischievous shenanigans of the Katzenjammer kids, Hans and Fritz, and the captain, who tried in vain to bring order to the household.

With 10 balloons being released, an increase from the five released the previous year, Macy's kept the total reward amount at $500 by offering $50 each for the balloons' return. Suburbanites located in the vicinity of Roosevelt Field on Long Island were given the heads-up, as newspapers noted that prevailing winds had sent the balloons in their direction.

On Wednesday, November 26, 1930, colorful blurbs appeared in newspapers previewing the next day's events. November 27, 1930, was a brisk day, and snow flurries were in the air (the first time snow fell on the event, but not the last), which gave the spectators a Currier and Ives helping of holiday cheer. The event was scheduled to begin at 110th Street and Amsterdam Avenue. That year, 15 comic character balloons were released in front of Macy's. As each balloon was released, shouts from the crowds were heard blocks away. The balloons danced and swayed in the breeze, taking on a life of their own. The concrete buildings of the city were hidden behind a rush of smaller colorful balloons, adding to the merriment. Music for the event was supplied by the bands of the 71st Regiment, the 9th Coast Artillery, and the 102nd Engineers. Wrapping up the event, Tony Sarg broadcast a message over the radio advising residents of the Eastern seaboard to watch the skies, as the balloons might be heading their way.

As the 1920s came to a close, it was clear the parade had been a major success. Originally envisioned as a thank-you from a group of Macy's employees and proudly sponsored by the biggest department store in the world, the parade became a cherished event unique to New York City. New Yorkers took the event to heart, and for a couple of hours on Thanksgiving Day, even the most cynical became believers in fantasy. After beginning as a kind of circus parade chock-full of ragamuffins (a term used to describe the clowns and various other merrymakers), it began to take shape as a truly wondrous and magical Macy's miracle.

Source: Grippo, Robert M., and Christopher Hoskins. "The 1920s: Bands, Clowns, and Merrymakers." *Macy's Thanksgiving Day Parade*. Charleston, SC: Arcadia Publishing, 2004.

President Herbert Hoover Proclaims Thanksgiving during the Great Depression (1930)

The Thanksgiving proclamation below, by President Herbert Hoover, was the first one to be made during the Great Depression. Hoover reminds the American people that they have much to be thankful for, despite the difficult economic times, and asks them to be particularly mindful of those "in need and suffering from forces beyond their control."

BY THE PRESIDENT OF THE UNITED STATES OF AMERICA

Notwithstanding that our forefathers endured the hardships and privations of a primitive life, surrounded by dangers and solaced only with meager comforts, they nevertheless bequeathed to us a custom of devoting one day of every year to universal thanksgiving to Almighty God, for the blessing of life itself and the means to sustain it, for the sanctuary of home and the joys that pervade it, and for the mercies of His protection from accident, sickness, or death.

Our country has many causes for thanksgiving. We have been blest with distinctive evidence of divine favor. As a nation we have suffered far less than other peoples from the present world difficulties. We have been free from civil and industrial discord. The outlook for peace between nations has been strengthened. In a large view we have made progress upon the enduring structure of our institutions. The arts and sciences that enrich our lives and enlarge our control of nature have made notable advances. Education has been further extended. We have made gains in the prevention of disease and in the protection of childhood.

Now, therefore, I, Herbert Hoover, President of the United States of America, do hereby designate Thursday, November 27, 1930, as a National Day of Thanksgiving, and do enjoin the people of the United States so to observe it, calling upon them to remember that many of our people are in need and suffering from causes beyond their control, and suggesting that a proper celebration of the day should include that we make sure that every person in the community, young and old, shall have cause to give thanks for our institutions and for the neighborly sentiment of our people.

In witness whereof, I have hereunto set my hand and caused the seal of the United States to be affixed.

Done at the City of Washington this 6th day of November, in the year of our Lord nineteen hundred and thirty, and of the Independence of the United States of America the one hundred and fifty-fifth.

HERBERT HOOVER

Source: Hoover, Herbert. *Thanksgiving Proclamation*, November 6, 1930. Available online at the Pilgrim Hall Museum, http://www.pilgrimhall.org/ThanxProc1930.htm.

Marble Workers Protest on Thanksgiving (1930s)

The following excerpt is taken from "Interview No. 7," which was conducted during the late 1930s as part of the Federal Writers' Project. The subject of the interview is a Norwegian immigrant in his mid-thirties, identified only as Mr. M, who lives in the marble quarry town of West Rutland, Vermont, in housing leased from his employer. A strong believer in workers' rights, Mr. M participated in a labor strike in 1936. The resolution of this labor dispute brought slight improvements in working conditions at the quarry and an increase in the pay of common laborers from 37.5 to 44 cents per hour. Mr. M recalls an incident that took place during the strike, when a group of workers took over the company town of Proctor and marched in protest outside of the marble company owner's house on Thanksgiving Day.

Q. Do you remember any mass movement of the workers in this town during the strike that could be called dangerous to life or property?

A. No. The time we took over Proctor we showed them our strength, though. It was Thanksgiving, and mighty little Thanksgiving for some of us. Some of the men and women wanted to go out to Proctor while the Proctors were enjoying their big dinner, and show them how little their workers had to be thankful for. I tried to discourage them, but when I found they were determined to go, I went along, with a lot of my friends, to keep them from getting tough. So hundreds of us landed into Proctor. The sheriffs and deputies tried to stop us, and we got the bunch of them and locked them up and took the town over. Then we paraded all afternoon through the streets. The next day the company unloaded a gang of deputies into Proctor and from then on nobody could stand on the corner, or collect in even twos or threes, without being busted up.

Source: "Interview No. 7." In Library of Congress Collection, *American Life Histories: Manuscripts from the Federal Writers' Project, 1936-1940.* Available online at http://memory. loc.gov/ammem/wpaintro/wpahome.html.

President Franklin D. Roosevelt
Changes the Date of Thanksgiving (1939)

For the first six years of his presidency, Franklin D. Roosevelt followed long-established tradition and proclaimed the last Thursday in November as the nation's Thanksgiving holiday. In 1939, however, Roosevelt instead followed the suggestion of a major industry group, the Retail Dry Goods Association, and moved the date of Thanksgiving forward one week, from November 30 to November 23. The President and the retailers hoped that extending the Christmas shopping season by a week would help stimulate the U.S. economy during the Great Depression. Instead, the President's decision caused confusion across the United States, and the holiday he created became known derisively as "Franksgiving." Roosevelt's controversial proclamation, which ironically makes several references to the historical traditions behind Thanksgiving, appears below.

BY THE PRESIDENT OF THE UNITED STATES OF AMERICA—
A PROCLAMATION

I, Franklin D. Roosevelt, President of the United States of America, do hereby designate Thursday, the twenty-third of November 1939, as a day of general thanksgiving.

More than three centuries ago, at the season of the gathering in of the harvest, the Pilgrims humbly paused in their work and gave thanks to God for the preservation of their community and for the abundant yield of the soil. A century and a half later, after the new Nation had been formed, and the charter of government, the Constitution of the Republic, had received the assent of the States, President Washington and his successors invited the people of the Nation to lay down their tasks one day in the year and give thanks for the blessings that had been granted them by Divine Providence. It is fitting that we should continue this hallowed custom and select a day in 1939 to be dedicated to reverent thoughts of thanksgiving.

Our Nation has gone steadily forward in the application of democratic processes to economic and social problems. We have faced the specters of business depression, of unemployment, and of widespread agricultural distress, and our positive efforts to alleviate these conditions have met with heartening results. We have also been permitted to see the fruition of measures which we have undertaken in the realms of health, social welfare, and the conservation of resources. As a Nation we are deeply grateful that in a world of turmoil we are at peace with all countries, and we especially rejoice in the strengthened bonds of our friendship with the other peoples of the Western Hemisphere.

Let us, on the day set aside for this purpose, give thanks to the Ruler of the Universe for the strength which He has vouchsafed us to carry on our daily labors and for the hope that lives within us of the coming of a day when peace and the productive activities of peace shall reign on every continent.

In witness whereof, I have hereunto set my hand and caused the seal of the United States of America to be affixed.

Done at the City of Washington this thirty-first day of October, in the year of our Lord nineteen hundred and thirty-nine, and of the Independence of the United States of America the one hundred and sixty-fourth.

FRANKLIN D. ROOSEVELT

Source: Roosevelt, Franklin D. *Thanksgiving Proclamation*, October 31, 1939. Available online at Pilgrim Hall Museum, http://www.pilgrimhall.org/ThanxProc1930.htm.

The U.S. Congress
Makes Thanksgiving a Legal Holiday (1941)

Despite the protests and confusion surrounding President Franklin Roosevelt's 1939 decision to move Thanksgiving forward by a week, he proclaimed the earlier date for the holiday again in 1940 and 1941. By this time, however, polls indicated that 62 percent of the American people disapproved of the change, and surveys showed no increase in retail sales that could be attributed to the earlier date of Thanksgiving. Confronted with this information, Roosevelt acknowledged that moving the holiday had been a mistake. On December 26, 1941, the U.S. Congress passed a joint resolution establishing Thanksgiving as a federal holiday to be held annually on the fourth Thursday in November, and Roosevelt signed it into law.

JOINT RESOLUTION

Making the fourth Thursday in November a legal holiday.

Resolved by the Senate and House of Representatives of the United States of America in Congress assembled, That the fourth Thursday of November in each year after the year 1941 be known as Thanksgiving Day, and is hereby made a legal public holiday to all intents and purposes and in the same manner as the 1st day of January, the 22nd day of February, the 30th day of May, the 4th day of July, the first Monday of September, the 11th day of November, and Christmas Day are now made by law public holidays.

APPROVED, December 26, 1941.

Source: U.S. Congress. *Joint Resolution Making the Fourth Thursday in November a Legal Holiday,* December 26, 1941. Available online at Center for Legislative Archives, U.S. National Archives and Records Administration, http://www.archives.gov/legislative/features/thanksgiving.

Thanksgiving in Wartime

U.S. troops during Thanksgiving dinner at the Forward Operating Base Marez
in Mosul, Iraq, November 25, 2004.

President Woodrow Wilson Gives Thanks
for the End of World War I (1918)

The armistice ending World War I took effect on November 11, 1918. Six days later, President Woodrow Wilson expressed his gratitude for the successful conclusion of the conflict in a Thanksgiving Proclamation, which is excerpted below. Wilson shares his hope that the end of war will result in a "new structure of peace and good will among the nations." Unfortunately, the peace only lasted for two decades before tensions left over from the armistice erupted into World War II.

A Proclamation of Thanksgiving for Victory

(November 17, 1918)

It has long been our custom to turn in the autumn of the year in praise and thanksgiving to Almighty God for His many blessings and mercies to us as a nation. This year we have special and moving cause to be grateful and to rejoice.

God has in His good pleasure given us peace. It has not come as a mere cessation of arms, a relief from the strain and tragedy of war. It has come as a great triumph of right. Complete victory has brought us, not peace alone, but the confident promise of a new day as well, in which justice shall replace force and jealous intrigue among the nations.

Our gallant armies have participated in a triumph which is not marred or stained by any purpose of selfish aggression. In a righteous cause they have won immortal glory and have nobly served their nation in serving mankind.

God has indeed been gracious. We have cause for such rejoicing as revives and strengthens in us all the best traditions of national history. A new day shines about us in which our hearts take new courage and look forward with open hope to new and greater duties.

While we render thanks for these things, let us not forget to seek the divine guidance in the performance of these duties, and divine mercy and forgiveness for all errors of act or purpose, and pray in all that we do we shall strengthen the ties of friendship and mutual respect upon which we must assist to build the new structure of peace and good will among the nations.

Wherefore, I, Woodrow Wilson, President of the United States of America, do hereby designate Thursday, the twenty-eighth day of November next, as a day of thanksgiving and prayer and invite the people throughout the land to cease upon that day from their ordinary occupations, and in their several homes and places of worship to render thanks to God, the Ruler of Nations.

Source: Wilson, Woodrow. "A Proclamation of Thanksgiving for Victory (November 17, 1918)." *Guarantees of Peace: Messages and Addresses to the Congress and the People, Jan. 31, 1918, to Dec. 2, 1918, Together with the Peace Notes to Germany and Austria.* New York: Harper & Brothers Publishers, 1919.

Alex Haley Discovers the Power of Gratitude (1943)

Long before he won a Pulitzer Prize for his 1976 historical novel Roots, *African-American author Alex Haley spent 20 years in the U.S. Coast Guard. He enlisted in 1939, at the beginning of World War II, and served as a cook onboard a transport ship that operated in the Pacific for the duration of that conflict. Haley looks back upon his wartime service in a 1982 article for* Parade *magazine entitled "Thank You: What's Most Important Is Often Too Easily Forgotten." He shares the valuable insights he gained on Thanksgiving Day 1943, by writing letters of gratitude to people back home who had influenced his life.*

It was 1943, during World War II, and I was a young U.S. coastguardsman, serial number 212-548, a number we never seem to forget. My ship, the USS *Murzim,* had been under way for several days. Most of her holds contained thousands of cartons of canned or dried foods. The other holds were loaded with 500-pound bombs packed delicately in padded racks. Our destination was a big base on the Island of Tulagi in the South Pacific.

I was one of the *Murzim's* several cooks and, quite the same as for folks ashore, this Thanksgiving morning had seen us busily preparing a traditional dinner featuring roast turkey.

Well, as any cook knows, it's a lot of hard work to cook and serve a big meal, and clean up and put everything away. But finally, around sundown, with our whole galley crew just bushed, we finished at last and were free to go flop into our bunks in the fo'c'sle [forecastle].

But I decided first to go out on the *Murzim's* afterdeck for a breath of open air. I made my way out there, breathing in great, deep draughts while walking slowly about, still wearing my white cook's hat and the long apron, my feet sensing the big ship's vibrations from the deep-set, turbine diesel and my ears hearing the slightly hissing sound the sea makes in resisting the skin of the ship.

I got to thinking about Thanksgiving. In reflex, my thoughts registered the historic imagery of the Pilgrims, Indians, wild turkeys, pumpkins, corn on the cob and the rest.

© 1982 Alex Haley. All rights reserved. Originally published in *Parade Magazine*. Reprinted by permission of the Estate of Alex Haley and Parade Publications.

Yet my mind seemed to be questing for something else—some way that I could personally apply to the waning Thanksgiving. It must have taken me a half-hour to sense that maybe some key to an answer could result from reversing the word "Thanksgiving"—at least that suggested a verbal direction, "Giving Thanks."

Giving thanks—as in praying, thanking God, I thought. Yes, of course. Certainly.

Yet my mind continued nagging me. Fine. But something else.

After a while, like a dawn's brightening, a further answer did come—that there were *people* to thank, people who had done so much for me that I could never possibly repay them. The embarrassing truth was that I'd always just accepted what they'd done, taken all of it for granted. Not one time had I ever bothered to express to any of them so much as a simple, sincere "Thank you."

At least seven people had been particularly and indelibly helpful to me. I realized, with a gulp, that about half of them had since died—so they were forever beyond any possible expression of gratitude from me. The more I thought about it, the more ashamed I became. Then I pictured the three who were still alive and, within minutes, I was down in the fo'c'sle.

Sitting at a mess table with writing paper and memories of things each had done, I tried composing genuine statements of heartfelt appreciation and gratitude to my dad, Simon A. Haley, a professor at the old AMNC (Agricultural Mechanical Normal College) in Pine Bluff, Ark., now a branch of the University of Arkansas; to my grandma, Cynthia Palmer, back in our little hometown of Henning, Tenn.; and to the Rev. Lonual Nelson, my grammar school principal, retired and living in Ripley, six miles north of Henning.

I couldn't even be certain if they would recall some of their acts of years past, acts that I vividly remembered and saw now as having given me vital training, or inspiration, or directions, if not all of these desirables rolled into one.

The texts of my letters began something like, "Here, this Thanksgiving at sea, I find my thoughts upon how much you have done for me, but I have never stopped and said to you how much I feel the need to thank you—" And briefly I recalled for each of them specific acts performed on my behalf.

For instance, something uppermost about my father was how he had impressed upon me from boyhood to love books and reading. In fact, this graduated into a family habit of after-dinner quizzes at the table about books read most recently and new words learned. My love of books never diminished and later led me toward writing books myself. So many times I have felt a sadness when exposed to modern children so immersed in the electronic media that they have little to no awareness of the wondrous world to be discovered in books.

I reminded the Reverend Nelson how each morning he would open our little country town's grammar school with a prayer over his assembled students. I told him that whatever positive things I had done since had been influenced at least in part by his morning school prayers.

In the letter to my grandmother, I reminded her of a dozen ways she used to teach me how to tell the truth, to be thrifty, to share, and to be forgiving and considerate of others. (My reminders included how she'd make me pull switches from a peach tree for my needed lesson.) I thanked her for the years of eating her good cooking, the equal of which I had not found since. (By now, though, I've reflected that those peerless dishes are most gloriously flavored with a pinch of nostalgia.) Finally, I thanked her simply for having sprinkled my life with stardust.

THE TEXTS OF MY LETTERS BEGAN SOMETHING LIKE, "HERE, THIS THANKSGIVING AT SEA, I FIND MY THOUGHTS UPON HOW MUCH YOU HAVE DONE FOR ME, BUT I HAVE NEVER STOPPED AND SAID TO YOU HOW MUCH I FEEL THE NEED TO THANK YOU."

Before I slept, my three letters went into our ship's office mail sack. They got mailed when we reached Tulagi Island.

We unloaded cargo, reloaded with something else, then again we put to sea in the routine familiar to us, and as the days became weeks, my little personal experience receded. Sometimes, when we were at sea, a mail ship would rendezvous and bring us mail from home, which, of course, we accorded topmost priority.

Every time the ship's loudspeaker rasped, "Attention! Mail call!" 200-odd shipmates came pounding up on deck and clustered about the raised hatch atop which two yeomen, standing by those precious bulging gray sacks, were alternately pulling out fistfuls of letters and barking successive names of sailors who were, in turn, hollering "Here! Here!" amid the jostling.

One "Mail Call" brought me responses from Grandma, Dad and the Reverend Nelson—and my reading of their letters left me not only astounded, but more humbled than before.

Rather than saying they would forgive that I hadn't previously thanked them, instead, for Pete's sake, they were thanking *me*—for having remembered, for having considered they had done anything so exceptional.

Always the college professor, my dad had carefully avoided anything he considered too sentimental, so I knew how moved he was to write me that, after having helped educate many young people, he now felt that his best results included his own son.

The Reverend Nelson wrote that his decades as a "simple, old-fashioned principal" had ended with grammar schools undergoing such swift changes that he had retired in self-doubt. "I heard more of what I had done wrong than what I did right," he said, adding that my letter had brought him welcome reassurance that his career had been appreciated.

A glance at Grandma's familiar handwriting brought back in a flash memories of standing alongside her white wicker rocking chair, watching her "settin' down" some letter to relatives. Frequently touching her pencil's tip to pursed lips, character by character, each between a short, soft grunt, Grandma would slowly accomplish one word, then the next, so that a finished single page would consume hours. I wept over the page representing my Grandma's recent hours invested in expressing her loving gratefulness to *me*—whom she used to diaper!

Much later, retired from the Coast Guard and trying to make a living as a writer, I never forgot how those three "thank you" letters gave me an insight into something nigh mystical in human beings, most of whom go about yearning in secret for more of their fellows to express appreciation for their efforts.

I discovered in time that, even in the business world, probably no two words are more valued than "thank you," especially among people at stores, airlines, utilities and others that directly serve the public.

Late one night, I was one of a half-dozen passengers who straggled weary and grumbling off a plane that had been forced to land at the huge Dallas/Fort Worth Airport. Suddenly, a buoyant, cheerful, red-jacketed airline man waved us away from the regular waiting room seats, saying, "You sure looked bushed. I know a big empty office where you can stretch out while you wait." And we surely did. When the weather improved enough for us to leave, "Gene Erickson" was in my notebook and, back home, I wrote the president of that airline describing his sensitivity and his courtesy. And I received a thank you!

I travel a good deal on lecture tours, and I urge students especially to tell their parents, grandparents, and other living elders simply "thank you" for all they have done to make possible the lives they now enjoy. Many students have told me they found themselves moved by the response. It is not really surprising, if one reflects how it must feel to be thanked after you have given for years.

Now, approaching Thanksgiving of 1982, I have asked myself what I will wish for all who are reading this, for our nation, indeed for our whole world— since, quoting a good and wise friend of mine, "In the end we are mightily and merely people, each with similar needs." First, I wish for us, of course, the simple common sense to achieve world peace, that being paramount for the very survival of our kind.

And there is something else I wish—so strongly that I have had this line printed across the bottom of all my stationery: *"Find the good—and praise it."*

Source: Haley, Alex. "Thank You." *Parade,* November 21, 1982

President Harry S. Truman Gives Thanks
for Peace at the End of World War II (1945)

World War II ended in victory for the United States and its allies in 1945, with the surrender of Germany in May and Japan in August. The conflict took the lives of over 400,000 American soldiers, however, and the nation also mourned the loss of its wartime commander-in-chief, President Franklin D. Roosevelt, to a brain hemorrhage in April 1945. His successor, President Harry S. Truman, makes reference to these events in his Thanksgiving proclamation. Truman credits national unity—as well as the American people's profound commitment to securing rights and freedoms for all mankind—for the successful war effort.

THANKSGIVING DAY, 1945

BY THE PRESIDENT OF THE UNITED STATES OF AMERICA—
A PROCLAMATION

In this year of our victory, absolute and final, over German fascism and Japanese militarism; in this time of peace so long awaited, which we are determined with all the United Nations to make permanent; on this day of our abundance, strength, and achievement; let us give thanks to Almighty Providence for these exceeding blessings. We have won them with the courage and the blood of our soldiers, sailors, and airmen. We have won them by the sweat and ingenuity of our workers, farmers, engineers, and industrialists. We have won them with the devotion of our women and children. We have bought them with the treasure of our rich land. But above all we have won them because we cherish freedom beyond riches and even more than life itself.

We give thanks with the humility of free men, each knowing it was the might of no one arm but of all together by which we were saved. Liberty knows no race, creed, or class in our country or in the world. In unity we found our first weapon, for without it, both here and abroad, we were doomed. None have known this better than our very gallant dead, none better than their comrade, Franklin Delano Roosevelt. Our thanksgiving has the humility of our deep mourning for them, our vast gratitude to them.

Triumph over the enemy has not dispelled every difficulty. Many vital and far-reaching decisions await us as we strive for a just and enduring peace. We will not fail if we preserve, in our own land and throughout the world, that same devotion to the essential freedoms and rights of mankind which sustained us throughout the war and brought us final victory.

NOW, THEREFORE, I, HARRY S. TRUMAN, President of the United States of America, in consonance with the joint resolution of Congress approved December 26, 1941, do hereby proclaim Thursday November 22, 1945, as a day of national thanksgiving. May we on that day, in our homes and in our places of worship, individually and as groups, express our humble thanks to Almighty God for the abundance of our blessings and may we on that occasion rededicate ourselves to those high principles of citizenship for which so many splendid Americans have recently given all.

IN WITNESS WHEREOF, I have hereunto set my hand and caused the seal of the United States of America to be affixed.

DONE at the City of Washington 12th day of November in the year of our Lord one thousand nine hundred forty-five and of the Independence of the United States of America the one hundred and seventieth.

HARRY S. TRUMAN

Source: Truman, Harry S. *Thanksgiving Proclamation*, November 12, 1945. Available online at Pilgrim Hall Museum, http://www.pilgrimhall.org/ThanxProc1940.htm.

The U.S. Navy Becomes Family
for a Sailor at Sea on Thanksgiving (2005)

*Sailor Hendrick Dickson recalls his first Thanksgiving at sea in this 2005
article for the U.S. Navy publication* All Hands. *He and his shipmates initially feel depressed about being away from their homes and families. But a
traditional turkey dinner, with all the trimmings, helps them pull together
and enjoy the holiday.*

When I was growing up, Thanksgiving was always my favorite holiday. It was
the one holiday that brought the family closer together. The rest of the year, up
to the fourth Thursday in November, was mediocre when it came to taking the
time out to appreciate family and being blessed for having them there for you.

In my family there is nothing hokey about Thanksgiving like some other holidays. No gimmicky gifts that overshadow the true meaning of the moment. And
no family cookouts that always seem to end with some kind of controversy.

On Thanksgiving we never just tolerated each other because it was a holiday
and it was the thing to do. The feeling of love was always genuine—we
always seemed really and truly "thankful" for each other.

But the first Thanksgiving I spent out at sea aboard USS *America* (CV 66),
"the Big Dawg," began as the most depressing "turkey day" ever. It was as
eerie as a climactic scene from an old Vincent Price horror flick. The way
everyone walked around in a daze, I swear, it was like watching zombies wander through a cemetery.

I missed home and my family, and my mom's turkey and dressing with the
cranberry sauce. And the pecan pies, and the potato salad, collard greens and
the cornbread. Everybody felt the same, you could see it in their eyes.

At the end of the watch, we dragged ourselves toward the mess decks. There
was supposed to be this big celebration to commemorate the day, but you
could read in everyone's face, "Yeah, right! I'm out to sea. What do I have to
be thankful for?"

When we got to the serving line, we couldn't help but notice the extra hands
working in the galley. The mess specialists were really turning to, but even

Reprinted by permission from *All Hands*.

more impressive was that familiar aroma of Thanksgiving classics—turkey and dressing, ham, roast beef, macaroni and cheese, cakes and pies. If you named it, they cooked it. Even shrimp cocktail. It was like a Thanksgiving buffet.

The mess decks were bustling like never before. Everyone joking and telling stories about home and holidays. I really couldn't put my finger on it, maybe it was the food and seeing how much the mess specialists had gone out of their way to make the day special for us. But it didn't take long to realize that even though we were not at home, we did have a lot to be thankful for.

Later that evening, we gathered on the hangar bay with the rest of our ship-mates and listened as the ship's choir belted out inspirational songs and the chaplain delivered a message of thanks before taps.

It wasn't the Thanksgiving I was used to at home, but it was truly special. I still missed my family, of course, but I realized I wasn't alone.

And that's just it—for those six months you are away from home, there is always someone there who is going through the same thing you are. No matter how tough things get out there, you always have each other to keep you going, cheer you up, look out for you or whatever. Somebody is always there to help you through the rough time. Kinda sounds like a family, huh?

Source: Dickson, Hendrick. "Underway Family." *All Hands* (U.S. Navy), November 2005.

Native American Perspectives on Thanksgiving

Wampanoag descendants attending the National Day of Mourning
observance in Plymouth, Massachusetts, on November 22, 2001.

A Native American Thanksgiving Address

Long before European colonists began arriving in America, indigenous peoples established their own thanksgiving and harvest festival traditions. Many Native American cultures made it a regular part of daily life to express gratitude for such necessities as food and shelter. The Thanksgiving address below, entitled "Greetings to the Natural World," originated among the Iroquois people. It offers thanks not only to the Creator, but also to the spirits of all the animals killed and plants harvested to provide food and clothing for their people.

The People

Today we have gathered and we see that the cycles of life continue. We have been given the duty to live in balance and harmony with each other and all living things. So now, we bring our minds together as one as we give greetings and thanks to each other as people.

Now our minds are one.

The Earth Mother

We are all thankful to our Mother, the Earth, for she gives us all that we need for life. She supports our feet as we walk about upon her. It gives us joy that she continues to care for us as she has from the beginning of time. To our mother, we send greetings and thanks.

Now our minds are one.

The Waters

We give thanks to all the waters of the world for quenching our thirst and providing us with strength. Water is life. We know its power in many forms—waterfalls and rain, mists and streams, rivers and oceans. With one mind, we send greetings and thanks to the spirit of Water.

Now our minds are one.

Reprinted with permission from the Mohawk Nation Council of Chiefs (MNCC), www.mohawk nation.org.

The Fish

We turn our minds to all the Fish life in the water. They were instructed to cleanse and purify the water. They also give themselves to us as food. We are grateful that we can still find pure water. So, we turn now to the Fish and send our greetings and thanks.

Now our minds are one.

The Plants

Now we turn toward the vast fields of Plant life. As far as the eye can see, the Plants grow, working many wonders. They sustain many life forms. With our minds gathered together, we give thanks and look forward to seeing Plant life for many generations to come.

Now our minds are one.

The Food Plants

With one mind, we turn to honor and thank all the Food Plants we harvest from the garden. Since the beginning of time, the grains, vegetables, beans and berries have helped the people survive. Many other living things draw strength from them too. We gather all the Plant Foods together as one and send them a greeting of thanks.

Now our minds are one.

The Medicine Herbs

Now we turn to all the Medicine herbs of the world. From the beginning they were instructed to take away sickness. They are always waiting and ready to heal us. We are happy there are still among us those special few who remember how to use these plants for healing. With one mind, we send greetings and thanks to the Medicines and to the keepers of the Medicines.

Now our minds are one.

The Animals

We gather our minds together to send greetings and thanks to all the Animal life in the world. They have many things to teach us as people. We are honored by them when they give up their lives so we may use their bodies as food for our people. We see them near our homes and in the deep forests. We are glad they are still here and we hope that it will always be so.

Now our minds are one.

The Trees

We now turn our thoughts to the Trees. The Earth has many families of Trees who have their own instructions and uses. Some provide us with shelter and shade, others with fruit, beauty and other useful things. Many people of the world use a Tree as a symbol of peace and strength. With one mind, we greet and thank the Tree life.

Now our minds are one.

The Birds

We put our minds together as one and thank all the Birds who move and fly about over our heads. The Creator gave them beautiful songs. Each day they remind us to enjoy and appreciate life. The Eagle was chosen to be their leader. To all the Birds—from the smallest to the largest—we send our joyful greetings and thanks.

Now our minds are one.

The Four Winds

We are all thankful to the powers we know as the Four Winds. We hear their voices in the moving air as they refresh us and purify the air we breathe. They help us to bring the change of seasons. From the four directions they come, bringing us messages and giving us strength. With one mind, we send our greetings and thanks to the Four Winds.

Now our minds are one.

The Thunderers

Now we turn to the west where our grandfathers, the Thunder Beings, live. With lightning and thundering voices, they bring with them the water that renews life. We are thankful that they keep those evil things made by Okwiseres underground. We bring our minds together as one to send greetings and thanks to our Grandfathers, the Thunderers.

Now our minds are one.

NOW WE TURN OUR THOUGHTS TO THE CREATOR, OR GREAT SPIRIT, AND SEND GREETINGS AND THANKS FOR ALL THE GIFTS OF CREATION. EVERYTHING WE NEED TO LIVE A GOOD LIFE IS HERE ON THIS MOTHER EARTH. FOR ALL THE LOVE THAT IS STILL AROUND US, WE GATHER OUR MINDS TOGETHER AS ONE AND SEND OUR CHOICEST WORDS OF GREETINGS AND THANKS TO THE CREATOR.

The Sun

We now send greetings and thanks to our eldest Brother, the Sun. Each day without fail he travels the sky from east to west, bringing the light of a new day. He is the source of all the fires of life. With one mind, we send greetings and thanks to our Brother, the Sun.

Now our minds are one.

Grandmother Moon

We put our minds together to give thanks to our oldest Grandmother, the Moon, who lights the night-time sky. She is the leader of woman all over the world, and she governs the movement of the ocean tides. By her changing face we measure time, and it is the Moon who watches over the arrival of children here on Earth. With one mind, we send greetings and thanks to our Grandmother, the Moon.

Now our minds are one.

The Stars

We give thanks to the Stars who are spread across the sky like jewelry. We see them in the night, helping the Moon to light the darkness and bringing dew to the gardens and growing things. When we travel at night, they guide us home. With our minds gathered together as one, we send greetings and thanks to the Stars.

Now our minds are one.

The Enlightened Teachers

We gather our minds to greet and thank the enlightened Teachers who have come to help throughout the ages. When we forget how to live in harmony, they remind us of the way we were instructed to live as people. With one mind, we send greetings and thanks to these caring teachers.

Now our minds are one.

The Creator

Now we turn our thoughts to the creator, or Great Spirit, and send greetings and thanks for all the gifts of Creation. Everything we need to live a good life is here on this Mother Earth. For all the love that is still around us, we gather our minds together as one and send our choicest words of greetings and thanks to the Creator.

Now our minds are one.

Closing Words

We have now arrived at the place where we end our words. Of all the things we have named, it was not our intention to leave anything out. If something was forgotten, we leave it to each individual to send such greetings and thanks in their own way.

Now our minds are one.

Source: "Iroquois Thanksgiving Address: Greetings to the Natural World." Mohawk Nation Council of Chiefs. Available online at http://www.mohawknation.org.

Wampanoag Perspectives on the Original Immigrants (1989)

The Wampanoag Indians suffered greatly as a result of the arrival of the Pilgrims in 1620. Through interviews with their descendants, including a historian at Plimoth Plantation, Washington Post *writer John S. Lang details the short- and long-term consequences.*

Thanksgiving just hasn't been the same in these parts since the Boat People came.

They washed ashore a ways up the beach, chilled and hungry, disease-ridden, dirty and stinking, not having bathed in six weeks. They couldn't speak the language and wouldn't learn it, belonged to an odd religious cult, had no respect for property rights and no job skills in the local economy. They survived the first year—by robbing graves and taking charity.

Some of the old families of Cape Cod took food baskets to the newcomers' first Thanksgiving—and never even got invited back. Now Amelia Bingham is so upset she won't celebrate the holiday. "I think maybe I'll just have a fish."

The old neighborhood's been going down ever since the illegal aliens arrived. That was 134,318 days ago, and Mrs. Bingham is still disgusted. On Thursday night, however, her table will have a distinction vital to early Thanksgiving feasts. The guests will be Indians, her family.

Despite her blue-nose Yankee name, Mrs. Bingham is clan mother ("the old lady of the tribe") of the Mashpee Wampanoags. Remember the Wampanoags? As the old grammar school texts have it, they were the guests, the happy natives, at the very first Thanksgiving dinner of those kindly Christians in white collars, the Pilgrims.

But not really. It was Indian largess that made the day. What happened is that a certain Wampanoag, name of Tisquantum, had been helping the Pilgrims get through their awful first year. He taught them how to hunt animals they'd never seen; he showed them which plants were edible, what the growing seasons were—"to plant the corn seeds when the oak leaves in spring were the size of squirrel ears"—and when to harvest.

© 1989 The Washington Post. Reprinted with permission.

Wampanoags did go to the Pilgrims' first celebration of giving thanks in 1621. They brought the meat. A letter written soon after by one Edward Winslow states: "Our harvest being gotten in, our Governor sent four men on fowling, that so we might after a more special manner rejoice together . . . many of the Indians amongst us, and amongst the rest their greatest king, Massasoit with some 90 men, whom for three days we entertained and feasted. And they went out and killed five deer, which they brought to the plantation and bestowed on our governor. . . . "

It is disputed, however, how many actually sat down with the Pilgrims. Slow Turtle, a.k.a. John Peters, brother of Mrs. Bingham and medicine man of the Wampanoags and executive director of the Massachusetts Commission on Indian Affairs, is the one who scorns the *Mayflower* forebears as "Boat People." And he opines that only one Wampanoag actually ate dinner with them. "The rest stayed well back, afraid of their nasty diseases."

Perhaps. From Pugwash to Patagonia, natives were showing newcomers how to find food and getting sick for their trouble. Indians introduced the Europeans to 80 percent of the foodstuffs Americans now take for granted today, including corn, turkey, pumpkins, cranberries, chili peppers, potatoes, yams, raspberries, blueberries, Concord grapes—and tobacco and chewing gum, too.

In exchange, according to University of Minnesota sociologist Russell Thornton in his book, "American Indian Holocaust and Survival," the Indians got introductions to bubonic plague, typhoid, cholera, smallpox, measles, scarlet fever, diphtheria, mumps, whooping cough, gonorrhea and common colds.

INDIANS INTRODUCED THE EUROPEANS TO 80 PERCENT OF THE FOODSTUFFS AMERICANS NOW TAKE FOR GRANTED TODAY, INCLUDING CORN, TURKEY, PUMPKINS, CRANBERRIES, CHILI PEPPERS, POTATOES, YAMS, RASPBERRIES, BLUEBERRIES, CONCORD GRAPES—AND TOBACCO AND CHEWING GUM, TOO.

Not that the Americas came close to French philosopher Rousseau's notion of a paradise of Noble Savages. Thornton says afflictions already present included bacillary and amoebic dysentery, viral fevers, roundworms, pellagra and salmonella. Recently, some scientists cited archaeological evidence that the Indians had nonvenereal syphilis and passed it to the Europeans, among whom it became a sexual disease.

Still, the Indians' end of the bargain was, as Thornton calls it, "a demographic collapse"—a holocaust proportionately as destructive as any the world has known. He counts up to 93 epidemics and pandemics of Old World pathogens wasting the Indians until the beginning of this century. They simply had no immunities to Eurogerms.

When Columbus bumped into some Caribbean island in 1492, Thornton calculates, there were five million Indians in what is now the United States. By 1850, only 250,000 could be counted. Today, their numbers are climbing back, toward two million, at a rate of growth twice that of this nation as a whole. Yet they make up little more than one half of one percent of the American population. And they remain among the poorest, least educated, shortest-lived of all Americans.

The Public Health Service reports the Indian death rate from alcoholism is 3.8 times that for all races in the U.S. They are 1.8 times more likely to be murdered, 1.3 times more likely to die of suicide. According to the 1980 census, median household income for Indians was $11,471, compared with $16,841 for the American population at large. Nearly one in three lives below the poverty level.

That's why Slow Turtle says today, "If you want to know what I'm doing for Thanksgiving, it's nothing. What have I got to be thankful for? Dirty air? Dirty water? It's not Indian air. It's not Indian water. It's for all of us. But look what these Boat People have done to the land and the water and the air! What kind of people are these who destroy the future of their own children and grandchildren? What are they giving thanks for?"

Another question Indians keep asking themselves: Why did old Massasoit even go to the Pilgrim's feast?

"Political expediency," says Nanepashemet, a historian and Wampanoag. "A plague, contracted from the crew of the European slaver Captain Thomas Hunt, who raided the coast in 1614, had greatly weakened us in the years just before the Pilgrims got here. Maybe one in five was left alive. The Wampanoag could muster only a few hundred warriors. Our enemies to the West, the Narragansetts, were far enough away to have escaped the epidemic and could field maybe five thousand. And the Europeans had the guns. We thought they would protect us."

It is arguable that the Pilgrims would never have been able to found Plimoth [sic] Plantation on the Cape had it not been for disease among the Indians that

216

wiped out whole tribes. As it was, they simply moved into the ruins of the Wampanoag village of Pawtuxet. All they had to do, says Bette Haskins of Harvard's American Indian Program, was sweep away the human bones that littered the ground because no Pawtuxet was alive to bury the dead. The advantage of being able to take possession of cleared ground was incalculable in a thickly forested land where an ordinary hardwood tree was three feet thick.

Even so, Haskins asserts, the Pilgrims were so ill-prepared, so lacking in tools and provisions, they were soon reduced to grave-robbing. "They found that Native people buried their dead with stores of corn and beans. The Pilgrims dug up many graves, taking the food." But that and the handouts from the Wampanoags weren't enough. Out of 103 who landed on the Mayflower, only 55 survived the winter. That first Thanksgiving dinner for 50 white and 90 Indian men invited along with Massasoit was cooked by just five women—the only ones left alive.

One thing sure about that dinner, the Pilgrims weren't giving thanks for Indian help. Governor William Bradford wrote in 1620 that America was unpeopled country, "being devoyd of all civil inhabitants, where there are only savage and brutish men, which range up and downe, litle otherwise than the wild beasts of the same."

This was an attitude repeated wherever the white people met the Indians. In Virginia in 1607, as the colonists were starving, Captain John Smith wrote: "Our provision being now within twentie dayes spent, the Indians brought us great store bothe of Corne and bread already made . . . With fish, oysters, bread and deere, they kindly traded with me and my men . . ."

> "IF YOU WANT TO KNOW WHAT I'M DOING FOR THANKSGIVING, IT'S NOTHING. WHAT HAVE I GOT TO BE THANKFUL FOR? DIRTY AIR? DIRTY WATER? IT'S NOT INDIAN AIR. IT'S NOT INDIAN WATER. IT'S FOR ALL OF US. . . . WHAT KIND OF PEOPLE ARE THESE WHO DESTROY THE FUTURE OF THEIR OWN CHILDREN AND GRANDCHILDREN?"

But within 15 years, he was calling them "hell-hounds" who "put on a more unnatural brutishness than beasts." Justifying a war on them, he wrote: "where before we were troubled in clearing the ground of great Timber, which was to them of small use; now we may take their own plaine fields and Habitations, which are the pleasantest places in the Countrey. Besides, the Deere, Turkies and other Beasts and Fowles will exceedingly increase if we beat the Salvages out of the Countrey."

Very efficiently they did just that. In his book, Thornton cites one recorded incident when the Virginia colonists negotiated a treaty with rebellious tribes in the Potomac River area: "After a toast was drunk symbolizing eternal friendship, the Chiskiack chief and his sons, advisers and followers, totaling two hundred, abruptly dropped dead from poisoned sack, and the soldiers put the remainder out of their misery."

Out on Cape Cod, the Wampanoags are remarkable for having been able to hang on right where they were when white colonists first arrived. They lost most of their population, lost their language, lost many of their traditions, lost almost all of their land and even lost their original looks, now showing traces of white and black blood. But they're still here, most notably at Mashpee and on the Gay Head cliffs of Martha's Vineyard. There are 7,000 to 13,000 Indians in Massachusetts. Maybe 3,000 of them are Wampanoag. Nobody even bothered to try to tally Indians until the 1980 census, and the true head count of Native Americans is still in dispute.

Yes, the Wampanoags survive all right, as something of a minor pain in the Back Bay. In Massachusetts, state spending on Indian matters is being cut by a third—to a not-so-grand total of $52,000 a year. As Slow Turtle's assistant, Burne Stanley, puts it: "Very soon, the Massachusetts Commission on Indian Affairs will consist of one Indian sitting at one desk in somebody else's office."

Academia is no more generous than government. For instance, the charter of Harvard College in 1650 states that it was created to provide "necessary provision that may conduce to the education of the English and Indian youths of this country in knowledge and godliness."

So how many Indians are being educated by Harvard? From Haskins, director of the university's American Indian Program: "Let's see, we've got one in the Kennedy School of Government, one in divinity school, one in the school of dentistry, six in law and 13 in the graduate school of education. And 24 undergrads." This out of total enrollment of 16,000.

Harvard "disfunded" the American Indian Program, which recruits and counsels Indian youths on campus, in 1987. Haskins' office gets by, for the time being, on a Ford Foundation grant. So why doesn't some Indian file suit, force the university to keep to the terms of its charter? Slow Turtle smiles and slowly shakes his head: "We'd just get some judge who went to Harvard."

The Wampanoags don't have a lot of luck in court. A few years back, they filed suit to gain title to the land around Mashpee. The case was dismissed. The U.S. Supreme Court declined to hear the appeal. As Amelia Bingham recalls it: "The judges say it would set a precedent all up and down the East Coast." Slow Turtle puts it this way: "You think a judge is going to give Indians the land the bank sits on?"

So today, in Mashpee, immigrants have found something that may prove more effective than disease and warfare for getting rid of the Wampanoags. It's called taxes. The natives had governed themselves from 1870 until 1967, when the influx of non-Indians tipped the voting balance and newcomers took over the local government. Mashpee, one of few towns missed by developers, became the site of several vast projects of shopping centers and summer homes.

"Property taxes are stacked against us," contends Mrs. Bingham. "Most Wampanoag own several acres. But because of the developers, half-acre lots are valued at $25,000. Most of our people work as laborers. They cannot afford those rates. Today, our young people are having to leave. Yes, yes, I know that happens in white communities where developers go in. But our young people have never left. I mean never. I mean in 10,000 years!"

Nanepashemet, the Wampanoag historian, sees no future for Indians on the Cape, and no point in Thanksgiving. He is wryly amused by the ironies of his life. He was born on November 26, on which Thanksgiving sometimes falls. He works at Plimoth Plantation, the tourist attraction that tries to re-create life here in the 1620s. Nanepashemet portrays the Indians who helped the Pilgrims get settled, but he doesn't make enough money to buy his own home.

"As far as setting aside one day of your life to give thanks, that's a sign of a very ungrateful people," he says. "Amongst our people, children are taught to give thanks every day for the simple fact of being alive. A lot of our ceremonies are of thanksgiving, not just one."

On Thursday, he's not sure what he'll do. He's got the day off, and maybe he'll drive to Plymouth and go to the statue of Massasoit that stands on the hill above Plymouth Rock. That's where, for the past 18 years, Indians from across America have gathered to mark Thanksgiving as a National Day of Mourning.

"The first year there were 500 of us. In recent years, there've been about 100. There are speeches about our past history, about present issues, about the rain forest. Unfortunately, most people have heard it all before. You see the same people every year."

From where they stand, the Indians cannot see the Rock. It is topped with an edifice that looks for some reason like a tiny Greek temple. But they make jokes about it. The Wampanoag have a saying, that the Pilgrims upon landing fell first upon their knees and then upon the aborigines.

"If only," Nanepashemet muses, "Plymouth Rock had landed on them."

Source: Lang, John S. "Guess Who's Not Coming to Thanksgiving Dinner; Those Who Were at the First Celebration See Little to Be Grateful for Today." *Washington Post*, November 21, 1989.

Some Native American Thanksgiving Observances (1998)

In the following article, published in the Washington Post *in 1998, Native Americans from various tribes across the nation share their complex feelings about, and ways of observing, the Thanksgiving holiday.*

Like millions of other families across the country, Billy Tayac and his family will sit down to a turkey dinner this afternoon.

At their farm in Southern Maryland, they will visit with friends and relatives they have not seen since the last big gathering, trade stories and reminisce. But unlike the celebratory mood that prevails in many households, a sense of loss holds sway as the clan gathers for Thanksgiving.

"It's really a national day of mourning," said Tayac, one of about 100 remaining members of a Native American tribe known as the Piscataway, which numbered in the thousands when Europeans first landed on this continent. "We're survivors. That's what it's about."

There is no simple way to characterize the range of feelings Native Americans bring to this holiday. Many celebrate it, others ignore it, and some use it as a time to reflect on a history marked by painful and costly encounters with the people who colonized the continent and since have written most of the history.

The way most school history books tell it, the holiday commemorates a feast that was a celebration of cooperation between newly arrived Europeans and indigenous people who helped them learn how to grow and harvest the foods that thrived in the New World.

For some Native Americans, that story is a sham. The holiday is a sharp reminder that many Native American tables are conspicuously shy of bounty and that many clans have been wiped off the Earth.

To add insult to injury, the traditional Thanksgiving foods—the turkey, the cranberries, the yams—have been appropriated: All are Indian foods. Far from cause for celebration, the arrival of the Europeans marked the beginning of what many see as genocide.

For others, the holiday evokes contradictory feelings. It is rooted in painful history, yes, but it is also a celebration of family and a time to take stock of what wealth fate has supplied.

© 1998 The Washington Post. Reprinted with permission.

Irene Herder grew up in Tuba City, Ariz., on the Navajo Indian reservation that was her family's traditional homeland. She remembers learning about Thanksgiving in school as a seven-year-old and recalls the pictures in her history textbooks: Indians wearing feathered headdresses and buckskin clothes, watching the Europeans arrive in boats.

"I didn't realize those Indians they were talking about were me," she said, explaining that she never saw Navajos wearing buckskin or headdresses. "Navajos wear velveteen blouses and gathered skirts."

> "WE'RE HERE BECAUSE SOME WHITE MAN DIDN'T KILL OUR ANCESTORS. I SEE IT AS A TIME OF MOURNING AND COMMEMORATION FOR THOSE PEOPLE WHO DIDN'T MAKE IT. AND ALSO A CELEBRATION FOR THOSE WHO HAVE SURVIVED," SAID SUZAN SHOWN HARJO, A CHEYENNE INDIAN.

Even so, the teachers at her school had children make headdresses from colored paper. She remembers her grandparents talking about how they were punished by teachers in their federally administered schools if they uttered a word of their native Navajo.

Yet, when Herder thinks back on how Indians were depicted in her grade school lessons about Thanksgiving, she feels neither anger nor sorrow.

"How it was portrayed to us, the Indians welcomed the Pilgrims because the Indians are naturally friendly," she said. "We do things communally. We care. . . . I hadn't learned that our ancestors were driven off their homelands."

Today, Herder lives in Falls Church, and her understanding of her people's history is more complex.

Still, she cherishes Thanksgiving as a time to gather with others. She plans to have a traditional turkey dinner with friends in Silver Spring this afternoon.

"I don't really have any hang-ups about the history," she said. "We sit down, we give thanks for what we have today. We just pray like other Americans. And then we eat."

Leslie Webb grew up on a military base in San Antonio, the daughter of a Cheyenne River Sioux father and a Mexican-American mother. Today, she lives in Silver Spring.

Though her father, a product of strict reservation schools, de-emphasized Thanksgiving, Webb's own schooling gave her the sense that the holiday was a celebration of trans-cultural cooperation.

"I think it was supposed to be about coming together, no matter what race," she said.

That view strikes her as naive today, as she raises her own daughter, but the positive feelings about the holiday remain.

Suzan Shown Harjo says she is a direct descendant of Chief Bull Bear, a Cheyenne Indian who was the first to sign an 1868 treaty that established the Cheyenne-Arapaho reservation in Oklahoma, where she was raised.

Today, she is a denizen of Capitol Hill, a professional Native American activist who is one of several plaintiffs suing to force the Washington Redskins to change their name, which she sees as a racist assault on her people.

Harjo plans to be in North Carolina today with her two children, digging into the usual feast with old friends—taking pleasure in community, even while cognizant of history.

"We're here because some white man didn't kill our ancestors," she said. "I see it as a time of mourning and commemoration for those people who didn't make it. And also a celebration for those who have survived.

"From native people's perspective," she added, "the day is about generosity, appreciation and sharing. And even though reason tells that you shouldn't ever again trust the people who are benefiting from the avarice of their ancestors, we still do."

Source: Goodman, Peter S. "For Native Americans, A Day of Mixed Emotions." *Washington Post,* November 26, 1998.

Thanksgiving in Modern Times

Modern American families continue to enjoy traditional Thanksgiving feasts.

"The Thanksgiving Day Parade," a Poem by Jack Prelutsky (1996)

Children's book author and poet Jack Prelutsky captures the magic of one of the holiday's most beloved traditions in this poem, entitled "The Thanksgiving Day Parade." In playful verse, he conveys the excitement that the annual spectacle of giant balloons, marching bands, clowns, and Santa Claus holds for children—regardless of the weather.

The Thanksgiving Day Parade

Thanksgiving Day is here today,
the great parade is under way,
and though it's drizzling quite a bit,
I'm sure that I'll see all of it.

Great balloons are floating by,
cartoon creatures stories high,
Mickey Mouse and Mother Goose,
Snoopy and a mammoth moose.

Humpty Dumpty, Smokey Bear
hover in the autumn air,
through the windy skies they sway,
I hope that they don't blow away.

Here comes Santa, shaking hands
as he waddles by the stands.
It's so much fun, I don't complain
when now it really starts to rain.

The bands are marching, here they come,
pipers pipe and drummers drum,

Text Copyright © 1982 Jack Prelutsky. Used by permission of HarperCollins Publishers.

hear the tubas and the flutes,
see the clowns in silly suits.

It's pouring now, but not on me,
I'm just as dry as I can be,
I watch and watch, but don't get wet,
I'm watching on our TV set.

Source: Prelutsky, Jack. "The Thanksgiving Day Parade." In *It's Thanksgiving*. New York: Harper-Collins, 1996. Available online at http://homepages.rootsweb.com/~homespun/tmtp.html.

Thanksgiving with Immigrant Parents (2000)

With its primary customs of gathering together and eating a good meal, Thanksgiving has been embraced by many immigrants, who add their own culinary traditions to the mix. Since early in the 20th century, when waves of immigrants began to move to the United States, the Thanksgiving holiday has served as an occasion to assist newcomers in becoming more familiar with American history and traditions. Still, as Samar Farah relates in the following article in Christian Science Monitor, *the holiday can present challenges, particularly to a child with immigrant parents.*

My mother had her first Thanksgiving in 1979, six weeks after she and my father arrived from Lebanon with their two small children. We were staying with my aunt in New Jersey while my father looked for work. My dad, who had gone to college in New York, was familiar with the annual rite of turkey. For my mother, it was an early lesson in American culture.

My aunt, who had immigrated from Lebanon about a decade before, prepared for the day with her usual busy anticipation: "Soon we'll have Thanksgiving. In November, there'll be Thanksgiving." A native Arabic speaker, my mother immediately took to the word "Thanksgiving." Its simple meaning warmed her to the holiday.

Years later, when my parents hosted their own Thanksgiving dinners, it continued to be her favorite holiday. She found it easy to adapt to—unlike the Fourth of July, which is pure patriotic romp, and Christmas, which featured a barrage of commercialism she wasn't accustomed to.

Thanksgiving was more modest in its traditions and open to interpretation. It could be anything from a religious event to the raison d'etre for Martha Stewart types. For my mother, it became a way for her to celebrate her new country without totally suppressing her heritage. This meant that we had turkey and mashed potatoes and cranberry sauce—with pita bread and spinach pies and rice stuffing.

As I was growing up, though, our Thanksgivings gave me the same sense of cultural crisis I felt when taking a seat next to my friends in the cafeteria and drawing from my lunch box a Capri Sun and a lebne sandwich.

The child of first-generation parents, I was greedy for evidence that we were just like every other American family. What I usually got was just the opposite.

Copyright © 2000 by the Christian Science Publishing Society. Reproduced with permission.

I remember one of my first mornings away from home after sleeping over at a third-grade classmate's house. There were four kids in Laura Kelly's boisterous clan. Sitting at their breakfast table one morning, as the only person fate had cruelly failed to endow with freckles, I finally understood the deeper meaning of the Sesame Street jingle, "Which of these things is not like the other?"

It got worse fast when Laura's mother passed around eggs cooked sunny-side up. Till then, I had only eaten eggs with pita bread, sponging the gooey yoke into li'mes—small bites. Now I had just a fork and a knife in front of me. I knew that if I poked the yoke with either, it would quickly spread like spilled paint over the entire plate. How would I possibly slop it up with these crude tools?

> NO MATTER WHAT MY PARENTS DID, IT FELT AS IF WE WERE HOLIDAY IMPOSTORS. MY MOTHER'S RICE STUFFING WITH GROUND BEEF AND PINE NUTS FED MY INSECURITIES. THE INTRICATE PERSIAN RUGS THAT FILLED OUR HALL AND DINING ROOM WERE AT ODDS WITH THE APPLE PIE.

Experiences like this left me with an acute need to impose some sort of cultural order on my life. Never was this need more evident than on Thanksgiving, a holiday steeped in Norman Rockwell Americana. As a kid, I wanted to rewrite my parents' ways to the American Thanksgiving script.

I wanted to spell things out for them: Green beans are supposed to be bland and overcooked. You can't try to galvanize them with lemon juice and garlic.

I wanted to keep the story simple for my mother, who was piecing together the history of Pilgrims and Indians from cutouts I pasted together in school. But historians, with their penchant for murdering myth, complicated my mission. They introduced disputes over the Pilgrims' intentions, and the actual date and place the first Thanksgiving celebration occurred.

Tell immigrants that the Pilgrims probably didn't eat turkey, and there'll be a lot of second-generation kids staring at Thanksgiving duck curry.

No matter what my parents did, it felt as if we were holiday impostors. My mother's rice stuffing with ground beef and pine nuts fed my insecurities. The intricate Persian rugs that filled our hall and dining room were at odds with the apple pie, I felt. I wanted nothing more than my relatives in Indian feathers and Pilgrim hats.

It was not until college that I finally got over my childish craving for absolutes. If anything, college taught me that weird is relative. But I am not completely cured. This year, as I get ready to head home to New Jersey, I find myself longing for bread stuffing, preferably Stovetop. The difference is, I am also really looking forward to those spinach pies.

Source: Farah, Samar. "Growing Up a Thanksgiving Impostor." *Christian Science Monitor,* November 22, 2000.

President George W. Bush Proclaims Thanksgiving in the Wake of the September 11 Attacks (2001)

Thanksgiving gained new significance and meaning in the lives of many Americans following the terrorist attacks of September 11, 2001. This shocking event increased the level of appreciation many people felt for family, community, and country. On November 16, 2001, two months after the attacks took place, President George W. Bush issued the annual Thanksgiving proclamation. In this document, he reminds the American people that they have many reasons to be grateful, even in the face of adversity.

BY THE PRESIDENT OF THE UNITED STATES OF AMERICA, A PROCLAMATION

Nearly half a century ago, President Dwight Eisenhower proclaimed Thanksgiving as a time when Americans should celebrate "the plentiful yield of our soil . . . the beauty of our land . . . the preservation of those ideals of liberty and justice that form the basis of our national life, and the hope of international peace." Now, in the painful aftermath of the September 11 attacks and in the midst of our resolute war on terrorism, President Eisenhower's hopeful words point us to our collective obligation to defend the enduring principles of freedom that form the foundation of our Republic.

During these extraordinary times, we find particular assurance from our Thanksgiving tradition, which reminds us that we, as a people and individually, always have reason to hope and trust in God, despite great adversity. In 1621 in New England, the Pilgrims gave thanks to God, in whom they placed their hope, even though a bitter winter had taken many of their brethren. In the winter of 1777, General George Washington and his army, having just suffered great misfortune, stopped near Valley Forge, Pennsylvania, to give thanks to God. And there, in the throes of great difficulty, they found the hope they needed to persevere. That hope in freedom eventually inspired them to victory.

In 1789, President Washington, recollecting the countless blessings for which our new Nation should give thanks, declared the first National Day of Thanksgiving. And decades later, with the Nation embroiled in a bloody civil war, President Abraham Lincoln revived what is now an annual tradition of issuing a presidential proclamation of Thanksgiving. President Lincoln asked God to "heal the wounds of the nation and to restore it as soon as may be consistent with the Divine purposes to the full enjoyment of peace, harmony, tranquillity, and Union."

As we recover from the terrible tragedies of September 11, Americans of every belief and heritage give thanks to God for the many blessings we enjoy as a free, faithful, and fair-minded land. Let us particularly give thanks for the self-less sacrifices of those who responded in service to others after the terrorist attacks, setting aside their own safety as they reached out to help their neighbors. Let us also give thanks for our leaders at every level who have planned and coordinated the myriad of responses needed to address this unprecedented national crisis. And let us give thanks for the millions of people of faith who have opened their hearts to those in need with love and prayer, bringing us a deeper unity and stronger resolve.

In thankfulness and humility, we acknowledge, especially now, our dependence on One greater than ourselves. On this day of Thanksgiving, let our thanksgiving be revealed in the compassionate support we render to our fellow citizens who are grieving unimaginable loss; and let us reach out with care to those in need of food, shelter, and words of hope. May Almighty God, who is our refuge and our strength in this time of trouble, watch over our homeland, protect us, and grant us patience, resolve, and wisdom in all that is to come.

NOW, THEREFORE, I, GEORGE W. BUSH, President of the United States of America, by virtue of the authority vested in me by the Constitution and laws of the United States, do hereby proclaim Thursday, November 22, 2001, as a National Day of Thanksgiving. I encourage Americans to assemble in their homes, places of worship, or community centers to reinforce ties of family and community, express our profound thanks for the many blessings we enjoy, and reach out in true gratitude and friendship to our friends around the world.

IN WITNESS WHEREOF, I have hereunto set my hand this sixteenth day of November, in the year of our Lord two thousand one, and of the Independence of the United States of America the two hundred and twenty-sixth.

GEORGE W. BUSH

Source: Bush, George W. Thanksgiving Day Proclamation, November 16, 2001. Available online at Pilgrim Hall Museum, http://www.pilgrimhall.org/ThanxProc2000.htm.

Thanksgiving for New York Firefighters (2001)

After the terrorist attacks of September 11, 2001, firefighters and other rescue, recovery, and clean-up crews toiled around the clock at the site of the former World Trade Center. Thanksgiving Day 2001 found area fire-fighters and others still employed on this wrenching duty. The New York Times *article below follows the day of squad members of a fire station in Brooklyn, New York, who had suffered the loss of twelve of their men in the attacks.*

The first call of the Thanksgiving Day shift came in at 9:18 a.m.

"10-26!" the call box bleated. The driver started the fire engine and the men jumped into their boots, pants and suspenders, which stood next to their lockers like mannequins.

"10-26!" the call box bleated again. A stove fire.

"They burned the turkey already," Firefighter Bob West said. "You shouldn't stuff the turkey until after you cook it." That's what his mother told him, anyway.

It was shaping up to be another normal holiday for the men of Squad 1, the elite fire and rescue company stationed in the Park Slope section of Brooklyn, which lost 12 men on the morning of Sept. 11. But normal is a relative concept nowadays.

Thanksgiving, it seemed, had come around to its original meaning, less about football and overeating and Christmas commercials than about an appreciation for life. In the aftermath of the ambushes on the World Trade Center and the Pentagon, people across the nation stopped to consider and appreciate what they had and what they had lost.

There is a mother in Mississippi with a son in Afghanistan. He is alive, and she was grateful for that. A war refugee from Guatemala has made a life for her children by shining expensive shoes on Wall Street, and she was grateful for that.

Then there were the six men working at the small brick firehouse, surrounded by grandparents and wives and children, and they, too, were grateful for a few hours of the regular life. Their evening would be spent combing the smoldering pile of the twin towers for bodies.

Copyright © 2001 by The New York Times Co. Reprinted with permission.

The firehouse is still decorated in purple bunting and wilting flowers from the funeral of Lt. Michael Esposito. Squad 1 lost 11 other men that dark Tuesday morning: Amato, D' Atri, Russo, Cordice, Bilcher, Siller, Carroll, Fontana, Box, Garvey and Butler.

Firefighter Robert Maddalone is one of the new men assigned to the house, and while basting the turkey, he perhaps said it best.

"I'm thankful I'm alive, but I feel guilty I'm alive," he said. "I'm trying to remember the guys who aren't here. Their wives and children. It's a hollow feeling. You try to laugh sometimes to keep your sanity, but you feel bad about laughing."

The turkey came out well, moist with crispy skin, despite the men's playing with the stove's thermostat as if it were a radio dial.

A typical phone conversation went something like: "Happy Thanksgiving, Dad, is Mom there? Hi Mom. How long do I cook this bird? Sixteen pounds."

In the corner, Sean Cummins was playing with some walnuts, making some anatomical references to them in the style of the barracks.

The past 10 weeks have been the worst in his life. There was the trade center collapse and the death of thousands. There were the weeks on end searching the wreckage. There were the funerals of his company comrades and at least a dozen more of other firefighters. There was a scaffolding collapse that killed five. A fire that took the lives of three children. And the airplane crash that hit his neighborhood, leaving 265 dead.

Even so, Mr. Cummins has things to be thankful for. There is his wife, Maureen, and his three children. There is also the work he does.

> THANKSGIVING, IT SEEMED, HAD COME AROUND TO ITS ORIGINAL MEANING, LESS ABOUT FOOTBALL AND OVEREATING AND CHRISTMAS COMMERCIALS THAN ABOUT AN APPRECIATION FOR LIFE. . . . [PEOPLE] ACROSS THE NATION STOPPED TO CONSIDER AND APPRECIATE WHAT THEY HAD AND WHAT THEY HAD LOST.

"Tuesday morning we found a man in the pile," he said. "We dug him out, and he had his wallet in his pocket. I was hoping they would notify his family by Thanksgiving. That would make me feel good."

Around noon, Daniel A. Nigro, the chief of department, the top-ranking uniformed fire official, stopped by on his own time. He came to check the men's morale. He came to say hello to their families. He came with a lump in his throat. "The department is going to get through this, men," he told them. "I don't know what the future holds, but we'll all get through this."

The room fell silent, and the turkey made the hissing sound of falling rain.

The turkey was pulled from the oven just after 1 p.m. The neighbors came by with fixings. A call came over the box about a drug overdose. A tattered woman on the graffiti-scarred corner of Degraw Street and Fourth Avenue in Brooklyn was slumped in a doorway with her forehead to her knees. She had just come from the soup kitchen.

"What'd you eat?" the men asked her as a priest looked on.

"Nothin'," she slurred. "Jus' turkey."

"Uh, huh," one man said. "That's an awful lot of turkey."

Off she went in the ambulance, and life in New York went on, just like the old days.

Back at the firehouse, the turkey was still warm.

Bart Codd, the new captain at Squad 1, said grace. "Personally we have things to be thankful for," he said, scratching his bowed head. "But others don't. Let's keep that in perspective. Amen."

The men ate, watched the Detroit Lions lose, piled into their engine around 5 o'clock and drove down to ground zero full of roast turkey, sauce and yams.

Theresa Russo called as the men were on their way out. She lost her husband, Michael, a lieutenant at Squad 1. He and eight others have yet to be found. She just called to wish the men a happy Thanksgiving and to thank them for the job they do.

The six firemen arrived at ground zero around 5:30 p.m. and to their disappointment were assigned a backup role. No action.

They watched with their hands in their overalls as other men picked and raked through the scrap and the black dirt that is not dirt at all but pulverized building.

A police dog sniffed, and tourists peeked over the barricades and took photographs with their cameras over their heads.

"Surreal," Mr. West said.

Floodlights and smoke and the unmistakable stench. In the sky stood the green splendor of the Woolworth Building, a beautiful testament to humankind, and the firemen stood to consider it for a time. Below, was the wreckage and horror.

"The very worst of mankind," Firefighter Billy Reddan said.

Cigarette embers glowed in the dark recesses, and more than 150 men and women spent Thanksgiving evening here, working.

The scene brought to mind an image that Firefighter Tom DeAngelis painted that morning at the firehouse as he was coming off the night shift and the turkey was put in the oven.

"There was a dark alley around ground zero, near Washington Street, I think," he said. "It was 4 o'clock in the morning and a man was there with a bucket and brush scrubbing the rescuers' boots. A regular guy stooped over in an alley doing that, just wanting to help in some way. Where's the glory? To me he's a hero. I'm thankful to that guy."

Bill Noesges, a night foreman of the operating engineers, was among the workers at the trade center site, talking about his wife and children and Thanksgiving.

"To a person, we are proud to do this job," he said. "You couldn't tear me away from here, not even for the holiday. When it's all over, though, someone is going to have to reintroduce me to my wife."

However it may have sounded, Firefighter Eddie Cowan said he would give his two legs to make everything back to the way it was on Sept. 10.

An impossible wish, but at least it wasn't raining.

Source: LeDuff, Charlie. "On Holiday Shift, Gratitude at the Firehouse. (Squad 1: The First Holiday)." *New York Times*, November 23, 2001.

Maintaining Tradition: Thanksgiving and Football (2002)

Football became a Thanksgiving tradition late in the 19th century. The first college game was played on the holiday in 1876. Before long, other colleges, as well as high schools and local groups of players, were enjoying the Thanksgiving game. In the article below, USA Today *writer Gary Mihoces surveys some neighborhood groups and families who have revived the community football tradition, now known as Turkey Bowls.*

On Thanksgiving morning, the pickup football matchup in this Philadelphia suburb will be Italians vs. Irish as old grade-school buddies face off in their annual "Turkey Bowl."

"It's tradition. These guys live and breathe it," says Anthony Paoletti, 33, who sells construction materials the rest of the year but slings passes as the 6-foot, 250-pound quarterback of the Italians.

Football and Thanksgiving go together like pumpkin pie and whipped cream, from the annual pro games in Detroit and Dallas to high school championship games between crosstown rivals. Then there are the do-it-yourself Turkey Bowls: The games played by friends, families and whoever has the urge to chuck it long that have become Thanksgiving rituals across the USA.

On fields near you, you may see footballs fly Thursday. It's mostly guys, teens to 40s, but little kids, sisters, moms and more are invited to join some huddles. A 70-year-old in Ohio throws passes to, among others, his 6-year-old grandson.

A group of California high school pals called "The Last Man" will play its 27th annual Turkey Bowl. Now in their 40s, they pledge the last survivor will toast the rest, presumably decades from now. A Georgia family prints programs. Some Turkey Bowls have Web sites.

But the degree of organization, like a recipe for stuffing, is a matter of taste. No practice required. Design plays as you go. Team jerseys are nice, but ragtag is fine. You don't have to keep score—but most do.

Turkey Bowls are a way to get together on a day made for just that. They're a way to return, if just for moments, to times when the gang was younger, fleeter and thinner.

From USA TODAY, a division of Gannett Co., Inc. Reprinted with permission.

The Irish vs. Italians game in Aldan was begun by some of the current play-ers' older brothers in the late 1970s. Whether the field behind Aldan Elemen-tary is muddy or frozen, they play for a slightly cracked plaque and yearlong trash-talking rights.

"It's the one time of year I know I see all my old elementary school buddies," Paoletti says.

The Italians want their fourth win in a row. But Bob Park, 33, of the Irish says no way.

"This year I'm going to try to get to bed more than an hour before the game," says Park, also a veteran of the big party the teams throw the night before the game.

The Last Man Toast

"Each year we will toast together the friendship we have shared, until the last man—and he shall toast alone."

Seventeen members of a group called The Last Man made that pledge when they played their first Turkey Bowl in 1976, a year many were seniors at Corona del Mar (Calif.) High.

They'd grown up together and surfed together, and some had been football teammates.

"We thought, 'You know, let's make sure no matter where we are and what we're doing in life, that during Thanks-giving we celebrate our friendship,'" says Greg Wilfahrt, 42, of San Diego, co-founder of a wireless technology firm.

> FOOTBALL AND THANKSGIVING GO TOGETHER LIKE PUMPKIN PIE AND WHIPPED CREAM, FROM THE ANNUAL PRO GAMES IN DETROIT AND DALLAS TO HIGH SCHOOL CHAMPIONSHIP GAMES BETWEEN CROSSTOWN RIVALS. THEN THERE ARE THE DO-IT-YOURSELF TURKEY BOWLS.

One year, two members were absent because of military duty in Operation Desert Storm. But typically all attend. Some have come from as far as Boston and Atlanta.

"The one thing everybody says without hesitation is that they look forward every year to being together for The Last Man," Wilfahrt says.

Thanksgiving eve, they meet at a tavern. The next morning, they play in their original blue or white football jerseys from Corona del Mar High.

"Way back then they fit nicely with shoulder pads," Wilfahrt says. "Now they fit nicely without pads."

For their first Turkey Bowl in high school, they had one dad buy a magnum of champagne. They affixed a "Last Man" label and vowed it would not be opened until the "Last Man" made his toast. Their champagne has gone bad. But they have kept the bottle as a symbol and have as a backup a bottle of cognac.

"It's going to be no prize being the Last Man because you are going to die drinking the bottle," says Tom Freeman, 43, of Lake Forest, Calif., a sales manager with IBM's software group.

They have a safe-deposit box into which each has placed letters and mementos over the years. Upon each man's death, his letters will be read by the survivors.

On game day at their old junior high school, wives, kids and parents root them on. They allow some friends to participate and usually get 25-30 players. Some years they choose up sides. This year they'll split up according to a theme: players with San Diego State ties vs. those with UCLA ties.

How many years will they play?

"I see us out there when we're all 70," Wilfahrt says. "You'll get six quarterbacks on a side."

Freeman says, "My wife will tell you that for as long as I'm able to move we'll plan our Thanksgiving meal around the Last Man."

More Turkey Bowls

There are many variations on the Turkey Bowl theme:

* The Jarrell family of Decatur, Ga., plays the Saturday after Thanksgiving. This is "Turkey Bowl VIII" in their game program. Their Web site shows a football-toting turkey running across the screen.

Perry Jarrell, 45, and his son, PJ, 24, captain the teams, which compete for the Jarrell Cup, made from softball trophies. It's eight to 10 friends and relatives on each side, males and females age 16 to near 50. PJ's twin sister, Mandi, plays.

"I usually play receiver or line," says Perry, an architect. "Once in a while I may play quarterback. I try not to hog. . . . But my goal is to win the game every year."

Dad has won five of seven.

* In Lisle, Ill., Brian Quick, 41, started playing Turkey Bowls with pals from high school in 1976. After his sister Lisa was diagnosed in about 1980 with multiple sclerosis, the game became a fundraiser for multiple sclerosis research. Players solicit donations.

"They have to raise at least a minimum of $50, but most of them raise substantially more," Quick says.

They play the day after Thanksgiving at a junior high on a regulation field with a scoreboard and down markers. It's Pilgrims vs. Indians. About 40 players in various age brackets are rotated in and out.

"I'm the ringmaster," Quick says. "I've got to make sure everything is running smoothly. . . . But I try to play with all the age groups just to have some fun."

Amanda Gregor, 18, a freshman at St. Ambrose University in Iowa, will be playing in her fourth Turkey Bowl in Lisle. She got into it as a high school sophomore through her uncle, Jeff Webster, one of the game's founding players.

"I wanted to play the year before," she says. "But (Webster) was like, 'No, you'll get killed. You'll be the only girl.' I said I could handle my own. So I played the next year, and I was the only girl."

She's held her own: "I think I've made a touchdown every year."

* For the 35th year, Lindsay Freshly of Westerville, Ohio, will catch Turkey Bowl passes from his father, Orlo, a retired minister now 70. The son's scouting report on Dad: "Incredibly fit. . . . I would put him up against any other 70-year-old for accuracy and leading his receivers up to 35 yards."

They'll play with relatives this year at a gathering in Sandusky, Ohio. "My dad has been throwing footballs to me all my life. He just throws it up, and I get it," says Lindsay, an agronomist whose son, Tristan, 6, will play his second game.

 * The Turkey Bowl in the Lincoln Place section of Pittsburgh goes back to the '40s. The Oldsters (25 and older) play the Youngsters (24 and younger). It's full-contact, full-pads, bring your own gear.

"We have a (betting) line on the game. We put it up at the VFW," says Rob Capozzolo, 33.

Capozzolo is a 5-7, 240-pounder who has won national titles as a powerlifter and has bench-pressed 715 pounds. Like his grandfather, he's played in many of the games, but he'll sit out this year.

"I've been involved in a lot of weightlifting competition, and I'm not going to go up and get hurt or do something silly," he says.

> *Turkey Bowls*
> ARE A WAY TO GET
> TOGETHER ON A
> DAY MADE JUST
> FOR THAT. THEY'RE
> A WAY TO RETURN,
> IF JUST FOR A FEW
> MOMENTS, TO
> TIMES WHEN THE
> GANG WAS
> YOUNGER,
> FLEETER, AND
> THINNER.

Capozzolo says the games get "very competitive." But, he adds, "It's really just a big social event. . . . You're going to see some old face you haven't seen all year."

Make It Up as You Go

The basic rule of Turkey Bowls: make your own rules.

"There is no method to the madness," says George Byers, 30, who has played the last five years with co-workers at a Wal-Mart in West Mifflin, Pa. They start with the national anthem (last year it was a CD of the Whitney Houston version) and play tackle with no pads.

Byers says they wear "whatever they can afford to get ripped up." Without team colors, there can be confusion. "Sometimes you end up on the other team and don't even know it," he says.

The score isn't a big deal. "If it's a rout, we'll split up and redo the teams," Byers says.

In Niskayuna, N.Y., longtime buddies will play their 10th Turkey Bowl. They play tackle behind the line of scrimmage and two-hand touch once a receiver or runner crosses it.

"It gives the defensive line a little more incentive to go after the quarterback," says Anthony Rizzi, 25, of Rochester, N.Y., a software engineer who plays quarterback and maintains the Web site.

Last year the Niskayuna players experimented with 10-yard, first-down markers.

"But it made the game less offensive because the quarterbacks just kept scrambling for first downs," Rizzi says. He figures they'll revert to the old system: two pass completions in four tries is a first down.

In Decatur, Ga., the Jarrells use first-down markers.

"I put together a couple of closet poles with a wire in the middle," Perry Jarrell says.

For some games, a touchdown is one point. Others use conventional scoring with extra points and field goals. In Niskayuna, they added kicking last fall.

"We've got a lot of soccer guys. We added kicking to get them involved," Rizzi says.

Some play tackle. Others go with two-hand touch. The latter applies in Aldan, where the Italians wear red jerseys and the Irish sport gold (with green numbers).

"In the original games, it was tackle football," recalls Tim Maguire, 32, of Mount Laurel, N.J., who rejoined the Irish last fall after not playing since 1988.

That was when they were teens. As they got older and the soreness after each game lingered longer, they switched rules.

"Now it's rough touch . . . a tackle every now and then," Maguire says.

The Physical Test

You can get hurt in a Turkey Bowl, and not just routine bumps.

In the Jarrell game in Georgia, a neighbor in his 40s tore his Achilles' tendon last year. "He's not playing this year. Perhaps he'll referee," Perry Jarrell says.

In Aldan, Tom Zimmerman, 31, of the Irish (he's part German) suffered a broken collarbone years ago when he was sandwiched by two guys.

Rob DiGregorio, 33, of the Italians recalls a year the field was frozen: "Sam Patterson (of the Irish) landed on his butt and had to go home. He was sore for two weeks. It was like hitting rock."

Being fit helps, but it's no requirement. "None of us is in shape. . . . We're overweight, the whole bunch," says Paoletti, the 250-pound Italian quarterback.

But some Aldan players are in better condition than others.

"I try to keep myself in half-decent shape and if you do that, you have a good shot at being better than anybody else out there," says Joe Spina, 32, whose receptions and defense have earned him MVP awards the last three years.

Turkey Bowl tips: Know your limits, and keep it fun.

Turkey Bowl spirit

John Tobin, 42, is the Aldan ironman. He was among the older brothers who originated the game, and he stills plays for the Irish.

"I just love the game. You're with friends, clowning around," he says.

The night before, they party at Tony's Bar in Collingdale, Pa. It's a long night, complete with soaping each other's cars and other pranks, such as placing old hot-water tanks in somebody's yard.

"One of the tough parts is the day of the game, calling people to get them up to play," Tobin says.

To the victors belong the spoils. Spina has his MVP plaques in his basement. "When my brother-in-law (Joe McBlain of the Irish) comes over, we'll go down there and I'll rub it in," he says.

Spina adds, "The guy who wins is a little less sore than the other guy at Thanksgiving dinner."

Source: Mihoces, Gary. "Pass the Turkey—and the Football." *USA Today*, November 27, 2002.

The Secret Joy of Eating Thanksgiving Dinner at the "Kids' Table" (2004)

For many contemporary Americans, homecoming is the most important fea-ture of Thanksgiving. Millions of people travel over the holiday weekend in order to share a special meal with friends and family members. A common feature of these large gatherings in homes across the country is the "kids' table"—a makeshift spot where the children eat Thanksgiving dinner togeth-er, separate from the adults. In this 2004 Country Living *article, entitled "Turning the Tables at Thanksgiving," Faith Andrews Bedford remembers the joy this tradition brought to her childhood.*

As a child, I had never heard of such a thing as a kids' table. Our holiday gatherings were very small—just my two sisters and my parents, my grand-mother, my Aunt Gertrude and Uncle George, and me. We could all fit around the dining room table together if we put in both leaves. Ellen and Beth and I had to be extra good, of course. We wore our Sunday best, sat up nice and straight, and never talked with our mouths full. But the year Uncle George and Aunt Gertrude moved away, we became a very tiny group. Mother wistfully observed that we wouldn't need any leaves at all in the table for Thanksgiving dinner.

"Only you folks and Grandmother this year?" our neighbor, Mrs. Bailey, exclaimed when she spied mother putting a tiny turkey into her cart at the A & P.

Mother nodded sadly. "You must come and join us." Mrs. Bailey declared.

"Oh, we couldn't possibly impose," Mother replied as I eagerly tugged at her skirt and tried to look very pleading.

Janie Bailey was my best friend, the youngest of seven children. They lived just down the road from us; something fun was always going on at their house. Janie shared a bedroom with her sister Judy, which sounded wonderful to me. I knew that she envied the bedroom I had all to myself, but I consid-ered company and security far more desirable. Surely, I thought, monsters in the closet would never come out if there were two girls in the room.

© 2004 Faith Andrews Bedford. All rights reserved.

"Don't be silly," Mrs. Bailey insisted. "We always have 20 or 30 for dinner. What are six more? We'd love to have you."

"Thank you," Mother relented at last. "But only if you let me bring something." I hugged her in delight.

"Two of your wonderful pies would be great," Mrs. Bailey said, as she briskly pushed her cart away down the aisle, piling in things from every shelf until we could barely see her behind an enormous mound of food.

On Thanksgiving afternoon, the Baileys' driveway was lined with cars and trucks; more had spilled out onto the fields. Dozens of cousins and aunts and uncles had driven out from Chicago or down from Wisconsin. We wondered how everyone could possibly fit in for dinner. When we opened the door we understood. Tables and chairs filled every nook and cranny. Sofas had been pushed back against the walls, and card tables were draped with cloths in autumn colors. Chairs, borrowed from the fire department hall, were snuggled as close together as possible.

As Mother took her pies to the kitchen, Janie and her sister Colleen grabbed our hands and pulled us out to the sunporch where their two oldest brothers, Thomas and Sean, were carefully positioning place cards. "We'll all be at this table," Janie said, putting her place card next to mine. A long yellow tablecloth covered three card tables topped with a huge piece of plywood. Fifteen chairs were set around it. My sisters and I stared at each other in astonishment. Everything was child-sized and perfect, from the plates and glasses to the table decorations. Janie's Aunt Kate brought out some small vases full of brightly colored mums and laughed at our wide-eyed wonder.

"Everyone wants to be at the kids' table," she said, putting the vases in our hands. "And everyone has a job." We eagerly set to work carefully placing the mums between pairs of tiny candlesticks.

After Mrs. Bailey's brother, Father Michael, said the blessing, we filled our plates at the buffet table and wondered how three turkeys could possibly have two big and six little drumsticks each. By the time we reached the kids' table, the sunporch was filled with children's laughter. To keep the little ones happy, Thomas and Sean had fashioned clown hats from their napkins. Cousin Patrick from Chicago was telling riddles, and Ellen was seeing how many peas she could balance on her knife. Hilarity reigned. We didn't have to eat our vegetables and no one made us sit up straight. Janie's big sister Margaret and her cousin Mary rolled their eyes at the jokes and whispered together during most of the meal. But I'd begun to notice that teenage girls did that sort of thing.

In the dining room, the low murmur of adult conversation was punctuated by an occasional burst of laughter. Every once in a while an uncle's voice would call out, "Quiet down out there." If that didn't work, one of the aunts would poke her head around the door and give us The Look. The noise level would drop a milli-decibel for a moment, and then someone would tell another joke or make a funny face and set us all off again. Eventually, the grown-ups wearied of trying to suppress our merriment.

A LONG YELLOW TABLECLOTH COVERED THREE CARD TABLES TOPPED WITH A HUGE PIECE OF PLYWOOD. FIFTEEN CHAIRS WERE SET AROUND IT. MY SISTERS AND I STARED AT EACH OTHER IN ASTONISHMENT. EVERYTHING WAS CHILD-SIZED AND PERFECT, FROM THE PLATES AND GLASSES TO THE TABLE DECORATIONS.

When dinner was over, the older children cleared off the plates and the younger ones brought out the desserts. Mother's pies won a round of applause and were followed by a carrot cake brought by Aunt Maureen and Uncle Mitchell's famous pumpkin cookies. After the last of the dishes had been dried and put back in the cupboards, we headed home beneath an autumn moon. As we shuffled through drifts of leaves, we begged our parents to let us have Thanksgiving with the Baileys forever and ever.

Dad laughed and said if we minded our manners we might be invited back again. "What manners?" Beth and I giggled.

Years of shared laughter and wonderful dinners followed. But when Janie and I were 14, the Baileys moved to Wisconsin. I cried for weeks.

Years later, we ran into each other at a school reunion. After a quick hug and a sharing of family photographs, I asked, "So, how long did you get to stay at the kids' table?"

Janie laughed, "By the time I was 14 it had seemed like forever. I thought the grown-ups were so much more interesting; their conversation appeared to be about such important things. The laughter at their table sounded so sophisticated." She rolled her eyes in mock teenage disgust. "By the time I was 15, I couldn't believe Mom was still seating me with the babies."

"When did you finally graduate to the grown-ups' table?" I asked.

"Not 'til I was 16," she said, smiling at the memory. "I had told Mom I would die if I had to stand another year of humiliation."

"And?" I asked expectantly. "Was it everything you hoped it would be?"

"It was awful!" Janie said, laughing. "I couldn't believe I'd waited so long for something so boring. Everything they talked about was incredibly dull—golf handicaps, stocks, bonds, politics. The jokes were corny and Uncle Peter even talked with his mouth full!"

"Horrors!" I gasped.

We dissolved in giggles just as dinner was being announced. Our classmates began filing into the banquet hall. "Come on," I said, linking my arm in hers. "Let's go blow bubbles in our milk and pile peas on our knives."

Source: Bedford, Faith Andrews. "Turning the Tables at Thanksgiving. *Country Living,* November 2004.

The Rewards of Extending Charity on Thanksgiving (2005)

As contemporary Americans count their blessings at Thanksgiving, many feel inspired to offer food and other forms of assistance to those less fortunate than themselves. For instance, many people spend a portion of the Thanksgiving holiday serving dinner to strangers at homeless shelters, veterans' hospitals, or senior citizen centers. In this 2005 article for the Indianapolis Business Journal, *entitled "Go Beyond the Turkey on Thanksgiving," Tawn Parent describes her rewarding experiences as a volunteer for Meals on Wheels and encourages others to view the holiday as an opportunity for charity.*

Too much enthusiasm can do you in.

Three years ago, my family volunteered to deliver Thanksgiving dinner for Meals on Wheels. In a moment of excessive gusto, I decided we should throw ourselves into the holiday spirit for the occasion. We spent days practicing "Over the River and Through the Woods," with which we planned to enchant recipients at each stop. On the big day, I stuffed my two-year-old into a fringed Indian costume, against his will. My husband, reluctantly, and I, with more eagerness, donned the ridiculously large Pilgrim headwear I had painstakingly crafted.

Once on the road, my son's mood turned from bad to worse. He kicked and screamed whenever we tried to remove him from the car, so we finally gave up. My husband and I took turns delivering the meals solo, sans musical accompaniment.

Although I was disappointed by the failure of my grand plans, I still enjoyed myself, and the clients seemed delighted with the meals, the visits and, to a lesser extent, the hats.

That is one of many memorable moments from the eight years I have volunteered for Meals on Wheels. I sit on the board as well as delivering meals with my family and/or with co-workers who are part of the IBJ [*Indianapolis Business Journal*] delivery squad.

Meals on Wheels' mission appeals to me because it's about much more than the food. It's about people who are elderly or disabled being able to remain in

© 2005 *Indianapolis Business Journal.* Reprinted with permission.

their homes instead of going into an institution. It's about couples being able to stay together. It's about dignity. And it's about connecting with people and having fun.

I have met some real characters over the years. One of our most colorful clients was "Elvira." Whenever I knocked on her door, she would shout, "Come on!" so vigorously that at first I feared I was interrupting a domestic dispute. But I soon learned it was her standard greeting. The first time I brought along my stepdaughter, then 6, Elvira shrieked with delight. "Get the baby a Coke! Get the baby a Coke!" she shouted to a visiting friend. We enjoyed the Coke and the conversation. Eight years later, my stepdaughter remembers it still. And an IBJ colleague will never forget the time Elvira answered the door in her birthday suit.

> *M*EALS ON WHEELS' MISSION APPEALS TO ME BECAUSE IT'S ABOUT MUCH MORE THAN THE FOOD. IT'S ABOUT PEOPLE WHO ARE ELDERLY OR DISABLED BEING ABLE TO REMAIN IN THEIR HOMES INSTEAD OF GOING INTO AN INSTITUTION. IT'S ABOUT COUPLES BEING ABLE TO STAY TOGETHER. IT'S ABOUT DIGNITY.

Other favorites are the two elderly sisters who live together in a stately house near The Children's Museum of Indianapolis. The ramp at their house has been an irresistible draw for my son. We made a delivery there when he was first learning to walk. We handed the packages of food to "Agnes" and then my son began his long, faltering walk down the ramp. After several minutes, he finally reached the bottom. As I took hold of his hand, I looked up and saw Agnes still standing there, smiling and waving. I think her day had just been made.

And there's "Joe," who listens to opera so loud he doesn't usually hear us until the third knock.

Then there are the times nobody answers the door. That typically happens at least once every time I deliver the route. So I dutifully call it in to the Meals on Wheels office, which contacts the client's family. Usually, it turns out the client was at the doctor or some other appointment. But about once a month, a call from a driver signals an emergency—a client has taken a bad fall or suffered a heart attack. I wonder sometimes whether a call from me has ever prompted such a discovery.

At its best, volunteer work involves much more than time. It creates relationships and memories that last. I'm grateful Meals on Wheels has given me that. What about you?

I invite you to make a Thanksgiving resolution: If you give time to a charitable effort that has real meaning for you, take this opportunity to deepen your involvement. And if you don't have such a connection, start looking for one....

Because Thanksgiving is about much more than the food, right?

Source: Parent, Tawn. "Go Beyond the Turkey on Thanksgiving." *Indianapolis Business Journal*, November 21, 2005.

Thanksgiving Thrives
Despite Pressures of the Modern World (2006)

Despite all of the changes that have occurred through the centuries, the Thanksgiving holiday still holds a deep emotional appeal for many Americans, as this 2006 New York Times *editorial makes clear.*

Is this the year Thanksgiving becomes nothing more than the prelude to tomorrow's shopping? Will we soon be calling the fourth Thursday in November Black Friday Eve? Probably not. But we may need a richer set of Thanksgiving traditions, an enlarged sense of the day, as a last defense against Christmas—perhaps even a bigger Thanksgiving songbook so that we don't find ourselves surprised by Bing Crosby singing "White Christmas" in a crosstown cab in early November. Lovely song, but heard too early in the season it causes private despair instead of commercial elation.

This is the day when all our impulses collide. We work hectically to fit the holiday in—hectic flying, hectic driving, hectic shopping and cooking—and yet we hope somehow that we will be sitting down, come dinner, to a full-fledged, old-fashioned Norman Rockwell "Freedom From Want" feast, with a roasted turkey that fulfills our emotional needs and embodies the permanence of our familial and communal bonds reaching right back to the 17th century. It may be too much to ask of one day and one bird and one set of relatives.

And yet all that fervor to be getting somewhere, to come to some quiet point of mutual celebration in the day suggests that Thanksgiving is still thriving. The light of late November registers deeply in nearly all of us. When dusk comes and yellow lights begin to shine out of the windows of houses upon a still largely snowless nation, you may begin to understand the force that has drawn us all together, bound by as much as love and as little as proximity.

Just when it feels as though we might be overlooking the meaning of this holiday—the peculiar value of Thanksgiving—it becomes clear that we have drawn together once again not to exchange the gifts our entire culture seems to be driving us to shop for but to share, simply, each other.

Source: *New York Times.* "Keeping Thanksgiving." November 23, 2006.

Copyright © 2006 by The New York Times Co. Reprinted with permission.

THANKSGIVING RECIPES

Appetizers

Stuffed Celery

INGREDIENTS

    1 bunch celery
    8 oz. package cream cheese
    small jar American cheese spread
    10-15 stuffed green olives, chopped

OPTIONAL ADD-IN:

    chopped green onions, to taste

DIRECTIONS

1. Separate stalks of celery, wash, slice off ends, then dry with paper towel.
2. Mix half of the cream cheese with half of the chopped green olives.
3. Mix half of the American cheese spread with the remaining chopped green olives.
4. Now there are four variations of stuffing for the celery: stuff 1/4 of the celery with plain cream cheese, 1/4 with cream cheese and olives, 1/4 with plain American cheese spread, and 1/4 with American cheese spread and olives.

Baked Pumpkin Seeds

INGREDIENTS

    2 cups pumpkin seeds
    2 teaspoons butter *or* margarine, melted
    salt to taste

DIRECTIONS

1. Heat oven to 300 degrees.
2. Place seeds, butter, and salt in a bowl and mix.
3. Spread seeds into a single layer on a cookie sheet and bake until golden, about 45 minutes. Stir about halfway through baking.

Seasoned Baked Pumpkin Seeds

INGREDIENTS

2 cups pumpkin seeds
2 teaspoons butter *or* margarine, melted
2 teaspoons Worcestershire sauce
¼ teaspoon garlic powder
salt to taste

DIRECTIONS

1. Heat oven to 300 degrees.
2. Place all ingredients in a bowl and mix.
3. Spread seeds into a single layer on a cookie sheet and bake about 45 minutes. Stir about halfway through baking.

Cheese Ball

INGREDIENTS

8 oz. package cream cheese
½ cup blue cheese, crumbled
1 cup sharp Cheddar cheese, shredded
½ small onion, finely chopped
1 teaspoon garlic powder
1 tablespoon Worcestershire sauce
½ cup chopped pecans

OPTIONAL ADD-INS:

¼ cup chopped green olives
¼ cup chopped parsley

DIRECTIONS

1. Place all ingredients, except pecans, into a bowl and beat together with mixer at medium speed until blended smoothly or place in a food processor and blend.
2. Shape mixture into a ball and roll in the pecans to coat.
3. Cover cheese ball and refrigerate for at least 4 hours.

Cheese Ball covered with nuts.

Sugar Coated Pecans

INGREDIENTS

1 egg white
1 tablespoon water
1 pound pecan halves
1 cup white sugar
¾ teaspoon salt
½ teaspoon ground cinnamon

DIRECTIONS

1. Preheat oven to 250° F (120° C). Grease one baking sheet.
2. In a mixing bowl, whip together the egg white and water until frothy. In a separate bowl, mix together sugar, salt, and cinnamon.
3. Add pecans to egg whites, stir to coat the nuts evenly. Remove the nuts, and toss them in the sugar mixture until coated. Spread the nuts out on the prepared baking sheet.
4. Bake at 250° F (120° C) for 1 hour. Stir every 15 minutes.

Turkey

Cooking and Handling Instructions

Twenty-first century cooks have popularized several methods of preparing turkey for the Thanksgiving meal. In addition to the traditional roasted turkey, other options include deep-fried, grilled, and smoked turkey, provided one has the necessary equipment. All guidelines and recipes for preparing turkey below, except for the Roasted Turkey recipe, are provided by the U.S. Department of Agriculture's Food Safety and Inspection Service. For more information about food safety (in English and Spanish), call:

USDA Meat and Poultry Hotline, 1-888-MPHotline (1-888-674-6854) or TTY: 1-800-256-7072, available 10:00 a.m. to 4:00 p.m. Eastern time, Monday through Friday, http://www.fsis.usda.gov.

Let's Talk Turkey— A Consumer Guide to Safely Roasting a Turkey

Fresh or Frozen?

Fresh Turkeys

- Allow 1 pound of turkey per person.
- Buy your turkey only 1 to 2 days before you plan to cook it.
- Keep it stored in the refrigerator until you're ready to cook it. Place it on a tray or in a pan to catch any juices that may leak.

Do not buy fresh pre-stuffed turkeys. If not handled properly, any harmful bacteria that may be in the stuffing can multiply very quickly.

Frozen Turkeys

- Allow 1 pound of turkey per person.
- Keep frozen until you're ready to thaw it.
- Turkeys can be kept frozen in the freezer indefinitely; however, cook within 1 year for best quality.

See "Thawing Your Turkey" for thawing instructions.

Thawing Your Turkey

There are three ways to thaw your turkey safely—in the refrigerator, in cold water, or in the microwave oven.

In the Refrigerator (40 °F or below)
Allow approximately 24 hours for every 4 to 5 pounds

4 to 12 pounds	1 to 3 days
12 to 16 pounds	3 to 4 days
16 to 20 pounds	4 to 5 days
20 to 24 pounds	5 to 6 days

Keep the turkey in its original wrapper. Place it on a tray or in a pan to catch any juices that may leak. A thawed turkey can remain in the refrigerator for 1 to 2 days. If necessary, a turkey that has been properly thawed in the refrigerator may be refrozen.

In Cold Water
Allow approximately 30 minutes per pound

4 to 12 pounds	2 to 6 hours
12 to 16 pounds	6 to 8 hours
16 to 20 pounds	8 to 10 hours
20 to 24 pounds	10 to 12 hours

Wrap your turkey securely, making sure the water is not able to leak through the wrapping. Submerge your wrapped turkey in cold tap water. Change the water every 30 minutes. Cook the turkey immediately after it is thawed. Do not refreeze.

In the Microwave Oven

- Check your owner's manual for the size turkey that will fit in your microwave oven, the minutes per pound, and power level to use for thawing.
- Remove all outside wrapping.
- Place on a microwave-safe dish to catch any juices that may leak.
- Cook your turkey immediately. Do not refreeze or refrigerate your turkey after thawing in the microwave oven.

REMINDER: Remove the giblets from the turkey cavities after thawing. Cook separately.

Frozen Pre-Stuffed Turkeys

USDA recommends only buying frozen pre-stuffed turkeys that display the USDA or State mark of inspection on the packaging. These turkeys are safe because they have been processed under controlled conditions.

DO NOT THAW before cooking. Cook from the frozen state. Follow package directions for proper handling and cooking.

Allow 1¼ pounds of turkey per person.

Roasting Your Turkey

- Set your oven temperature no lower than 325 °F.

- Place your turkey or turkey breast on a rack in a shallow roasting pan.

- For optimum safety, stuffing a turkey is not recommended. For more even cooking, it is recommended you cook your stuffing outside the bird in a casserole. Use a food thermometer to check the internal temperature of the stuffing. The stuffing must reach a safe minimum internal temperature of 165 °F.

- If you choose to stuff your turkey, the ingredients can be prepared ahead of time; however, keep wet and dry ingredients separate. Chill all of the wet ingredients (butter/margarine, cooked celery and onions, broth, etc.). Mix wet and dry ingredients just before filling the turkey cavities. Fill the cavities loosely. Cook the turkey immediately. Use a food thermometer to make sure the center of the stuffing reaches a safe minimum internal temperature of 165 °F.

- A whole turkey is safe when cooked to a minimum internal temperature of 165 °F as measured with a food thermometer. Check the internal temperature in the innermost part of the thigh and wing and the thickest part of the breast. For reasons of personal preference, consumers may choose to cook turkey to higher temperatures.

- If your turkey has a "pop-up" temperature indicator, it is recommended that you also check the internal temperature of the turkey in the innermost part of the thigh and wing and the thickest part of the breast with a food thermometer. The minimum internal temperature should reach 165 °F for safety.

261

Basting the turkey.

- For quality, let the turkey stand for 20 minutes before carving to allow juices to set. The turkey will carve more easily.

- Remove all stuffing from the turkey cavities.

Optional Cooking Hints

- Tuck wing tips under the shoulders of the bird for more even cooking. This is referred to as "akimbo."

- Add 1/2 cup of water to the bottom of the pan.

- If your roasting pan does not have a lid, you may place a tent of heavy-duty aluminum foil over the turkey for the first 1 to 1 1/2 hours. This allows for maximum heat circulation, keeps the turkey moist, and reduces oven splatter. To prevent overbrowning, foil may also be placed over the turkey after it reaches the desired color.

- If using an oven-proof food thermometer, place it in the turkey at the start of the cooking cycle. It will allow you to check the internal temperature of the turkey while it is cooking. For turkey breasts, place thermometer in the thickest part. For whole turkeys, place in the thickest part of the inner thigh. Once the thigh has reached 165 °F, check the wing and the thickest part of the breast to ensure the turkey has reached a safe minimum internal temperature of 165 °F throughout the product.

- If using an oven cooking bag, follow the manufacturer's guidelines on the package.

REMEMBER! Always wash hands, utensils, the sink, and anything else that comes in contact with raw turkey and its juices with soap and water.

- Discard any turkey, stuffing, and gravy left out at room temperature longer than 2 hours; 1 hour in temperatures above 90 °F.
- Divide leftovers into smaller portions. Refrigerate or freeze in covered shallow containers for quicker cooling.
- Use refrigerated turkey and stuffing within 3 to 4 days. Use gravy within 1 to 2 days.
- If freezing leftovers, use within 2 to 6 months for best quality.

Reheating Your Turkey

Cooked turkey may be eaten cold or reheated.

In the Oven

- Set the oven temperature no lower than 325 °F.
- Reheat turkey to an internal temperature of 165 °F. Use a food thermometer to check the internal temperature.
- To keep the turkey moist, add a little broth or water and cover.

In the Microwave Oven

- Cover your food and rotate it for even heating. Allow standing time.
- Check the internal temperature of your food with a food thermometer to make sure it reaches 165 °F.
- Consult your microwave oven owner's manual for recommended times and power levels.

Timetables for Turkey Roasting
(325 °F oven temperature)

Use the timetables below to determine how long to cook your turkey. These times are approximate. Always use a food thermometer to check the internal temperature of your turkey and stuffing.

Unstuffed

8 to 12 pounds	2¾ to 3 hours
12 to 14 pounds	3 to 3¾ hours
14 to 18 pounds	3¾ to 4¼ hours
18 to 20 pounds	4¼ to 4½ hours
20 to 24 pounds	4½ to 5 hours

Stuffed

8 to 12 pounds	3 to 3½ hours
12 to 14 pounds	3½ to 4 hours
14 to 18 pounds	4 to 4¼ hours
18 to 20 pounds	4¼ to 4¾ hours
20 to 24 pounds	4¾ to 5¼ hours

It is safe to cook a turkey from the frozen state. The cooking time will take **at least 50 percent longer** than recommended for a fully thawed turkey. Remember to remove the giblet packages during the cooking time. Remove carefully with tongs or a fork.

Roasted Turkey

INGREDIENTS

> 1 thawed turkey with giblets removed
> 1 stick butter

DIRECTIONS

1. Heat oven to 325 degrees.
2. Rinse turkey with water, then place it breast side up into a large roasting pan.
3. If stuffing the turkey, place stuffing into both ends, but stuff the turkey loosely, since the stuffing will expand during baking.
4. Melt 1 stick butter and brush or drizzle all over the turkey.
5. Baste the turkey about every half hour with the butter and juices from the bottom of the roasting pan.
6. See timetable above, in **Guide to Safely Roasting a Turkey**, for cooking time.

Deep-Fried Turkey

A whole turkey can be successfully cooked by the deep fat frying method provided the turkey is **not** stuffed and has been completely thawed. The turkey should be 12 pounds or less in size.

There are safety concerns when working with such a large amount of oil. Select a cooking vessel large enough to completely submerge the turkey in oil without it spilling over. The oil should cover the turkey by 1 to 2 inches. To determine the amount of oil needed, do a preliminary test using water. Place the turkey in the cooking utensil and add water to cover. Then remove the turkey and measure the amount of water. This is the amount of oil needed.

Select a safe location outdoors for deep fat frying a turkey. Heat the cooking oil to 350° F. Slowly and carefully lower the turkey into the hot oil. Monitor the temperature of the oil with a thermometer constantly during cooking. Never leave the hot oil unattended. Allow approximately 3 to 5 minutes per pound cooking time. Remove turkey from the oil and drain oil from the cavity. Check the temperature of turkey with a food thermometer. The turkey is safely cooked when the food thermometer reaches a minimum internal temperature of 165° F in the innermost part of the thigh and wing and the thickest part of the breast.

Stuffed Roasted Turkey.

If the turkey is not done, immediately return the turkey to the hot oil for additional cooking. When the turkey is done, remove it from the oil and place it on a sturdy tray lined with paper towels. The skin can be golden to dark brown to almost black. Let it rest about 20 minutes before carving.

Allow the used oil to cool before pouring it into containers for refrigerator storage. The oil can be reused if it is strained, covered, and used within a month.

Grilled Turkey

Outdoor cooking of a big bird for the holiday meal is becoming a popular cooking method. During grilling, a turkey cooks by indirect heat in an outdoor covered gas or charcoal grill and a pan of water is placed beneath the grilling surface to catch the fat and juices that drip from the turkey as it cooks. Cooking is done by the hot, smoky, steamy air.

Covered Charcoal Grill

Turkeys that are 16 pounds or less are the recommended size for safe grilling. A larger turkey remains in the "Danger Zone"—between 40 and 140 °F—too long. **Do not stuff the turkey.** Because cooking is at a low temperature, it can take too long for the temperature of the stuffing to reach 165 °F. Also, smoked stuffing has an undesirable flavor.

Begin with clean equipment and a good quality charcoal. Build a pyramid of charcoal to one side. Ignite the charcoal, and let the coals get red hot. Place an appliance thermometer on the food rack to monitor the air temperature inside the grill. When the charcoal has developed white powdery ash—about 20 to 30 minutes—and the air temperature reaches 225 to 300 °F, place a drip pan (with water in it to create moist, hot steam for cooking), in the center of the grill beneath where the turkey will be set and carefully push the hot coals evenly around the edge. Position the grill rack and place the prepared turkey on it (breast side up). Then place the cover on the grill.

Replenish with about 15 briquettes every hour as needed to maintain 225 to 300 °F. If desired, add water-soaked hardwood or fruitwood, in the form of chunks or chips, to add flavor to the turkey as it is cooking. **Do not** use a softwood (pine, fir, cedar, or spruce) because it gives the food a turpentine flavor and coats it with a black pitch or resin.

Cooking times depend on many factors: the size and shape of the turkey, the distance from the heat, temperature of the coals, and the temperature of the outside air. Always use a food thermometer. The turkey is done when the food thermometer reaches a safe minimum internal temperature of 165 °F in the innermost part of the thigh and wing and the thickest part of the breast. Estimate 15 to 18 minutes per pound if using a covered grill. A whole turkey can be successfully cooked, provided the turkey is not stuffed and has been completely thawed.

Covered Gas Grill
Gas grills have become very popular in the last few years. The gas heat can be supplied by either propane tanks or by natural gas piped from the home.

If your gas grill has only one large burner, place a pan of water under the grate to create indirect heat. Place the turkey in a roasting pan and place on top of the grill.

If the grill has two or three burners, the turkey should be placed away from the flame. This can be done by turning off one of the burners and placing the turkey in that area. When using a gas grill, always follow manufacturer's directions for cooking times.

Smoked Turkey

Most smokers are cylinder-shaped devices and use either electricity, gas, or charcoal for heat. Follow manufacturer's directions for gas or electric smokers.

Charcoal smokers have two pans—one for charcoal and one for liquid. Smokers require a liquid to create the moist, hot smoke needed for cooking. When using a charcoal smoker, fill the pan for liquid with water, wine, apple juice, or the liquid you desire. Fill the charcoal pan with a good quality charcoal. Light the charcoal and place the cover on the smoker. When the smoker has reached an internal temperature of 225 to 300 °F, quickly place the turkey on the smoker rack and replace the cover. (Some smokers have built in temperature indicators. If yours does not, place an appliance thermometer on the smoker rack before starting your heat source.) Add charcoal every 1 to 2 hours, as necessary, to maintain 225 to 300 °F. Replenish the liquid as necessary. Heat and liquid are critical to maintaining the hot smoke that cooks the turkey.

When cooking with a smoker, start with clean equipment. Place the smoker in an area shielded from winds to maintain a safe cooking temperature. If desired, add water-soaked hardwood or fruitwood, in the form of chunks or chips, to add flavor to the turkey. **Do not** use a softwood (pine, fir, cedar, or spruce) as it gives the food a turpentine flavor and coats it with a black pitch or resin.

Cooking times depend on many factors: the size and shape of the turkey, the distance from the heat, temperature from the coals, and temperature of the outside air. Completely thaw the turkey before cooking. Estimate 20 to 30 minutes per pound if using a smoker. **Do not stuff the turkey.** Because smoking cooks at a low temperature, it can take too long for the temperature of the stuffing to reach 165 °F. Also, smoked stuffing has an undesirable flavor. Always use a food thermometer. The turkey is safely cooked when the food thermometer reaches a safe minimum internal temperature of 165 °F in the innermost part of the thigh and wing and the thickest part of the breast.

Turducken

The "turducken" is a deboned stuffed chicken inside a deboned stuffed duck inside a deboned stuffed turkey. The name is comprised of syllables from the words "turkey," "duck," and "chicken." Usually the tip end of the turkey leg bones and the first two wing joints are left on the turkey so that after assembly, the finished product resembles a whole turkey. Alternatively, the finished turducken can be a completely boneless roll with stuffing layered between each bird.

Stuffings may include cornbread dressing, sausage stuffing, oyster dressing, alligator, crawfish and shrimp. To serve, the roasted turducken is sliced crosswise so that servings consist of all the layers.

The idea for this multilayered, deboned fowl came from Louisiana, where thousands of them are commercially prepared yearly. Turduckens are prepared in other states as well, and consumers also debone poultry and assemble them in home kitchens.

Critical control points involved in handling this risky assemblage are many, especially if the dish is made by a consumer and not in a USDA-inspected plant. Safe steps in food handling, cooking, and storage are essential to prevent foodborne illness. You can't see, smell, or taste harmful bacteria that may cause illness. In every step of food preparation, follow the four Fight BAC!® guidelines to keep food safe:

- Clean—Wash hands and surfaces often.
- Separate—Don't cross-contaminate.
- Cook—Cook to proper temperatures.
- Chill—Refrigerate promptly.

As when cooking any meat or poultry product, USDA strongly recommends using a food thermometer to ensure the turducken has reached a safe minimum internal temperature of 165 °F throughout the product. Here are specific recommendations from the USDA Meat and Poultry Hotline for safely handling and cooking turduckens.

Safe Handling of Turducken Ingredients

- When creating a turducken at home, bring the raw birds directly home from the store and refrigerate (40 °F or below) immediately—within 2 hours (1 hour when the temperature is above 90 °F).

- Make sure the raw poultry is wrapped securely and place it on a plate or casserole dish to prevent cross-contamination, or raw juices from getting onto ready-to-eat food.

- Store the raw turkey, duck, and chicken no longer than 2 days before deboning, assembling and cooking.

- If the turducken has been purchased through mail order, make sure it arrives frozen with a cold source in an insulated carton. Transfer it immediately to the freezer. If the turducken arrives warm, notify the company. **Do not use the product.**

Creating a Turducken

- Before and after handling any raw meat or poultry, always wash hands in warm, soapy water for 20 seconds.

- While handling and deboning the three birds, keep the raw poultry and their juices away from other food.

- Make the stuffing immediately before assembling the turducken.

- Make sure the birds and stuffing are not out of the refrigerator in the "Danger Zone"—between 40 and 140 °F—more than 2 hours while assembling the turducken.

- Pack the stuffing loosely, not too tightly, to promote efficient heat transfer during cooking.

- After cutting raw poultry, wash cutting board, knife, and counter tops with hot, soapy water.

- After washing, you may choose to sanitize cutting boards by using a solution of 1 tablespoon of unscented, liquid chlorine bleach per 1 gallon of water.

- Another good and easy way to wash the cutting board is to run it through the dishwasher after use. Non-porous acrylic, plastic, glass and solid wood boards can be washed in a dishwasher (laminated boards may crack and split).

Roasting the Turducken and Handling Leftovers

- For home-prepared turducken, roast immediately after assembly.

- Roast the turducken in an oven set no lower than 325 °F.

- When roasting a purchased USDA-inspected turducken, follow the package directions.
- When roasting a purchased frozen turducken without package directions, cook from the frozen state in an oven set no lower than 325 °F to a safe minimum internal temperature of 165 °F to ensure a safely cooked product.
- Use a food thermometer to ensure that all layers of the turducken and stuffing reach a minimum safe internal temperature of 165 °F. The thermometer should be placed at the center of the thickest part of the turducken to determine the safe internal temperature.
- Slice and serve the cooked turducken within 2 hours after cooking. If it is not intended to be served within 2 hours then slice and cut in smaller portions before putting in the refrigerator to cool fast. A whole cooked turducken may not cool to a safe temperature within the time needed to prevent bacterial growth.
- After slicing and serving the turducken, refrigerate any leftovers in a shallow container within 2 hours of cooking. Perishable food should not be left out more than 2 hours at room temperature (1 hour when the temperature is above 90 °F).
- Use the leftovers within 3 to 4 days after cooking or freeze for longer storage.

Gravy

Homemade Turkey Gravy

INGREDIENTS

Drippings and broth from turkey in roasting pan
4 to 6 tablespoons flour
Giblets, finely chopped
Salt and pepper to taste

DIRECTIONS

1. Remove turkey from roasting pan after fully cooked.
2. Pour broth into a separate bowl and leave solid drippings in pan.
3. Over low medium heat, gradually stir flour, tablespoon by tablespoon, into pan and mix well with drippings.

4. Add giblets and keep stirring for 1-2 minutes.
5. Slowly add turkey broth, stirring constantly.
6. Stir in salt and pepper.
7. Bring to a boil and stir until smooth and thickened.

17ᵗʰ-Century Onion Gravy

INGREDIENTS

5-6 onions, chopped or sliced thin
1 tablespoon sugar
¼ cup red vinegar
2 teaspoons pepper
1 teaspoon salt
2 cups water

DIRECTIONS

1. Boil onions and salt in water until tender.
2. Remove cooked turkey from roasting pan and place pan over medium heat and stir up drippings.
3. Add boiled onions, sugar, vinegar, and pepper and heat to desired consistency.

Stuffings

Sage Stuffing

This recipe makes enough stuffing to both stuff a turkey (for moist stuffing) and fill a 3-quart casserole (for crustier stuffing).

Ingredients

½ loaf white bread
½ package seasoned stuffing croutons
1 lb. pork sausage
1 onion, diced
4 stalks celery, diced
1 large egg
1 can chicken broth
1 stick butter *or* margarine, melted
2 tablespoons ground sage

Optional add-ins:

2 chopped apples
1 cup raisins
1 cup dried cherries
1 cup walnuts *or* pecans

Directions

1. Tear slices of bread into smaller pieces and divide evenly into two large bowls. Mix seasoned stuffing croutons into each bowl and set aside.
2. In large skillet fry pork sausage, onion, and celery until sausage is cooked through and vegetables are tender.
3. In medium bowl mix egg, chicken broth, butter, and sage.
4. Pour half the sausage, vegetables and any optional add-ins into one bowl and half into the other.
5. Pour half the egg mix into each bowl.
6. Mix both bowls of stuffing.
7. Stuff turkey and place remaining stuffing into casserole to bake separately. Bake casserole stuffing at 350 degrees for 30-40 minutes.

Cornbread Stuffing

Ingredients

8 cups crumbled cornbread
4 slices white bread torn into pieces *or* seasoned stuffing croutons
1 onion, chopped
4 stalks celery, chopped
½ green pepper, chopped
2 tablespoons ground sage
1 stick butter *or* margerine
½ cup cooked turkey giblets
1 teaspoon thyme
1 can chicken broth
water

Directions

1. Mix cornbread, white bread (or croutons), and giblets in large bowl and set aside.

Ingredients for making cornbread stuffing: onions, eggs, cornbread.

2. Saute onion, celery, green pepper and spices in butter in large skillet until tender.
3. Mix vegetables and chicken broth into bread mixture. Add water if desired.
4. Place stuffing into turkey or bake in casserole at 400 degrees for 25-30 minutes.

Wild Rice Stuffing

INGREDIENTS

2 packages instant wild and long grain rice
4 slices bacon
1 onion, chopped
3 stalks of celery, chopped
1 package fresh mushrooms, sliced
1 egg, beaten
½ teaspoon garlic powder

DIRECTIONS

1. Cook rice according to package instructions.
2. Fry bacon until crisp, then remove and crumble into pieces.
3. Saute onion, celery, and mushrooms in bacon drippings.
4. Sprinkle garlic into vegetables.
5. Mix all ingredients in large bowl.
6. Place stuffing in turkey or lightly grease a 13x9x2 baking dish, place stuffing in baking dish, cover, and bake at 325 degrees for 25-30 minutes or until lightly browned.

Hawaiian/Chinese-American Rice Stuffing

INGREDIENTS

2½ cups Chinese or Japanese mochi rice (sticky sweet rice)
2½ cups water (for cooking rice)
½ lb. Chinese sausage (lup cheong), chopped
1 onion, chopped
6-8 green onions, chopped
1 cup water chestnuts, cooked, peeled, and chopped

1 tablespoon peanut oil

2 tablespoons soy sauce

OPTIONAL ADD-INS:

½ cup black-eyed peas, cooked

1 cup shiitake mushrooms, chopped

3 slices bacon, cooked crisp and chopped

DIRECTIONS

1. In large bowl soak rice in enough cold water to cover it by 1 inch. Soak rice for at least one hour.
2. After soaking, drain rice, rinse with fresh water, and drain again.
3. Place rice in large saucepan, and add 2½ cups water. Bring to a boil, cover, and reduce heat to simmer for about 20 minutes, or until rice is tender.
4. In a large skillet or wok heat peanut oil and sauté sausage and white onion (and mushrooms and peas, if including) about 5 minutes, or until sausage is cooked and onion is tender.
5. Stir in green onions and water chestnuts (and bacon, if including), then remove from heat.
6. Mix in rice and soy sauce.
7. Mix well and serve as is or place into turkey as stuffing.

Oyster Stuffing

INGREDIENTS

1 pint raw oysters, chopped (save about ½ juice)

10-12 slices bread, torn up

1 stick butter *or* margarine

1 onion, chopped

3 stalks celery, chopped

1 teaspoon thyme

1 teaspoon poultry seasoning

DIRECTIONS

1. Saute onions and celery in butter until tender.
2. In large bowl, mix sautéed vegetables, spices, oysters and juice, and bread crumbs.
3. Place stuffing in turkey or into greased 13x9x2 baking dish and bake at 350 degrees for 30 minutes.

Side Dishes

Mashed Potatoes

INGREDIENTS

8-10 potatoes, peeled and quartered
½ cup milk
¼ cup butter *or* margarine

DIRECTIONS

1. Boil potatoes in water until tender.
2. Drain water from saucepan.
3. Add milk and butter, then mash to desired consistency.

Garlic Mashed Potatoes

INGREDIENTS

8 medium red potatoes, quartered
3 cloves garlic, peeled
2 tablespoons butter
½ cup milk, warmed
½ teaspoon salt
¼ cup grated Parmesan cheese

DIRECTIONS

1. Place potatoes and garlic in a large saucepan; cover with water. Bring to a boil. Reduce heat; cover, and simmer for 20-25 minutes or until the potatoes are very tender. Drain well.
2. Add the butter, milk and salt; mash. Stir in Parmesan cheese.

Green Bean and French-Fried Onion Casserole

INGREDIENTS

4 lbs fresh green beans, ends snipped, cut in 1 inch pieces
2 cans cream of mushroom soup
milk

Green Bean and French-Fried Onion Casserole
using fresh green beans is a frequent part of the Thanksgiving feast.

2 teaspoons soy sauce
1½ cups French-fried onions

DIRECTIONS

1. Parboil green beans for about 4 minutes.
2. In 3-quart casserole mix soup, 2 soup cans full of milk, and soy sauce.
3. Mix in green beans and 1 cup French-fried onions.
4. Bake at 350 degrees for 20 minutes.
5. Sprinkle remaining onions on top and bake 10 more minutes.

Succotash

INGREDIENTS

2 cups frozen lima beans

278

2 cups frozen corn
1 can creamed corn
½ cup red pepper, chopped
1 tablespoon butter *or* margarine
Salt and pepper, to taste

DIRECTIONS

1. In a saucepan saute red pepper in butter until tender.
2. Add remaining ingredients and cook until tender.

Candied Yams

INGREDIENTS

6 yams or sweet potatoes
½ cup brown sugar
2 tablespoons butter *or* margarine
3 tablespoons water
½ teaspoon salt

DIRECTIONS

1. Boil potatoes in enough water to cover them. Cook until tender, about 30 minutes.
2. Remove yams or sweet potatoes from pan, remove skins, and slice.
3. Mix brown sugar, butter, water, and salt into a skillet and cook over medium heat until bubbly.
4. Stir in yams or sweet potatoes until covered with glaze and heated.

Sweet Potato Casserole

INGREDIENTS

4 cups sweet potato, cubed
½ cup white sugar
2 eggs, beaten
½ teaspoon salt
4 tablespoons butter, softened
½ cup milk

½ teaspoon vanilla extract
½ cup packed brown sugar
⅓ cup all-purpose flour
3 tablespoons butter, softened
½ cup chopped pecans

DIRECTIONS

1. Preheat oven to 325° F (165° C). Put sweet potatoes in a medium saucepan with water to cover. Cook over medium high heat until tender; drain and mash.
2. In a large bowl, mix together the sweet potatoes, sugar, eggs, salt, butter, milk and vanilla. Mix until smooth. Transfer to a 9x13 inch baking dish.
3. In medium bowl, mix the sugar and flour. Cut in the butter until the mixture is coarse. Stir in the pecans. Sprinkle the mixture over the sweet potato mixture.
4. Bake in the preheated oven 30 minutes, or until the topping is lightly brown.

Cranberry Sauce

INGREDIENTS

1 lb. fresh cranberries
2 cups sugar
2 cups water
zest from 1 orange

DIRECTIONS

1. In a saucepan heat sugar and water to boiling, stirring and boiling for about 5 minutes.
2. Add cranberries and orange zest; continue stirring and boiling until cranberry skins begin to pop.
3. Remove from heat and chill for about 3 hours.

Breads and Rolls

Baking Powder Biscuits

INGREDIENTS

2 cups flour
3 teaspoons baking powder
¾ cup milk
½ cup shortening *or* margarine
1 tablespoon sugar
1 teaspoon salt

DIRECTIONS

1. Combine dry ingredients in a large bowl.
2. Cut shortening into mixture with a pastry blender until well combined and crumbly.
3. Stir in milk until dough is soft and sticky.
4. On a floured surface knead dough 10 times.
5. Roll out dough or pat down to about ½-inch thick.
6. Cut dough into 12 pieces.
7. Place biscuits onto ungreased cookie sheet.
8. Bake in 450-degree oven for 10-12 minutes, until golden brown.

Corn Bread

INGREDIENTS

1 cup all-purpose flour
1 cup yellow corn meal
¼ cup brown sugar (be generous!)
2 teaspoons baking powder
½ teaspoon salt (optional)
1 cup skim milk
¼ cup vegetable oil
2 egg whites *or* 1 egg, beaten

DIRECTIONS

1. Heat oven to 400 degrees.

Pumpkin Bread.

2. Grease 8-inch or 9-inch pan.
3. Combine dry ingredients.
4. Stir in milk, oil, and egg, mixing just until dry ingredients are moistened.
5. Pour batter into prepared pan.
6. Bake 20 to 25 minutes until golden brown and a wooden toothpick inserted in the center comes out clean. Serve warm.

Pumpkin Bread

INGREDIENTS

3 cups sugar
1 cup salad oil
4 eggs
2 cups pumpkin
⅔ cup water

3½ cups flour
2 teaspoons baking soda
1½ teaspoon salt
1 teaspoon cinnamon
1 teaspoon nutmeg

DIRECTIONS

1. Beat eggs in medium bowl.
2. In a large bowl mix sugar, salad oil, pumpkin and water, then add in eggs slowly.
3. In a separate bowl combine and sift flour, baking soda, salt, cinnamon, and nutmeg.
4. Mix wet and dry ingredients thoroughly.
5. Pour batter into 3 greased and floured bread pans.
6. Bake at 350 degrees for one hour.

Cranberry Corn Muffins

INGREDIENTS

1 package of cornbread mix
1 cup whole cranberry sauce

DIRECTIONS

1. Prepare cornbread mix according to package instructions.
2. Stir in cranberry sauce
3. Spoon mixture into paper muffin liners in muffin tin.
4. Bake according to package instructions.

Thanksgiving Dinner Rolls

INGREDIENTS

1 package (.25 ounce) active dry yeast
¼ cup warm water
1 pinch white sugar
½ cup white sugar
2 eggs

1 cup warm water
½ cup vegetable oil
1 teaspoon salt
4 cups all-purpose flour

DIRECTIONS

1. In a large bowl, stir yeast, ¼ cup warm water, and a pinch of sugar.
2. In another bowl, beat eggs in 1 cup warm water; add oil and salt. Mix egg mixture into yeast, and add sugar. Gradually add flour.
3. Cover with a damp cloth, and allow to stand at room temperature for 1 hour, then place in the refrigerator and allow to rise overnight. This dough is rather sticky, and will raise to at least twice its size.
4. Divide the dough into 4 equal parts. Roll each section out into a circle on a floured board or wax paper. Cut into pizza slice shapes, and roll slices large end to small end. Place on greased flat baking pans, and allow to rise for 2 hours.
5. Bake at 375° F (190° C) for 8 minutes.

Desserts

Apple Pie

INGREDIENTS

2 9-inch refrigerated pie crusts
6 medium apples, peeled, cored, and thinly sliced
2 tablespoons butter *or* margarine
¾ cup sugar
¼ cup flour
½ teaspoon ground cinnamon
½ teaspoon ground nutmeg

DIRECTIONS

1. Heat oven to 425 degrees.
2. Mix dry ingredients.
3. Stir in apple slices.

Apple pie still life.

4. Arrange 1 pie crust into 9-inch pie pan.
5. Pour filling into pie pan and spread evenly.
6. Dot butter on top of filling.
7. Place second pie crust on top and cut a few slits into top crust.
8. Connect the top and bottom crusts and flute.
9. Bake 40-50 minutes or until crust is golden brown and filling is bubbly.

Sweet Potato Pie

INGREDIENTS

1 9-inch pie crust
4-5 sweet potatoes, peeled
1 12-oz. can evaporated milk
2 eggs
¾ cup sugar
2 tablespoons butter *or* margarine, melted
1 teaspoon cinnamon
½ teaspoon salt
½ teaspoon ground ginger
¼ teaspoon ground cloves

DIRECTIONS

1. Heat oven to 425 degrees.
2. Boil sweet potatoes until they can be mashed.
3. Mash sweet potatoes.
4. Beat eggs in large bowl.
5. Mix in remaining ingredients.
6. Pour mixture into pie crust.
7. Bake 40-50 minutes.

Pecan Pie

INGREDIENTS

1 9-inch pie crust
1 cup pecan pieces

3 eggs

1 cup corn syrup

⅔ cup sugar

⅓ cup butter *or* margarine, melted

½ teaspoon salt

DIRECTIONS

1. Heat oven to 375 degrees.
2. In large bowl beat all ingredients (except pecans) well.
3. Stir in pecan pieces.
4. Pour into pie shell.
5. Bake 45 minutes or until set.
6. Chill for at least two hours.

Pumpkin Pie

INGREDIENTS

1 9-inch pie crust

1 16-oz. can pumpkin pie filling

1 12-oz. can evaporated milk

2 eggs

¾ cup sugar

2 tablespoons butter *or* margarine, melted

1 teaspoon cinnamon

½ teaspoon salt

½ teaspoon ground ginger

¼ teaspoon ground cloves

DIRECTIONS

1. Heat oven to 425 degrees.
2. Beat eggs in a large bowl.
3. Mix remaining ingredients into bowl with eggs.
4. Pour mixture into pie crust.
5. Bake for 40-50 minutes.

A beautiful Pumpkin Pie ready to serve with whipped cream.

Ambrosia

INGREDIENTS

8-10 oranges, peeled and split into sections
1 20-oz. can pineapple chunks, drained
½ cup maraschino cherries, cut in half
⅓ cup sugar
1 cup flaked coconut

OPTIONAL ADD IN:

1 cup small marshmallows

DIRECTIONS

1. Mix all ingredients and chill.

Pumpkin Ice Cream

INGREDIENTS

½ gallon vanilla ice cream

1 16-oz. can pumpkin pie filling

1 teaspoon vanilla extract

¼ cup sugar

DIRECTIONS

1. Mix all ingredients in a large bowl.
2. Freeze for 2 hours.
3. Beat mixture on medium speed for 30 seconds.
4. Freeze for another 2 hours or until firm.

Cranberry Cheesecake

INGREDIENTS

1 9-inch graham cracker pie crust

1 8-oz. package cream cheese, softened

2 cups frozen whipped topping, thawed

1 cup fresh or frozen cranberries

½ cup sugar

⅛ teaspoon vanilla extract

DIRECTIONS

1. Beat cream cheese, whipped topping, sugar, and vanilla.
2. Stir in cranberries.
3. Pour mixture into pie crust.
4. Chill at least 2 hours.

Cranberry Orange Jell-O Salad

INGREDIENTS

1 can whole cranberry sauce

1 package orange-flavored gelatin

2 cups boiling water

1 cup sour cream

DIRECTIONS

1. Mix water and gelatin until gelatin is dissolved.

2. Stir in cranberry sauce.
3. Refrigerate until partially thickened.
4. Mix in sour cream and pour mixture into a 5-cup mold.
5. Chill until firm.

Beverages

Mulled Apple Cider

INGREDIENTS

1 gallon apple cider
2 cinnamon sticks
2 teaspoons whole cloves
2 teaspoon whole allspice
⅔ cup sugar
1 lemon *or* orange, thinly sliced

DIRECTIONS

1. Heat all ingredients except lemon (or orange) to boiling, then reduce heat and simmer for 15-20 minutes.
2. Strain punch and pour into heatproof punch bowl.
3. Float lemon or orange slices on top.

Apple Cranberry Cider

INGREDIENTS

1 quart apple cider
2 cups cranberry juice
⅓ cup packed brown sugar
4 whole cloves
2 cinnamon sticks (3 inches)

DIRECTIONS

1. In a large saucepan, combine the cider, cranberry juice and brown sugar. Place cloves and cinnamon sticks on a double thickness of cheesecloth; bring up corners of cloth and tie with kitchen string to form a bag. Add to pan.
2. Bring to a boil over medium heat. Reduce heat; simmer, uncovered, for 15-20 minutes. Discard spice bag before serving.

Mulled Apple Cider, shown with cinnamon sticks.

Cranberry Punch

INGREDIENTS

    2 quarts cranberry juice
    1 6-oz. can frozen pink lemonade, thawed
    1 32-oz. bottle sparkling water

DIRECTIONS

    1. Mix cranberry juice and lemonade into punch bowl.
    2. Mix in sparkling water just before serving.

Creamy Hot Chocolate

INGREDIENTS

    ⅓ cup unsweetened cocoa powder

¾ cup white sugar

1 pinch salt

⅓ cup boiling water

3½ cups milk

¾ teaspoon vanilla extract

½ cup half-and-half cream

DIRECTIONS

1. Combine the cocoa, sugar and pinch of salt in a saucepan. Blend in the boiling water.
2. Bring this mixture to an easy boil while you stir. Simmer and stir for about 2 minutes. Watch that it doesn't scorch.
3. Stir in 3½ cups of milk and heat until very hot, but do not boil! Remove from heat and add vanilla. Divide between 4 mugs.
4. Add the cream to the mugs of cocoa to cool it to drinking temperature

Mocha Coffee

INGREDIENTS

1 cup hot brewed coffee

1 tablespoon unsweetened cocoa powder

1 tablespoon white sugar

2 tablespoons milk

DIRECTIONS

1. Pour hot coffee into a mug. Stir in cocoa, sugar and milk.

Eggnog

INGREDIENTS

6 eggs, beaten

2¼ cups milk

⅓ cup white sugar

1 teaspoon vanilla extract

1 cup heavy whipping cream

2 teaspoons white sugar

1 pinch ground nutmeg

DIRECTIONS

1. In a large saucepan, combine the eggs, milk and ⅓ cup sugar. Cook and stir over medium heat until mixture coats a metal spoon.
2. Remove from heat. Cool quickly by placing pan in a sink or bowl of ice water and stirring 1 to 2 minutes. Stir in the vanilla. Chill 4 to 24 hours.
3. Before serving, whip the cream and 2 tablespoons sugar until soft peaks form. Transfer chilled egg mixture to a punch bowl. Fold in whipped cream mixture and serve at once. Sprinkle each serving with nutmeg.

Leftover Ideas

Turkey Tetrazzini

INGREDIENTS

2½ cups leftover turkey, chopped

½ lb. spaghetti or vermicelli, cooked and drained

2 cups fresh mushrooms, sliced

5 tablespoons butter *or* margarine

3 tablespoons olive oil

2 cups chicken broth

1 cup heavy cream *or* half-and-half

4 tablespoons flour

2 tablespoons dry cooking sherry

⅛ teaspoon ground nutmeg

¾ cup grated Parmesan cheese

¼ cup Italian-flavored bread crumbs

DIRECTIONS

1. Heat oven to 375 degrees.
2. In large saucepan or skillet heat 4 tablespoons butter and 3 tablespoons oil until melted.
3. Add mushrooms to pan and sauté about 5 minutes.
4. Remove mushrooms with slotted spoon and set aside.
5. Stir flour into the pan and cook until bubbly.
6. Pour in broth slowly and stir constantly. Cook until smooth and thickened.
7. Remove pan from heat and add cream, sherry, nutmeg, and cheese. Stir until cheese melts.
8. Add turkey and mushrooms and stir in well.
9. Toss in pasta.
10. Grease 3-quart baking dish and place mixture into dish.
11. Melt 1 tablespoon butter and mix with bread crumbs.
12. Top casserole with bread crumbs.
13. Bake about 30 minutes.

Turkey Pot Pie

INGREDIENTS

2 9-inch refrigerated pie crusts
2 cups leftover turkey, chopped
1 can cream of chicken soup
milk
⅓ cup onion, chopped
2 cups frozen peas and carrots
¼ teaspoon pepper

DIRECTIONS

1. Heat oven to temperature recommended on pie crust package.
2. In saucepan heat turkey, soup, a soup can full of milk, vegetables, and pepper until boiling. Reduce heat and simmer about 2 minutes.
3. Arrange one pie crust in 9-inch pie pan.
4. Pour in turkey mixture and spread evenly in pie.
5. Make a top crust with the second pie crust. Turn edges under and flute.
6. Bake until golden brown, according to pie crust package baking time.

Turkey a la King

INGREDIENTS

2 cups leftover turkey, chopped
1 package refrigerated biscuits
1 can cream of chicken soup
milk
1 cup fresh mushrooms, chopped
2 cups frozen mixed vegetables

DIRECTIONS

1. Bake biscuits according to package directions.
2. In saucepan heat turkey, soup, a soup can full of milk, and vegetables over medium heat until boiling.
3. Reduce heat and simmer until vegetables are cooked.
4. Spoon turkey mixture over biscuits.

Turkey Panini Sandwich: delicious crusty sourdough bread, grilled panini-style, filled with cheese, turkey, tomato, and lettuce. Also known as a grilled or pressed sandwich.

Turkey Panini Sandwich

INGREDIENTS

    2 slices sourdough bread
    turkey
    cheese (any kind)
    sliced tomato
    arugula *or* romaine lettuce *or* fresh spinach leaves

DIRECTIONS
    1. Assemble sandwich.
    2. If you have a panini grill, grill sandwich according to instructions. Otherwise, place sandwich in a skillet lightly greased with olive oil and brown lightly on both sides; or, cook in a waffle iron.

Turkey Enchiladas

INGREDIENTS

    4 cups leftover turkey

10 6-inch flour *or* corn tortillas
1 18 oz. bottle enchilada sauce
2 cups green onion, chopped
2 cups shredded cheddar cheese

DIRECTIONS

1. Heat oven to 350 degrees.
2. In large bowl mix turkey, 1 cup green onions, ½ cup sauce, and 1 cup cheese
3. Warm tortillas according to package directions.
4. Spread ½ cup sauce in a 13x9x2 baking dish.
5. Fill each tortilla with about 2 tablespoons of the turkey mixture, fold, and place seam side down in the baking dish.
6. Cover enchiladas with remaining sauce.
7. Sprinkle with remaining cheese and green onions.
8. Bake for 20-30 minutes or until enchiladas are heated through and cheese melts.

Turkey Pasta Salad

INGREDIENTS

1 cup of leftover turkey, chopped
6 oz. pasta, cooked according to package directions then chilled
½ cup onion, chopped
½ cup celery, chopped
½ cup cucumber, chopped
½ cup carrots, chopped
½ cup frozen peas, cooked and chilled
¾ cup Miracle Whip
⅓ cup milk

OPTIONAL ADD-IN

shredded cheddar cheese

DIRECTIONS

1. In a small bowl mix Miracle Whip and milk (add a bit more of either if thicker or thinner consistency is desired).
2. Blend all other ingredients in a large bowl.
3. Mix in dressing and chill.

CHRONOLOGY

CHRONOLOGY OF DATES RELATED TO THANKSGIVING

1521   Juan Ponce de León and his exploring party observe a mass of thanksgiving upon reaching North America.

1541   May 23 – Francisco Vasquez de Coronado and 1,500 other Spanish explorers hold a thanksgiving service in the Texas Panhandle.

1564   June 30 – A small settlement of French Huguenots hold a thanksgiving service near present-day Jacksonville, Florida.

1565   September 8 – Pedro Menéndez de Avilés and 800 other Spanish colonists share a thanksgiving feast with Seloy Indians in St. Augustine, Florida.

1598   April – Juan de Oñate and 400 other Spanish colonists are said to have held a thanksgiving feast along the Rio Grande in Texas.

1607   August 9 – English colonists hold a thanksgiving service upon reaching Maine.

1608   Spring – A group of English Separatists, better known as the Pilgrims, leaves England for Holland in search of religious freedom.

1610   Spring – English settlers at Jamestown celebrate a feast of thanksgiving when a supply ship arrives; they had suffered a famine over the winter.

1614   Tisquantum (better known as Squanto) is kidnapped from his village, Patuxet, Massachusetts, along with at least 28 other Wampanoag Indian men, and sold into slavery in Spain.

1619   Squanto, having escaped slavery, finds a return voyage from England to North America. Upon arrival, he finds a plague has taken the lives of 90 percent of the people in his village.

           December 4 – The Berkeley Hundred settlement in Virginia observes a service of thanksgiving when they reach the James River. They intend to make this an annual event, but Indians destroy the settlement in 1622.

1620   July 22 –English Separatists who had lived in Holland since 1608 leave Holland for the New World. They travel in two ships, the Speedwell and the Mayflower, and make a brief stopover in England.

September 6 – After a brief stay in England, 106 Separatists set sail aboard the *Mayflower* for America.

November 11 – The *Mayflower* arrives near Cape Cod, Massachusetts. Before leaving the ship, the 41 adult male passengers draft and sign the Mayflower Compact. (*See Primary Sources for the text of the Compact.*)

1621   March 16 – An Abenaki Indian named Samoset is the first Native American to formally meet the Pilgrims at their settlement in Plymouth.

March 22 – Wampanoag leader Massasoit and Plymouth colonial governor John Carver sign a peace treaty, pledging to assist each other in case of attack. (*See Primary Sources for the text of the treaty.*)

Between September 21 and November 9 – The three-day celebration known as the "first Thanksgiving" takes place at Plymouth.

November 10 – The *Fortune* arrives at Plymouth, carrying 37 new English settlers.

1622   *Mourt's Relation*, a collection of writings by and about the Pilgrims, is published in London. The book contains colonist Edward Winslow's account of the first Thanksgiving. (*See Primary Sources for Winslow's description.*)

1675   June – King Philip's War begins when Metacom, a Wampanoag leader and son of Massasoit (whom the colonists called Philip), leads an alliance of Native warriors to force the English colonists out. The war lasts 14 months and kills about 5,000 people; about 75 percent of the dead were Native peoples.

1676 June 29 – The governing council of Charlestown, Massachusetts, proclaims a day of thanksgiving for the end of King Philip's War. *(See Primary Sources for the text of the proclamation.)*

August 12 – Colonial leaders in Connecticut declare a day of public thanksgiving to celebrate the end of King Philip's War.

1723 November 6 – Governor William Dummer of Massachusetts Bay Colony issues a proclamation to celebrate thanksgiving on November 28; the original printed document is one of the earliest thanksgiving proclamations to survive into the 21st century. *(See Primary Sources for the text of the proclamation.)*

1769 December 21 – Residents of Plymouth, Massachusetts, first celebrate Forefathers' Day, the anniversary of the Pilgrims' landing.

1774 October 22 – John Hancock, president of the Continental Congress, issues an early "independent" thanksgiving proclamation; it is the first to conclude without the words "God Save the King."

1776 July 4 – The Continental Congress issues the Declaration of Independence, formally proclaiming independence from Britain.

1777 November 1 – The Continental Congress issues a proclamation designating December 18 to be a day of thanksgiving for the Americans' victory over the British at Saratoga. *(See Primary Sources for the text of the proclamation.)*

1783 September 3 – The Revolutionary War officially ends with the Treaty of Paris.

1784 October 19 – The Continental Congress sets this day aside in thanksgiving for the end of the Revolutionary War.

1789 November 26 – As the first president of the United States, George Washington proclaims this date as the first national thanksgiving holiday. *(See Primary Sources for the text of the proclamation.)*

1802 January 1 – President Thomas Jefferson sends the now famous Danbury letter to a Baptist association in Connecticut, in which he explains his opposition to proclaiming an official national day of thanksgiving. (*See Primary Sources for the text of the letter.*)

1815   President James Madison proclaims a national day of thanksgiving in gratitude for the U.S. victory in the War of 1812.

1817   New York is the first U.S. state to designate Thanksgiving Day as a legal state holiday.

1820   December 22 – The 200th anniversary of the Pilgrims' landing is celebrated in Plymouth. (*See Primary Sources for an excerpt of the speech delivered by Daniel Webster for the occasion*).

1824   The Pilgrim Hall Museum opens in Plymouth.

1841   The first published scholarly reference to the Pilgrims having observed the "first Thanksgiving" appears in historian Alexander Young's *Chronicles of the Pilgrim Forefathers.* (*See Primary Sources for excerpts.*)

1846   Sarah Josepha Hale begins her years-long campaign to make Thanksgiving Day a legal national holiday.

1849   December 31 – King Kamehameha III of Hawaii proclaims this date to be Thanksgiving Day for the island nation.

1861   October 31 – Confederate President Jefferson Davis issues the first thanksgiving proclamation asking the Confederate States to observe the holiday on November 15. (*See Primary Sources for the text of the proclamation.*)

1863   October 3 – President Abraham Lincoln issues a proclamation declaring the last Thursday in November to be a national day of Thanksgiving, in apparent response to Sarah Josepha Hale's letter of September 28 asking Lincoln to declare the holiday. (*See Primary Sources for the text of Hale's letter and Lincoln's proclamation.*)

1876   November – The Intercollegiate Football Association holds its first championship game – between Yale and Princeton (Yale won) – on Thanksgiving Day.

1921   July 13, 14, 15, 16, 30, August 1, 2, 3, 10, 11, 12, 13 – The 300th, or tercentenary, anniversary of the Pilgrims' landing is celebrated with an elaborate pageant at Plymouth Rock.

November – The first Thanksgiving Day parade is held in Philadelphia, Pennsylvania, sponsored by Gimbel's department store.

1923   November – The J. L. Hudson Company holds the first Thanksgiving Day parade in Detroit, Michigan.

1924   November – The first Macy's Thanksgiving Day parade is held in New York City. *(See Primary Sources for a history of the parade.)*

1934   November – The first National Football League game is played on Thanksgiving Day when the Detroit Lions host the Chicago Bears.

1939   October 31 – President Franklin D. Roosevelt announces that he will move the holiday up one week and proclaim the Thanksgiving holiday to be observed on the third Thursday in November. Roosevelt maintains the controversial date change through 1941. *(See Primary Sources for the text of the proclamation.)*

1941   November 26 – The U.S. Congress establishes Thanksgiving as a federal holiday to be held on the fourth Thursday of November each year. The new law takes effect in 1942. *(See Primary Sources for the text of the law.)*

1947   November – The National Turkey Federation begins its annual tradition of presenting a live turkey to the president of the United States.

1956   November – The Detroit Lions' annual Thanksgiving Day football game is televised for the first time.

1970   November – The first National Day of Mourning is organized by Native Americans in Plymouth, Massachusetts. This Thanksgiving counter-observance began when organizers of a banquet to celebrate the 350th anniversary of the Pilgrims' landing refused to allow invited speaker Wamsutta (Frank) B. James, president of the Federated Eastern Indian League, to deliver a speech presenting a critical perspective on the Pilgrims.

1973   November – Astronauts Gerald Carr, Edward Gibson, and William Pogue celebrate the first Thanksgiving in space aboard the Skylab space station.

1982   November –Ronald Reagan is the first modern president to formally pardon a live turkey presented to him by the National Turkey Federation, inaugurating a new twist to the annual ceremony.

2001   November 16 – President George W. Bush issues the first Thanksgiving proclamation after the terrorist attacks of September 11. *(See Primary Sources for the text of the proclamation.)*

BIBLIOGRAPHY

BIBLIOGRAPHY:
BOOKS, ARTICLES, AND WEB SITES

This bibliography lists all sources consulted in the preparation of this volume. Sources are organized under the following categories: Books, Articles, and Web Sites.

Books

Alford, Henry. "Come, Ye Thankful People, Come." In *It's Time for Thanksgiving,* by Elizabeth Hough Sechrist and Janette Woolsey. 1957. Reprint, Detroit: Omnigraphics, 1999. Available online at http://www.cyberhymnal.org/htm/c/o/comeytpc.htm.

Appelbaum, Diana Karter. *Thanksgiving: An American Holiday, an American History.* New York: Facts on File, 1984.

Baldwin, Margaret. *Thanksgiving.* New York: Franklin Watts, 1983. (young adult)

Bates, Mrs. D.B. "Chapter V. A South Sea Rookery," pp. 39-45. *Incidents on Land and Water, or Four Years on the Pacific Coast. Being a Narrative of the Burning of the Ships Nonantum, Humayoon and Fanchon, Together with Many Startling and Interesting Adventures on Sea and Land.* Boston: J. French and Company, 1857. Available online at Library of Congress, http://memory.loc.gov/ammem/cbhtml/cbhome. html.

Bigelow, Bill, and Bob Peterson. *Rethinking Columbus: The Next 500 Years.* Milwaukee: Rethinking Schools, Ltd., 1998.

Bradford, William. *Of Plymoth Plantation, 1620-1647.* Edited by Samuel Eliot Morison. New York: Knopf, 1970.

Brumfield, Allaire Chandor. *The Attic Festivals of Demeter and Their Relation to the Agricultural Year.* Salem, NH: Ayer, 1981.

Buck, Franklin Agustus. "Letter from Sacramento," November 25, 1849, pp. 55, 57. *A Yankee Trader in the Gold Rush; The Letters of Franklin A. Buck, Compiled by Katherine A. White.* Boston: Houghton Mifflin Company, 1930. Available online at Library of Congress, http://memory.loc.gov/ammem/cbhtml/cbhome.html.

Child, Lydia Maria. "The New-England Boy's Song about Thanksgiving Day." *Flowers for Children.* Vol. 2. New York: C. S. Francis, 1845. Available online at Representative Poetry Online, University of Toronto Libraries, http://rpo.library.utoronto.ca/poem/473.html.

Curtin, Kathleen, and Sandra L. Oliver, with Plimoth Plantation. *Giving Thanks: Thanksgiving Recipes and History, from Pilgrims to Pumpkin Pie.* New York: Clarkson Potter, 2005.

Eberhard, Wolfram. *Chinese Festivals.* New York: Henry Schuman, 1952.

Grace, Catherine O'Neill, and Margaret M. Bruchac, with Plimoth Plantation. *1621: A New Look at Thanksgiving.* Washington, DC: National Geographic Society, 2001. (young adult)

Grippo, Robert M., and Christopher Hoskins. "The 1920s: Bands, Clowns, and Merrymakers." In *Macy's Thanksgiving Day Parade.* Charleston, SC: Arcadia Publishing, 2004.

Hale, Edward Everett. "Thanksgiving at the Polls: A Thanksgiving Story." In *The Brick Moon and Other Stories.* Boston: Little, Brown, 1899. Available online at http://www.gutenberg.org/etext/1633.

Hemans, Felicia Dorothea. "The Landing of the Pilgrim Fathers in New England." In *The League of the Alps, The Siege of Valencia, The Vespers of Palermo, and Other Poems.* Boston: Hilliard, Gray, Little, and Wilkins, 1826. Available online at Representative Poetry Online, Department of English, University of Toronto, http://rpo.library.utoronto.ca/poem/937.html.

Hodgson, Godfrey. *A Great and Godly Adventure: The Pilgrims and the Myth of the First Thanksgiving.* New York: Public Affairs Books, 2006.

Houghton, Eliza Poor Donner. "Chapter XXIX—Thanksgiving Day in California," pp. 260-62. *The Expedition of the Donner Party and Its Tragic Fate.* Chicago: A. C. McClurg and Co., 1911. Available online at the Library of Congress, http://memory.loc.gov/ammem/cbhtml/cbhome.html.

Hutton, Ronald. *The Stations of the Sun: A History of the Ritual Year in Britain.* Oxford: Oxford University Press, 1996.

Philbrick, Nathaniel. *Mayflower.* New York: Viking, 2006.

Prelutsky, Jack. "The Thanksgiving Day Parade." In *It's Thanksgiving.* New York: Harper Collins, 1996. Available online at http://homepages.rootsweb.com/~homespun/tmtp.html.

Scullard, H. H. *Festivals and Ceremonies of the Roman Republic.* Ithaca, NY: Cornell University Press, 1981.

Seale, Doris, Beverly Slapin, and Carolyn Silverman. *Thanksgiving: A Native Perspective.* Berkeley, CA: Oyate, 1998.

Stowe, Harriet Beecher. "Chapter XXVII—How We Kept Thanksgiving at Oldtown." *Oldtown Folks.* Boston: Fields, Osgood, 1869.

Thorpe, Francis Newton, ed. *The Federal and State Constitutions, Colonial Charters, and Other Organic Laws of the States, Territories, and Colonies Now or Heretofore Forming the United States of America.* Compiled and edited under the Act of Congress of June 30, 1906. Washington, DC: Government Printing Office, 1909.

Trepp, Leo. *The Complete Book of Jewish Observances: A Practical Manual for the Modern Jew.* New York: Behrman House/Summit Books, 1980.

U.S. Congress. *Annals of Congress,* House of Representatives, 1st Cong., 1st sess., September 25, 1789. Vol. I, pp. 949-50. Washington, DC: Gales and Seaton, 1834. Available online at the Library of Congress, http://memory.loc.gov/ammem/amlaw/lwac.html.

Waters, Kate. *Giving Thanks: The 1621 Harvest Feast.* New York: Scholastic, 2001. (young adult)

Webster, Daniel. "First Settlement of New England." Speech delivered in Plymouth, Massachusetts, December 22, 1820. In *The Great Speeches and Orations of Daniel Webster with an Essay on Daniel Webster as a Master of English Style* by Edwin P. Whipple. Boston: Little, Brown, & Co., 1889.

Whittier, John Greenleaf. "The Pumpkin." In *The Poetical Works of John Greenleaf Whittier.* Edited by W. Garrett Horder. London: Henry Frowde, 1898. Available online at http://www.potw.org/archive/potw209.html.

Wilson, Woodrow. "A Proclamation of Thanksgiving for Victory (November 17, 1918)." In *Guarantees of Peace: Messages and Addresses to the Congress and the People, Jan. 31, 1918, to Dec. 2, 1918, Together with the Peace Notes to Germany and Austria.* New York: Harper & Brothers Publishers, 1919.

Winslow, Edward. Letter reprinted in *Mourt's Relation: A Journal of the Pilgrims at Plymouth 1622.* Edited by Dwight B. Heath. Boston: Applewood Books, 1963.

Young, Alexander. *Chronicles of the Pilgrim Fathers of the Colony of Plymouth, from 1602 to 1625.* Boston: Little, Brown, 1841.

Articles

Alcott, Louisa May. "An Old-Fashioned Thanksgiving." *St. Nicholas Magazine,* November 1881.

Baker, Eggy, and James Baker. "Thanksgiving: A Brief History." *Early American Life,* December 2001.

Barovick, Harriet, et al. "We Gather Together." *Time,* November 19, 2001.

Barton, Jo Anne. "Thanksgiving Foods." *Virginia Culinary Thymes,* Winter 2004.

Bedford, Faith Andrews. "Turning the Tables at Thanksgiving: Every Child Has Special Rites of Passage—Going Away to Camp, Getting a Driver's License. For One Youngster, It Was Moving to the Grownups' Table at Thanksgiving." *Country Living,* November 2004.

Currivan, Gene. "Hot Turkey Cheers Third Army Squad." *New York Times,* November 24, 1944.

David, Lester. "Thanks, Squanto: A Remarkable Man Rescues the Pilgrims from Starvation during Their First Year in the New World." Boys' *Life,* November 1995.

Dickson, Hendrick. "Underway Family." *All Hands* (U.S. Navy), November 2005.

Farah, Samar. "Growing Up a Thanksgiving Impostor." *Christian Science Monitor*, November 22, 2000.

Fussell, James A. "Americans' Thanksgiving Feast Tradition for the Birds?" *Kansas City Star,* November 24, 2006.

Goodman, Peter S. "For Native Americans, A Day of Mixed Emotions." *Washington Post,* November 26, 1998.

Hale, Sarah Josepha. "Editor's Table: Our National Thanksgiving." *Godey's Lady's Book*, November, 1858. Available online at http://womenshistory.about.com/od/thanksgiving/a/hale_thanksday.htm.

Haley, Alex. "Thank You: What's Most Important Is Often Too Easily Forgotten." *Parade*, November 21, 1982.

Harshman, Terry Webb. "Pilgrims' Progress." *Child Life,* October-November 1994.

Jefferson, Thomas. "Letter to the Danbury Baptists," January 1, 1802. *Library of Congress Information Bulletin,* Vol. 57, No. 6, June 1998. Available online at Library of Congress, http://www.loc.gov/loc/lcib/9806/danpre.html.

Jewett, Sarah Orne. "The Lost Turkey." *Youth's Companion,* November 27, 1902. Available online at Jewett Texts, http://www.public.coe.edu/~theller/soj/unc/turkey.htm.

"Keeping Thanksgiving." *New York Times*, November 23, 2006.

Kirkpatrick, Melanie. "A Hymn's Long Journey Home: The Surprising Origins of 'We Gather Together,' a Thanksgiving Standard." *Wall Street Journal,* November 22, 2005.

Koch, Carole Christman. "Thanksgiving: A Holiday with a History Stretching across the Atlantic." *Capper's,* November 2005.

Lang, John S. "Guess Who's Not Coming To Thanksgiving Dinner; Those Who Were at the First Celebration See Little to Be Grateful for Today." *Washington Post,* November 21, 1989.

LeDuff, Charlie. "On Holiday Shift, Gratitude at the Firehouse. (Squad 1: The First Holiday)." *New York Times,* November 23, 2001.

Loewen, James W. "The Truth about the First Thanksgiving." *Monthly Review,* November 1992.

Mehren, Elizabeth. "In America's Boom Time, a Record Cry for Food." *Los Angeles Times,* December 18, 2000.

Meline, Megan. "The Founding Mother of Thanksgiving." *Chronicle of Higher Education,* November 28, 2003.

Mihoces, Gary. "Pass the Turkey – and the Football." *USA Today,* November 27, 2002.

Miller, Charles. "In Virginia: First Thanksgiving Festival Stresses Berkeley's Importance in History." *Richmond Times-Dispatch,* November 20, 2005.

Miller, Neil. "Of Pilgrims and Progress." *Boston Globe Magazine,* October 4, 1998.

Parent, Tawn. "Go Beyond the Turkey on Thanksgiving." *Indianapolis Business Journal,* November 21, 2005.

Pleck, Elizabeth. "The Making of the Domestic Occasion: The History of Thanksgiving in the United States." *Journal of Social History,* Summer 1999.

Schwarz, Frederic D. "1621: The First Thanksgiving, Sort Of." *American Heritage,* November 1996.

Shapiro, Walter. "Why We've Failed to Ruin Thanksgiving." *Time,* November 27, 1989.

Web Sites

America's Second Harvest. "For 38 Million Americans, Thanksgiving Is a Struggle," November 23, 2005. Available online at http://www.secondharvest.org/news_room/2005_News_Releases/112305.html.

Baker, James. "The Pilgrims as People: Understanding the Plymouth Colonists." Plimoth Plantation. Available online at http://www.plimoth.org/learn/history/thanksgiving/PilgrimPeople.asp.

Baker, Theodore, trans. "We Gather Together," 1894. First published as "Wilt heden nu treden" in the Dutch songbook Nederlandtsche Gedenckclanck, collected by Adrianus Valerius, Haarlem, Holland: 1626. Available online at http://www.cyberhymnal.org/htm/w/e/wegattog.htm.

Belcher, Jonathan. "Proclamation for a General Fast," February 26, 1735. Available online at This Common Feast: The South Atlantic Thanksgiving Project, http://www.southatlanticcenter.org/tgiving/proclaim.html.

Bush, George W. Thanksgiving Day Proclamation, November 16, 2001. Available online at Office of the Press Secretary, the White House, http://www.whitehouse.gov/news/releases/2001/11/20011116-3.html.

Camas, Joanne. "The First Thanksgiving: Just How Did the Pilgrims Give Thanks?" Epicurious.com. Available online at http://www.epicurious.com/cooking/holiday/thanksgiving/first.

Chaudhry, Maahum. "Not Your Average Pilgrims' Feast: Immigrants Transform Holiday Traditions." The Lowell [Lowell (San Francisco, CA) High School journalism class], November 2006. Available online at http://www.thelowell.org/content/view/1944/27.

Continental Congress. Thanksgiving Proclamation, November 1, 1777. Available online at This Common Feast: The South Atlantic Thanksgiving Project, http://www.southatlanticcenter.org/tgiving/proclaim.html.

Curtin, Kathleen A. "Partakers of Our Plenty." Plimoth Plantation. Available online at http://www.plimoth.org/learn/history/thanksgiving/plenty.asp.

Davis, Jefferson. Thanksgiving Proclamation for the Confederate States of America, October 31, 1861. Available online at South Atlantic Thanksgiving Project, http://www.southatlanticcenter.org/tgiving/proclaim.html.

Dow, Judy, and Beverly Slapin. "Deconstructing the Myths of 'The First Thanksgiving'." Oyate, June 12, 2006. Available online at http://www.oyate.org/resources/shortthanks.html.

Dummer, William. Thanksgiving Proclamation 1723. Available online at Pilgrim Hall Museum, http://www.pilgrimhall.org/GivingThanks3a.htm.

Eldredge, Nancy. "Native Traditions of Giving Thanks." Plimoth Plantation. Available online at http://www.plimoth.org/learn/history/thanksgiving/nativetrad.asp.

Elliott, Stephen. Extract from a Sermon Preached by Bishop Elliott, on the 18th of September, Containing a Tribute to the Privates of the Confederate Army. Savannah: [s.n.], 1862. Available online at Documenting the South, University of North Carolina at Chapel Hill, http://docsouth.unc.edu/elliotts1/elliott.html.

Food Network. "The History of Thanksgiving Foods," October 18, 2004. Available online at http://www.foodnetwork.com/food/et_hd_thanksgiving/article/0,1972,FOOD_9845_3263081,00.html.

Franklin D. Roosevelt Presidential Library. "The Year We Had Two Thanksgivings." Available online at http://www.fdrlibrary.marist.edu/thanksg.html.

Goldstein, Karin. "As American as Pumpkin Pie." Plimoth Plantation. Available online at http://www.plimoth.org/learn/history/thanksgiving/pumpkinpie.asp.

Governing Council of Charlestown, Massachusetts. Thanksgiving Proclamation, June 20, 1676. Available online at The University of Oklahoma College of Law, Chronology of U.S. Historical Documents, http://www.law.ou.edu/ushistory/thanksgiv.shtml.

Hale, Sarah Josepha. Letter to Abraham Lincoln, September 28, 1863. Transcribed and annotated by the Lincoln Studies Center, Knox College, Galesburg, Illinois. From the Abraham Lincoln Papers at the Library of Congress, 1863. Available online at http://memory.loc.gov/ammem/alhtml/malhome.html.

The History Channel. "The History of Thanksgiving." Available online at http://www.history.com/minisites/thanksgiving/.

Hoover, Herbert. Thanksgiving Proclamation, November 6, 1930. Available online at the Pilgrim Hall Museum, http://www.pilgrimhall.org/ThanxProc1930.htm.

"Interview No. 7." In Library of Congress Collection, American Life Histories: Manuscripts from the Federal Writers' Project, 1936-1940. Available online at http://memory.loc.gov/ammem/wpaintro/wpahome.html.

"Iroquois Thanksgiving Address: Greetings to the Natural World." Mohawk Nation Council of Chiefs. Available online at http://www.mohawknation.org.

Ives, Sarah. "The Truth behind Thanksgiving Dinner." *National Geographic Kids News*, November 24, 2003. Available online at http://news.nationalgeographic.com/kids/2003/11/thanksgiving.html.

Lincoln, Abraham. Thanksgiving Proclamation, October 3, 1863. Available online at the Library of Congress, http://memory.loc.gov/cgi-bin/ampage?collId=llsl&fileName=013/llsl013.db&recNum=764.

Muhlenberg, William Augustus. "The President's Hymn." Music by Joseph W. Turner. Boston: Oliver Ditson & Co., 1863. Sheet Music from the Alfred Whital Stern Collection of Lincolniana. Held in the Rare Book and Special Collections Division, Library of Congress. Available online at http://memory.loc.gov/ammem/scsmhtml/scsmhome.html.

National Aeronautics and Space Administration. "Out of This World Thanksgiving," November 24, 2003. Available online at http://www.nasa.gov/vision/space/livinginspace/Space_Thanksgiving.html.

Pilgrim Hall Museum. "Thanksgiving." Available online at http://www.pilgrimhall.org/thankg.htm.

Roosevelt, Franklin D. Thanksgiving Proclamation, October 31, 1939. Available online at Pilgrim Hall Museum, http://www.pilgrimhall.org/ThanxProc1930.htm.

Strester, George. "A Preacher Tries Farming." In American Life Histories: Manuscripts from the Federal Writers' Project, 1936-1940. Available online at the Library of Congress, http://memory.loc.gov/ammem/wpaintro/wpahome.html.

"Texas History Highlights: The First Thanksgiving?" *Texas Almanac* 2006-2007. Edited by Elizabeth Cruce Alvarez and Robert Plocheck. Available online at http://www.texasalmanac.com/history/highlights/thanksgiving.

"Thanksgiving Special." PBS Online NewsHour, November 1996. Available online at http://www.pbs.org/newshour/thanksgiving.

Travers, Carolyn Freeman. "Fast and Thanksgiving Days." Plimoth Plantation. Available online at http://www.plimoth.org/learn/history/thanksgiving/fastandthanks.asp.

Trivedi, Bijal P. "Where Do Turkeys Go after Being Pardoned by the President?" *National Geographic News,* November 20, 2001. Available online at http://news.national geographic.com/news/2001/11/1120_TVprezturkeys.html.

Truman, Harry S. Thanksgiving Proclamation, November 12, 1945. Available online at Pilgrim Hall Museum, http://www.pilgrimhall.org/ThanxProc1940.htm.

U.S. Congress. *Joint Resolution Making the Fourth Thursday in November a Legal Holiday,* December 26, 1941. Available online at Office of the Clerk, U.S. Capitol, http://clerkkids.house.gov/laws/inspectLaw/inspect_TextAll.html.

Washington, George. Thanksgiving Proclamation, October 3, 1789. Available online at the Library of Congress, http://memory.loc.gov/ammem/gwhtml/gwhome.html.

PHOTO CREDITS

PHOTO AND ILLUSTRATION CREDITS

Essays

Page 2: *The Landing of the Pilgrims at Plymouth Mass, Dec 22nd, 1620.* Library of Congress, LC-USZ62-3461

Page 6: Mark Aplet/Shutterstock

Page 9: *The Pilgrims Signing the Compact, Onboard the Mayflower, Nov. 11th, 1620.* Library of Congress, LC-DIG-ppmsca-07842

Page 13: *Landing of the Pilgrims.* Library of Congress, LC-USZ62-108110

Page 15: Kean Collection/Getty Images

Page 18: Library of Congress, Documents from the Continental Congress and the Constitutional Convention, 1774-1789

Page 21: *Uncle Sam's Thanksgiving Dinner.* Library of Congress, LC-USZ62-85882

Page 24: Sarah Josepha (Buell) Hale. Library of Congress, LC-USZ62-35926A

Page 29: *Castle Garden--their first Thanksgiving dinner.* Library of Congress, LC-USZ62-99401

Page 31: *Royal Progress.* Library of Congress, Panoramic Photographs, LC Digital ID: pan6a27464

Page 34: Andrew McDonough/Shutterstock

Page 36: Tom Pidgeon/Getty Images

Page 39: Lyndon Baines Johnson Library photo by Frank Wolfe, WHPO Collection

Page 43: Steven Senne/AP Photo

Page 50: David M. Albrecht/Shutterstock

Page 55: First Thanksgiving. Library of Congress, Detroit Publishing Company Photograph Collection, LC-D416-90423

Page 58: Ted Curtin/Plimoth Plantation/AP Photo

Page 61: Library of Congress, George Grantham Bain Collection, LC-DIG-ggbain-11154

Page 65: Library of Congress, George Grantham Bain Collection, LC-USZ62-70874

Page 67: Library of Congress, Farm Security Administration—Office of War Information Photograph Collection, LC-USW3-011874-D

Page 70: Photobar/Shutterstock

Primary Sources

Page 75: *The May Flower, 1620.* Library of Congress, Detroit Publishing Company Photograph Collection, LC-D416-14152

Page 89: Library of Congress, Rare Book and Special Collections Division, Printed Ephemera Collection, Portfolio 40, Folder 14

Page 99: Time Life Pictures/Getty Images

Page 109: *Home to Thanksgiving.* Library of Congress, LC-USZ62-15

Page 149: *American Progress.* Library of Congress, LC-DIG-ppmsca-09855

Page 165: Library of Congress, Rare Book and Special Collections Division, Sheet Music from the Alfred Whital Stern Collection of Lincolniana

Page 181: Library of Congress, LC-USZ62-96803

Page 193: Jim MacMillan/AP Photo

Page 207: Steven Senne/AP Photo

Page 225: Shutterstock

Recipes

Page 257: Mark Stout/iStockphoto

Page 262: Shawn Campbell/iStockphoto

Page 266: Steve Cukrov/Shutterstock

Page 274: Pamela Moore/iStockphoto

Page 278: Scott Roberts/Shutterstock

Page 282: Michael Ledray/Shutterstock

Page 285: Brenda McEwan/iStockphoto

Page 288: Lisa F. Young/Shutterstock

Page 292: Jaimie Duplass/Shutterstock

Page 297: Kelly Cline/iStockphoto

INDEX

INDEX

RIDGEMONT PUBLIC LIBRARY
MT. VICTORY, OHIO